Introducing Language and Cognition

In this accessible introduction, Michael Sharwood Smith provides a working model or 'map' of the mind, with language as its centrepiece. Drawing on cutting-edge research across linguistics, psychology and neuroscience, it allows students to quickly grasp how each separate aspect of the mind's operations can be related. This 'big picture' view includes the way the mind makes, stores and loses memories of all kinds as well how its various 'expert systems' combine and collaborate to solve, typically beyond our conscious awareness, the myriad tasks we face every millisecond of our existence. The book also focuses on language, that is, of the minds of monolingual, bilingual and multilingual speakers. It will be of interest to all students wishing to learn more about the complex relationship between language – one of the most important ways in which we define ourselves as human – and the mind.

MICHAEL SHARWOOD SMITH, Emeritus Professor at Heriot-Watt University and Honorary Professorial Fellow at Edinburgh University, has worked in many countries across the world, teaching applied linguistics, the English language and second language acquisition. He has more than a hundred publications and is known for terms such as *grammatical consciousness-raising*, *crosslinguistic influence* and *input-enhancement*. His major interests are the cognitive processes underlying the use and acquisition of languages. With John Truscott, he pioneered a crossdisciplinary framework for framing explanations of many diverse aspects of language acquisition and is also founding editor of the leading journal *Second Language Research*.

Introducing Language and Cognition
A Map of the Mind

MICHAEL SHARWOOD SMITH
Heriot-Watt University, Edinburgh

CAMBRIDGE UNIVERSITY PRESS

CAMBRIDGE
UNIVERSITY PRESS

University Printing House, Cambridge CB2 8BS, United Kingdom

Cambridge University Press is part of the University of Cambridge.

It furthers the University's mission by disseminating knowledge in the pursuit of education, learning, and research at the highest international levels of excellence.

www.cambridge.org
Information on this title: www.cambridge.org/9781316606704
DOI: 10.1017/9781316591505

© Michael Sharwood Smith 2017

This publication is in copyright. Subject to statutory exception and to the provisions of relevant collective licensing agreements, no reproduction of any part may take place without the written permission of Cambridge University Press.

First published 2017

Printed in the United Kingdom by Clays, St Ives plc

A catalogue record for this publication is available from the British Library.

Library of Congress Cataloging-in-Publication Data
Names: Sharwood Smith, Michael, author.
Title: Introducing language and cognition : a map of the mind / Mike Sharwood Smith.
Description: Cambridge, United Kingdom : Cambridge University Press, [2017] |
Includes bibliographical references and index.
Identifiers: LCCN 2016036246| ISBN 9781107152892 (hardback : alk. paper) |
ISBN 9781316606704 (pbk. : alk. paper)
Subjects: LCSH: Language acquisition–Psychological aspects. | Cognitive learning. | Brain–Physiology. | Psycholinguistics.
Classification: LCC P118.2 .S53 2016 | DDC 401/.9 – dc23 LC record available at https://lccn.loc.gov/2016036246

ISBN 978-1-107-15289-2 Hardback
ISBN 978-1-316-60670-4 Paperback

Cambridge University Press has no responsibility for the persistence or accuracy of URLs for external or third-party Internet Web sites referred to in this publication and does not guarantee that any content on such Web sites is, or will remain, accurate or appropriate.

To Ewa

Contents

Figures	*page* xiii
Preface	xv
Annotated Abbreviations	xvii

Introduction	1
Overview	1
Language as a Biological and Psychological Phenomenon	3
The World 'Outside' versus the World 'Inside'	3
The Role of Language	4
The 'Framework'	4
Mind and Brain Contrasted and Compared	5
Two Levels of Description	5
Mind and Brain Together	7
What Is a Representation?	8
Representations and Equivalent Terms	9
Knowledge as a Relative Concept	10
The Mind as a Network	11
Alternative Views and Close Relatives	13
What Is Special about Language?	16
Summary	17

PART I Mechanisms of the Mind	19

1 The Basic Design	21
In This Chapter	21
The Module or 'Processing Unit'	21
How Many Experts?	24
The Store's 'Primitives'	25
Interfaces	26
Summary	28

2 Perception	30
In This Chapter	30
From Sensory Experience to Representation	30
Perception as Illusion, of a Kind	32
The Perceptual 'Group'	33
Five Senses Extended	35

	Synaesthesia	35
	Perceptual Systems Are Not Equal	37
	Perceptual Experience without External Cause	38
	Making Sense	38
	Processing Is Bidirectional	41
	The Auditory System	42
	Taste and Smell	42
	Body Sense	43
	Perceptual Structures without Meaning or Value	44
	Summary	44
3	**Motion**	**45**
	In This Chapter	45
	Interconnectivity	45
	Imagined Movement	47
	The Language of Our Ancestors	48
	Integrating Motor Structures with the Perceptual Systems	48
	Summary	49
4	**Meaning**	**50**
	In This Chapter	50
	Conceptual Representations	50
	Thinking, Imagining and Sensing	52
	The Conceptual System and the Brain	52
	Integrating Conceptual Structures with the Perceptual and Motor Systems	53
	Summary	54
5	**Affect**	**56**
	In This Chapter	56
	Evaluation	56
	Neuroscientific Views	57
	Valence and Appraisal	60
	Basic Emotions	61
	Integrating Affect with Perceptual, Motor and Conceptual Systems	62
	Summary	63
6	**Memory, Processing and Activation**	**65**
	In This Chapter	65
	Memory	65
	Communication between Modules	67
	Working and Long-Term Memory	68
	Indexing	71
	Competition	72
	'Construction' versus 'Association'	74
	Processing Goes Both Ways and at the Same Time	75
	Every Module Is Both Expert and Stupid	76
	Summary	76

7 Consciousness and Attention — 78
In This Chapter — 78
Activation-Based Explanations of Consciousness — 78
Thinking Consciously Works Slowly and Sequentially — 80
Attention, Awareness and Activation — 80
Perception as the Engine of Consciousness — 82
Awareness of Emotion — 83
Summary — 84

8 Developing Knowledge and Ability — 85
In This Chapter — 85
Knowledge and Ability Combined — 85
Knowledge as Relative — 86
Knowledge and Ability Distinguished — 86
APT and Bidirectional Development — 87
Resting Level as a Relative Concept — 90
Growth and Affect — 90
Summary — 91

PART II Language(s) in the Mind — 93

9 Defining Language — 95
In This Chapter — 95
The Broad and Narrow Definitions of Language — 95
Organising Speech Sounds — 96
Organising Words and Parts of Words — 96
The UG-Controlled Zone — 97
Producing and Interpreting Utterances — 98
Summary — 99

10 The Core System — 100
In This Chapter — 100
What's Special about Language and What Isn't — 100
The Two Core Modules — 101
Phonological Structure (PS) — 103
Syntactic Structure (SS) — 105
Complex Linguistic Structures — 106
Processing in Parallel, Bidirectionally and Not Always Successfully — 108
Summary — 109

11 Language beyond the Core — 110
In This Chapter — 110
Language Sounds outside the Core — 110
Language Meanings outside the Core — 111
Language out of Context — 112
Language in Context — 114

	Language Articulation	116
	Language Perception	117
	The 'Colonising' Core	120
	Communicating *without* Using the Core System	122
	Summary	123
12	**Two Ways of Knowing a Language**	**125**
	In This Chapter	125
	Conceptual Knowledge of Grammar	126
	Metacognition	129
	Metalinguistic Ability and the Perceptual System	130
	Summary	131
13	**Language and Affect**	**133**
	In This Chapter	133
	The Relevance of Affect to Language	133
	Affect within the Core Language System	134
	Affect beyond the Core Language System: Sounds and Meanings	136
	Affect and the Auditory System (AfS and AS)	137
	Affect and the Conceptual System (AfS and CS)	138
	Grammaticality Judgements and AfS	139
	Expanding the Connections: Affective, Visual and Motor Structures	141
	Affect and the Visual System (AfS and VS)	142
	Affect and the Motor System	143
	Affect as an Inhibitor of Language	143
	Summary	146
14	**Language Development in the Monolingual**	**148**
	In This Chapter	148
	One Size Fits All	150
	The Tower of Babel	150
	Language 'Input': A Misleading Term	151
	Early Speech	152
	Babies, Birds and Monkeys	153
	Babies and Dogs	154
	Acquisition: The Early Stages	155
	The Silent Period and Baby Signing	156
	Language Acquisition by Processing	158
	Early Grammars	161
	Applying the Framework	162
	Conceptual Bootstrapping	163
	Acquiring Language by Interpreting Utterances	163
	Building Core Linguistic Structure from Speech Input	165
	Language Acquisition outside the Core System	167
	Simple Linguistic Systems	169
	Language Acquisition and Age	171
	Summary	172

15	**Becoming Multilingual**	173
	In This Chapter	173
	Accommodating Different Language Systems	174
	Escaping the Tower	175
	APT Applied to More Than One Language	178
	Competition Revisited	179
	Crosslinguistic Effects	180
	Code-Switching and Code-Mixing	184
	Heritage Languages	186
	The Growth of Metalinguistic Knowledge in Multilinguals	188
	Multilingualism and the Ageing Mind	190
	Summary	192
	Conclusion	194
	Overview	194
	Fixed, Flexible and Dynamic	194
	The Relationship between Language and Vision	195
	On the Myth of the Human Mind	196
	Social Context and the World Inside	196
	Closing Summary	197
	Glossary	199
	References	211
	Index	221

Figures

I.1	Mind and brain: the subway analogy.	*page* 7
1.1	A module or 'processing unit'.	23
1.2	Two interfaced modules.	27
2.1	The perceptual group.	34
2.2	'Making sense' of perceptual experience.	41
3.1	The motor store and interfaces with the perceptual systems.	49
4.1	Sound and meaning matched up.	51
4.2	The conceptual store and interfaces with the perceptual and motor systems.	54
5.1	The affect module.	60
5.2	The affect (AfS) system and its network of interfaces.	63
6.1	Two interfaced memory stores.	66
6.2	Two working memories with an interface connection.	68
6.3	Coactivated structures in two working memories.	69
6.4	Constructing and associating.	74
8.1	Different resting levels of activation.	89
9.1	Language: the core system and adjacent modules.	98
10.1	The core language system connections.	101
11.1	A visible language network (writing).	119
11.2	A visible language network (sign language).	120
11.3	The colonising core.	121
11.4	Two ways to understand 'horse'.	123
12.1	Two ways of knowing grammar.	128
13.1	Affect interface options for the core language system.	135
13.2	The AfS store interfaced with the sound and meaning structures.	137
13.3	Affect interfaced with motor and visual systems (MoS and VS).	142
13.4	Example of a 'taboo word' network.	144
13.5	Overview of the affective memory store and related connections.	146
14.1	Raw input, not 'words and sentences'.	149
14.2	All language systems stored and processed the same way.	150
14.3	A recipe for confusion?	151

14.4	Nonlinguistic comprehension.	155
14.5	Luke's signs.	157
14.6	Matching perceptual and phonological representations.	159
14.7	Matching activated auditory representations with phonological ones: comparisons of resting level status at two different times.	160
14.8	The banana network.	168
15.1	The Tower of Babel: two escape options.	177
15.2	Competition between alternative syntactic structures with hypothetical resting levels of activation.	184
C.1	The framework: stores and interfaces.	195

Preface

The original plan for this book was to present a more widely accessible version of *Multilingual Mind: A Processing Perspective* (Sharwood Smith & Truscott, 2014). While it mostly fulfils this basic task, it has also given me the opportunity to explore a few things in more detail as well as discuss human cognition in general before focusing on language.

I would like to put on record with gratitude the contribution of my reviewers, who cannot of course bear any responsibility for my interpretation of their helpful comments. Special thanks go to John Truscott, fellow creator of the MOGUL framework, for his many comments and suggestions. Thanks are also due to Ellen Bialystok and more generally to my friends and colleagues at Edinburgh and beyond who have always been willing to listen patiently to my proselytising about the merits of the framework for their own research. Thanks also to Ewa, Kirsty and Ania for their valuable support and, finally, to those outstanding scholars who have influenced the way this framework has developed, not least Ray Jackendoff, whose broad vision on the relationship of language and cognition has been particularly inspiring.

On a practical note, there is a glossary at the end of the book, although readers may also use the slightly more comprehensive online glossary available at http://www.mogulframework.com/. This one is updated from time to time.

Abbreviations

AfS	affective structure
AS	auditory structure
C	consonant
CS	conceptual structure
ERP	event-related potential
fMRI	functional magnetic resonance imaging
GS	gustatory structure
MOGUL	Modular Online Growth and Use of Language framework
MoS	motor structure
N	noun
OfS	olfactory structure
POpS	perceptual output structure
PS	phonological structure
PU	processing unit
SmS	somatosensory structure
SS	syntactic structure
UG	universal grammar
V	verb
VS	visual structure

Introduction

Overview

This book provides a particular perspective on how the mind is organised. This perspective is based on research in different areas of cognitive science. The result is a basic working model of the mind which can function as a shared resource for researchers in different areas to apply their particular expertise. This theoretical framework is explained in this book piece by piece like a jigsaw puzzle that is built up gradually in the ensuing chapters. Each chapter introduces one of the various parts that make up the whole, topics such as perception, emotion and consciousness. The chapters should be regarded as 'tasters' and not as comprehensive overviews of a given field of research. In other words they are designed to intrigue as much as inform. The focus will always be on how each topic contributes to a coherent conceptualisation of the mind. Once readers arrive in Part II, which is entirely devoted to how language fits into the framework, they should have become familiar with the way the mind is being described and the basic terminology being used. There will then be a modest increase in the more technical aspects of the discussion.

If readers at the outset of the book do not feel that they have much of a grasp of how all the bits fits together, they should not be surprised. Many specialist researchers are no different from anyone else in this regard. Being expert in one area of the mind is perfectly compatible with being very inexpert in others: delving deeply into just one research domain cannot provide an overall understanding of the mind as a whole. The book, once read from cover to cover, should provide the reader with one particular way of viewing both the whole and the parts that make up the whole.

The mind is presented as a network of interacting systems. Each of them is, in varying degrees, independent of the others but at the same time all of them are capable of collaborating with others to solve complex tasks. The various ways in which the framework draws on the research literature are detailed in Sharwood Smith and Truscott (2014). A large number of publications that focus on particular aspects of the framework described in this book have already appeared.[1]

---

[1] See the bibliography at http://www.mogulframework.com.

There are two important aspects of the big picture to be sketched out. In one sense, the mind is seen as being composed of specialised systems each of which has a unique set of tasks to perform independently of other systems. In other words, it has a *modular* architecture. As just mentioned, the different parts of the mind, the 'modules', are still interconnected in that they can collaborate with one another in various ways; in this way, they can therefore be seen as forming a whole, an integrated 'family' of systems. This makes the mind similar to the physical brain which supports the mind even though a corresponding map of the central nervous system might itself look very different, more complex. In the map of the mind being built up in the course of this book, a system like, for example, the visual system, is constructed out of a few basic parts whereas displaying the visual system in the eyes and brain would present readers with a much more complex network of pathways and locations stretching from the light-sensitive receptors in the eye via the optic nerve through to the five areas that make up the visual cortex.

Modularity, that is to say splitting up a complete system into largely independent subsystems certainly has its negative side when applied to the way in which academia is split up into separate research fields. While it makes sense to concentrate exclusively on a given class of phenomena and develop special methodological and technical tools for doing so, a less desirable side-effect of this specialisation is the appearance of large fences separating one area from others, areas that could be quite closely related and have a significant contribution to make to their neighbours but which are hampered by conceptualisations and terminology that are difficult to understand by anyone outside any one of the research areas concerned. The natural conclusion is that, where there are fences, they need to be breached for useful interdisciplinary research to take place. The study of *brain* and the study of *mind* provide a good example of this. Even though many accept that, in principle, they must be related, they can often be treated in practice as though they are quite unrelated. In that light, it therefore seems acceptable to study one without taking much or any account of the other. In the same way, and especially where language is concerned, the study of brief millisecond-by-millisecond moments of mental processing is seen as quite separate from accounts of cognition that deal with longer-term, relatively stable knowledge in the abstract, divorced from time and space. Again, for a coherent picture of how one is related to the other to emerge, researchers on both sides need to be sufficiently interested in each other's field to become familiar with the basic concepts and terminology that each side uses.

Ever increasing specialisation has certainly encouraged the further compartmentalisation of research fields. It is easier to study one type of phenomenon in isolation and delay any integration of research across disciplines until some later date. This 'separate development' strategy might make a lot of sense, especially with fields of research that are relatively new but there is a growing sense nowadays across many disciplines that there have to be limits. The natural sciences have long since abandoned this single-minded approach: interdisciplinary work is now very much the norm as a survey of Nobel Prize winners will confirm. Notable examples include Crick and Watson, a physicist and a biologist sharing the Nobel Prize in Medicine with Wilkins, both a biologist and a physicist, and two biologists, Lefkowitz and Kobika, winning in the chemistry category in 2012 after which Michael Levitt, also a biologist won the same prize the following year. Happily, in 'cognitive science', a label already designating an interdisciplinary group of disciplines, the collaborative approach to framing and exploring research questions is now on the increase. This short introductory book will not, therefore, have to break new ground; it will, however, aim to contribute a little to this wider context approach by providing a coherent and integrated view of mind and language. It is best read in advance of any book going into the fine detail of one or other of the areas covered.

Language as a Biological and Psychological Phenomenon

Even though this book ultimately places language centre stage, it is, as already suggested, about much more than that. A quick look at the table of contents will show you that language only comes into focus in Part II. Language is a vital part of any respectable account of the way we see the world through our mind's eye. From both a biological and a psychological point of view, facts and theories about language need to be understood within this wider perspective. Language grows in each human being from a very early age and is deeply involved in much of human behaviour.

The World 'Outside' versus the World 'Inside'

Although it is easy to talk about the world 'outside' us, the focus in this account will not be on the *physical* environment in which we exist. The outside world includes not only the immediate environment, everything we see and hear but also, more generally, the social world we move in with all the people with whom we interact. That world constitutes the *outer context* that we take for granted, a fascinating object of study in its own right but not the main topic of this book. Rather, what will be discussed in the following chapters is focussed on the world inside our heads where all these things we experience are interpreted, represented and stored. This is the *inner context*, the individually constructed world *inside*. The second chapter on perception will already make clear how important this inner context really is.

This unique, individual reconstruction of the external environment is, effectively, the actual world that we inhabit and experience, both consciously and subconsciously. We continue to experience it as an 'objective' world outside us largely unaware for most of the time that it is actually an inner reconstruction that depends on the resources we have, as individuals and as a species, to achieve it. The reconstruction will differ from one individual to another: it certainly differs dramatically from the experienced environments of other species living together with us in the same outside world. You can appreciate this difference a little better if you have seen simulations of what, for example, a cat sees both in the dark and in broad daylight compared to what we see.[2] This example shows us how even basic visual perception of what lies in front of and around us can differ when the eyes and associated visual brain areas are differently constructed and differently interconnected. The full picture of how the cat's brain makes sense of the same immediate environment we inhabit we can only guess at although it is already clear that the same external world that we share with the cat is a very different inner world by virtue of the different ways in which cats and humans reconstruct it. Even where only vision is taken into account, our reconstructed version of the outside world and that of the cat is consequently quite different and it is even more the case when we add the effect of other senses like smell and hearing.

The Role of Language

The whole of Part I will be devoted to the inner world in its widest sense. That said, anyone setting out to describe and explain the architecture of the human mind in a truly representative way cannot fail to ascribe a major role for human language ability. This becomes the theme of the second part of the book and so adding language will complete our map of the mind. The grand entrance of language in our Act II is particularly appropriate precisely because language ability is a key factor in defining us as members of the *human* species.

The 'Framework'

It might have been enough, in an account of the mind, to list and discuss in turn the different aspects of mental life. That in itself might contribute to some sort of big picture. However, some way of integrating the topics is required. The chapters that make up Part I, will indeed provide the reader with a picture of different mental systems but they will also describe how these systems interact as we cope with daily life on a millisecond-by-millisecond basis. This involves dealing with current tasks as well as planning for the future and reflecting on the past.

With each successive chapter, then, an integrated picture of the mind will gradually be built up. The account will be based on much current thinking in modern cognitive science. In other words, even though the framework itself has something special to offer, it is not a completely new model of the mind: much

---

[2] See http://www.livescience.com/40459-what-do-cats-see.html.

of what it is based on is the result of theories, hypotheses and empirical findings reported in the scientific literature. The framework also leaves open much detail to be filled in by people working in different research fields in ways they see fit. The main intended contribution is to draw separate strands of research into one integrated perspective. This is to be achieved by using the *Modular Online Growth and Use of Language* framework, otherwise known as the MOGUL framework (Truscott & Sharwood Smith 2004; Sharwood Smith & Truscott 2014). What will henceforth generally be referred to as 'the framework', does reflect a set of established views selected from various fields of research but it is impossible to be completely uncontroversial: there are naturally alternative views on the mind in general and about the different aspects of it, including those concerned directly with language.

Mind and Brain Contrasted and Compared

This book might well have been described as being about the brain. We could, of course, ask many questions about the mind and its relationship with the physical brain, both philosophical and ideological. These are topics for another book but using the framework, given the present assumption that brain and mind are indeed interrelated, should certainly prompt some interesting questions about the nature of their interaction. In any case, for the purposes of this discussion, we will be treating the brain, as opposed to mind, as a physical entity, three pounds of incredibly complex matter situated in the head and, together with the spinal cord, making up the central nervous system. We are only at the very beginning of understanding and making claims about the intricacies of the human brain and, making similar assumptions about progress in making sense of the human mind, we must approach the task with appropriate humility. At the same time, advances in understanding the brain can prompt interesting and useful questions for those who focus on how the mind is organised. The reverse is also true. This means it is important for researchers working on both sides of this particular fence to keep a weather eye on how research in the other field is developing to spot useful ways of improving and enriching their own accounts.

Two Levels of Description

Talking about the mind is talking at a different, abstract level of description. The functional map or 'architecture' of the mind does not give you the anatomical and physiological make-up of the brain. Both have to do with the systems that control our mental and physical activities. Although much emphasis in this book will be placed on the *knowledge* aspect of cognition, it will also include a description of what plays a crucial role in the *formation and implementation of knowledge*, namely

a.   our perceptual systems that process the sensory signals from the outside world and from our own bodies (Chapter 2);
b.   our articulatory systems (Chapter 3);
c.   our affective system that assigns positive or negative values and forms the basis of our conscious and subconscious emotional lives (Chapter 5).

There will be reference to brain systems throughout the discussion in the chapters that follow. This makes it especially important to keep firmly in mind the two distinct levels at which all these systems can be described and accounted for, in other words the neural (brain) level and the psychological (mind) level. There is an important proviso to this separation, however which will be mentioned later.

Some people take a popular analogy from the world of computers, calling the mind the 'software' that runs the hardware (the brain) but you might wish to see it the other way round, as the brain running the mind. Either way, the intimate connection between the two is hard to deny. The map of the New York subway serves as a guide to explain the difference in very simple terms. If we consider the actual, physical rail network as it twists and turns through the city and the myriad physical details that the passengers and staff encounter and deal with at first hand, only a very few aspects are represented in the map. What is more, these are shown on the map in a simplified, stylised manner. What the map does is show you the basic connections and how the whole system hangs together in a manner that makes it useful to the general public who are not all interested in cables, signalling systems, tunnel dimensions and the like. It is not an analogy that you can take very far but it gives some sense of the distinction between the two very different ways of thinking about the subway. You might argue that the map could better be compared to a very simplified representation of the brain, one that ignores physical shapes, pathways and relative sizes but still shows the basic parts and the way they function as a complete system. This map would be used differently, as a guide to the internal functions of the physical brain. In this sense, the 'mind' framework used in this book could be thought of as a working model of brain function but at a very abstract level and with explanations of human behaviour as its focus of interest (see Figure I.1).

We should keep the two descriptive levels of *brain* and *mind* distinct even though they are essentially two sides of the same coin.

A final point to be made in this context is that the mind/brain distinction should be seen as a matter of convenience. The distinction explained and illustrated thus far should not be taken as an adoption of radical *dualism* which assumes a disconnect between brain and mind (see Chomsky 2000, 75–105). Ultimately we are talking here about not two but *one* entity, seen and studied from two different perspectives, in other words two sides of the same coin. A fitting label for the approach adopted here might be *neuropsychology* except that people working in this field of research appear to stay very close to the physical brain level and

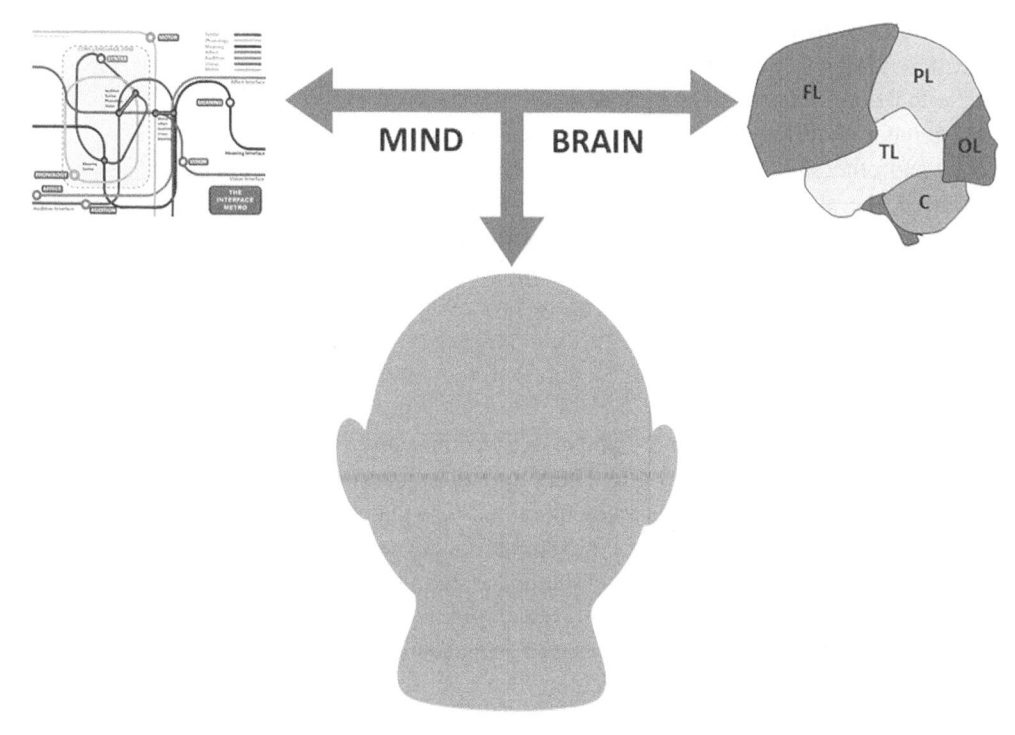

Figure I.1 *Mind and brain: the subway analogy.*

proceed from there to psychological function. It also tends to be clinical and experimental rather than theoretical in orientation.[3]

Note also that the mind taken as a whole is not to be identified as the conscious 'us', that, as it were, lives in the physical body that 'we' inhabit. In fact, very little in the mind, as will be shown later, is actually identifiable as what we might call the conscious 'us'. Most mental activity goes on behind the scenes and we are not and *cannot* become aware of it. The explanation of what actually is 'us' is a fascinating area which goes beyond the scope of this book. The framework adopted here, however, does provide one way of exploring the notion of self.

Mind and Brain Together

The problem, and importance of creating explicit links between these two distinct levels of description, brain and mind is what David Poeppel calls the 'mapping problem'. Mind and brain functions are indeed related but one

---

[3] A similar limitation holds for the field called *psycholinguistics*, which could refer to much more than it actually does. The narrower definition of both these research fields does not imply a lack of interest in theory but simply the chosen preferences of most researchers currently studying within them.

thing is certain: there is seldom any one-to-one relationship. When we talk about the visual system at the abstract level, for example, we can picture it in a single location. However if we ask where this is handled in the brain we will find a number of different interconnected locations are involved including the primary and other areas of the visual cortex located in the rear and lower parts of the head, the photoreceptors in the eyes, the thalamus, the optic nerves and various connections to other parts of the brain handling for example head and eye movement and the pupils' responses to light and Circadian rhythms. It is a similar story with the auditory system in the brain which connects up the ears, and particularly the receptors in them via the cochlear nerve to the auditory cortex in the temporal lobe crossing various locations en route including the brain stem and the thalamus.

One psychological system may involve activity in many physical locations in the brain. The opposite is also true. One physical system occupying just one location in the brain may also have many functions. The thalamus and its various parts located in the midbrain is a good example having several different major functions one of which is to act as a relay station for signals coming from different sources and going to different locations, visual and auditory signals providing two examples of this. In other words the brain's visual and auditory systems will each look more like subway systems in their own right with numerous pathways and waypoints.

The way in which the framework attempts to throw light on the workings of the mind should gradually become clearer in the successive chapters of this book. However, a few basic concepts need to be taken care of up front. Let us first begin with the notion 'representation'.

What Is a Representation?

In Victorian times, there was a belief that the eyes of murder victims might contain the image, imprinted and retained on the retinas, of the last person they had seen. This would provide vital, scientific evidence in a criminal investigation. As absurd as this idea now sounds, we still have to account for how the memory of a face, or anything else we encounter, can stay with us, seconds, hours, months even years after we encountered it. Logically these visual events must be stored, if not in our eyeballs, then somewhere in our minds as memories of some kind. The same goes for anything else we perceive using any of our various senses.

At a more abstract level, the question arises as regards the status of abstract thoughts and ideas, that is to say, things we have not directly perceived in the way we experience an image, a sound, a smell or a pain. Thoughts and ideas, constructed as they are during our lifetime, go to make up our accumulated knowledge of, and beliefs about the outside world. These too, must be 'represented' somewhere in our inside world so that we can use them on repeated occasions to make sense of what we experience whether awake or when dreaming. And there must be systems in our minds (and brains) that take care of all this complicated representing.

To take examples from perception, representations that result from things we perceive in the outside world are not literal copies, in the sense of the murderer's image retained in the eye of the victim, but perhaps more like files on a computer. You might say that a sound memory is a kind of mental MP3 file created in response to perceptual input from the environment, that is, signals registering on hair cells on the basilar membrane (in the inner ear). The same goes for a visual memory resulting from signals coming from photoreceptor cells on the retina (in the eye). The visual memory created this way is like a mental JPG file. These memories, which can be seen as the *output* of perceptual processing, followed by perceptual *input* of one kind or other, are stored and used again and again in interpreting instances of the same or similar input.

How these memory 'files', as we have called then, are realised physically in the brain as ensembles of neurons in different locations need not detain us here. Suffice it to say that they are not structured so as to mimic literally the sound or image they are representing. The memory files would not themselves provide evidence for a murder investigation, except in the world of science fiction. They are not completely reliable even when 'run' in order for us to experience consciously the given sights or sounds concerned and then verbally report them to an investigator. The running of the file, to stay with this computing metaphor, and the resulting conscious experience of the sound or object in question may be triggered by a stimulus from the outside environment: this is how you recognise an apple. Alternatively, it may also be invoked in the course of reflection, imagining or dreaming. So, in other words, I can recognise an apple on encountering an example of one in the environment or I can draw on my auditory or visual memory to re-create it in a deliberate act of imagining or, often much more convincingly, in a dream.

Representations and Equivalent Terms

The individual stores in the various modules contain items that, in this framework, are referred to in the most neutral way as 'structures'.[4] Very often the term 'representation' may also be used.[5] A visual structure is the mind's way of representing something visual. A conceptual structure is the mind's way of representing a particular meaning and so on. These abstract structures may be

---

[4] The framework reflects Ray Jackendoff's clear preference as regards the most appropriate and least misleading term for what are elsewhere called representations although the latter term is also used in this book as well (Jackendoff 2002, 20,199).
[5] In the case of motor structures (MoS) that determine how parts of the body behave, retaining the generic term 'structures' rather than calling them 'representations' might seem to some less confusing.

contrasted with the equivalent physical structures in the brain which can look very different. We can conclude from the preceding discussion that a mental representation is a structure that is encoded in a particular way peculiar to the store it inhabits. It will be implemented one way or another in the brain, involving various neural locations and pathways. A representation is also something that can be more or less available for processing at any given moment and it can become so inaccessible that we treat it as lost, in other words as completely forgotten. Whether memories can actually undergo complete extinction or not in the normal course of affairs is a separate matter.

As just indicated, the default term, namely *structure*, to be used in the book for an item in a store is the most theoretically neutral one. Sometimes a particular focus of interest will suggest the use of another equivalent term. For example, if you are thinking in mental processing terms, structures can be referred to as a *memory*, one which can be constructed and stored somewhere and duly retrieved during on-line performance to accomplish some task. On the other hand, if you are not interested in processing and are thinking purely in terms of more or less stable systems of knowledge whose properties you wish to describe and explain, as a descriptive or theoretical linguist would, you may prefer to use the term *representation*.

If you are interested in the neural correlates of structures, you will be talking about particular configurations of neurons in the brain and require more detailed terminology to do so. For example, Damasio's 'dispositional representation', which is expressed in terms of *brain* structure, meshes easily with the notion of a *mental* representation, otherwise called a structure in this book. A dispositional representation, according to Damasio is a potential pattern of neuron activity in *small ensembles of neurons* and it may be distributed over a number of different locations in the cortex, the precise locations depending on the type of representation and whether it is innate or acquired as a result of experience (Damasio 1994, 102–105). This reflects what was said earlier, namely that there is usually either a one-to-many or a many-to-one relationship between something in the brain and its equivalent in the mind. It should help, when talking in the abstract about the various mental structures to be discussed in this book, to keep in mind this very physical, neural version of a representation. This helps to get a feel of the kind of connections mind and brain may have. Both the more neutral term 'structure' and the term 'representation' (as in 'auditory' or 'visual' representation) will be used in this book to mean the same thing, that is something that is stored in memory, activated and manipulated and subject to growth or decline over time.

Knowledge as a Relative Concept

In everyday use, the word 'knowledge' refers to things that are 'true' and 'correct'. Someone who does not know their way round the streets of London is understood to lack knowledge and when giving directions to someone else can therefore say things that are 'wrong'. Gaining knowledge means eliminating what is incorrect and so avoiding error. You either know something or you do not. So much for the standard everyday understanding of the term. However, in this book, knowledge will be treated in a different way, as a relative concept and as a *set of interconnected representations or structures in the mind*. Someone's knowledge of London may not be totally in accordance with what others regard to be the facts but his or her ignorance will still be based on some system of mental representations which will be no different in nature from the system of representations in the minds of, say, a London taxi-drivers for example, who can be said to 'know' their way around the city. Knowledge is based on a particular network of representations that an individual has in his or her possession. These representations exist separate from the world outside on which they were, to some extent, originally based. We can certainly describe one person's knowledge as being not in accordance with facts that many people agree about but it is still knowledge of a kind.

Another example of knowledge in the relative sense would be one taken from language learning. A young child or a second language learner can regularly produce utterances like 'she runned to school' that we might label as 'ungrammatical' or 'incorrect'. The fact that they are regular constructions ('runned' instead of 'ran', 'goed' instead of 'went', etc.) indicates that the individual is operating a system of rules which reflects their current representation of the grammar of the language concerned.[6] If it were not confusing to do so, you could even call the constructions 'correct for that individual at that time'. This is, in a sense, their current 'knowledge' of the language, in other words. It is not wrong: it just happens to be 'nonnative' or different from the grammar of those judged to be, say, native adult speakers.

The attribution of rightness or wrongness to someone's knowledge is the result of a further evaluation process that is applied externally by social groups and usually accepted even by the individual concerned: positive or negative values as established externally are not relevant for the description of knowledge representations themselves, in the sense used here. The only inherent value they can have is their internal value to the user. This will be a topic that is discussed in the chapter on 'affect'. Where an individual comes to accept that something they thought be correct or incorrect according to the general consensus of opinion on the matter is not so, they will certainly re-evaluate it. The type of re-evaluation they then apply will be relevant in the parts of the book that deal with consciousness, e.g. Chapter 13.

The Mind as a Network

One thing that everyone can readily agree on is that the mind is a network of connections. The devil is, as they say, in the detail and the detail

---

[6] This was essentially the view adopted by the researchers in the early years of second language acquisition research and marked a clean break with those working in the area of second/foreign language instruction (Selinker 1972).

begins immediately we start describing what that network should be, what is connected to what and the nature of the connections. This is where the different schools of thought on how the mind is structured differ. Connectionists use the neural network as their chosen analogy for the mind which, in the simplest, 'classical' version of this approach to modelling the mind, consists of a network of simple, uniform units and connections between them. These units are conceived on analogy with the neurons in the brain and the connections on analogy with the synapses that connect them, synapses in fact being gaps across which electrochemical signals are passed between neurons in the brain. This approach differs from the one adopted in this book in that it does away with the need for rules and symbols in explaining how the mind works.

Although there are many forms of connectionism used to model mental activity, anything like this classical version is nothing like the map of the mind described in this book where, as we shall see, the nature of connections and the nature of the units to be connected exhibit great variety. It should be added that neural networks as used in artificial intelligence were biologically inspired but not intended to accurately represent the way neural pathways behave. The framework used in this book does represent the mind as a network but not as a single uniform system but as a *system of systems*, that is one composed of various experts specialising in one particular type of task. Each expert system has its own code so one would expect at the neural level to see distinctions between the encoding of, for example, visual signals and various different ways of encoding elsewhere, in other systems. This means that information built up within the different parts of the 'system of systems' is the product of *multiple encoding*.[7] Put another way, neither in the network that makes up the mind nor the network in the physical brain is knowledge written in one uniform code.

In sum, what characterises the present framework is the existence of various interconnected but in many ways independent *expert systems*, each of which has a specific function and uses its own unique code. In other words each carries out a specific set of tasks that no other expert system can perform. This is like different systems in the brain or like the other organs of the body with the liver, for example, performing different functions in a different manner than the kidneys. Mental networks are thus comparable to networks of neurons in exhibiting this functional specialisation.

Presenting the mind as a network of expert systems reveals one key characteristic of the framework used in this book and that is *modularity*. Just as there are different versions of the connectionist approach to the mind, so too there are different versions of modularity but the basic idea is that the mind is composed of various specialised 'modules' which collaborate in many different ways to

---

[7] This extends and redefines Paivio's dual coding theory which asserted that information was stored in both linguistic (verbal) code and in imagery (non-verbal code). In this case the imagery code is different depending on which perceptual system is involved (vision, sound smell, etc.) (Paivio 1986). Also, as will be discussed in Part II, the equivalent of Paivio's verbal code is split into multiple codes including two that are unique to language.

manage all the complex tasks it is faced with. These systems have their own unique set of operating principles but, as will be shown in more detail later, cooperate via the set of *interfaces* that link them together.

Alternative Views and Close Relatives

Since the mental architecture employed in this book provides a fairly open-ended model of the mind, a framework which can be engineered in different ways, rather than a fixed theory, it is difficult to compare it straightforwardly to anything except another framework with a similar type of scope. It has been devised using, and integrating many different theories and hypotheses concerning language in the mind, and indeed the mind in general. It is interesting, nevertheless, to briefly consider some other approaches which have varying degrees of compatibility with the approach set out in this book. In a way, each individual approach contributes insights about how the mind appears to work and is reflected in different aspects of the MOGUL framework.

Biolinguistics

Biolinguistics is an interdisciplinary area viewing language as part of the study of human biology (Chomsky 2004; Jackendoff 2011). Although its definition does not require adherence to the tenets of the most recent Chomskyan perspective on language,[8] at the moment many of the researchers who regard themselves as biolinguists do happen to adopt it when studying language, its acquisition and its evolution. There is good reason to suppose, however, that the framework is quite compatible with the biolinguistic enterprise as are Jackendoff's views on the language faculty which have influenced the design of the framework. In fact, one major advantage of the Jackendoff approach is to facilitate an approach where representational issues and processing issues can be easily discussed within a common framework. An orthodox Chomskyan approach as currently implemented views language from a strictly representational angle, studying abstract properties of grammar in isolation from the way they are deployed in real time. The abstract level of description and explanation in theoretical linguistics has its own distinct advantages but it is not legitimate, without making entirely new claims, to interpret the formal abstract concepts used in generative linguistic research as if they refer to millisecond-by-millisecond processes taking place in real time. This cautionary note is important since metaphors of space and time as exemplified by terms such as merge, movement and checking are part and parcel of the minimalist terminological repertoire. Finally, what the

---

[8] This is the Minimalist Program (Chomsky 1995). The details need not concern us here but, very briefly, it retains the essential claim that we are born with an innate capacity for language and seeks to encourage detailed studies of this capacity that are characterised by, as the name suggests, by great economy and simplicity and to a much greater degree than previous versions of his theory.

nature of the human language faculty might be and indeed whether it even exists is still a matter of lively controversy. This will not be debated in this book and the basic assumption will be that the map of the mind being sketched out here must reserve a special place for human linguistic ability.

Competition

Competition is a notion often employed in description of mental activity taking place in real time. It is sometimes associated with highly *non*modular processing theories also described as *connectionist*. These approaches hypothesise an unrestricted flow of information across an uncompartmentalised mind. Aimed at explaining language acquisition, MacWhinney's *Competition Model* (as developed with Elizabeth Bates) is an example of this (Bates & MacWhinney 1982). The framework in this book, however, is highly modular despite the fact that competition is a crucial notion in the way in which mental activity is explained. Information flow is not free. There are interfaces that control the limited interaction between different systems. Consequently, the treatment of which items compete with which other ones is constrained by each particular module and its unique properties. This means that, say, in the module that handles meaning (the conceptual system), conceptual representations will only compete with other conceptual representations in conceptual working memory: they will never have to compete with representations outside that conceptual system, even those with which they are associated. Only structures written in the same code compete with one another. The details concerning this type of competition should become clear in Part I of this book.

Connectionism

Connectionism has been referred to already. The most widely held interpretation seems to be what is in fact a radical connectionism of the sort pioneered by McClelland and Rumelhart (Rumelhart et al. 1986). This does away with symbolic representations and assumes unrestricted information flow within a system the properties of which are supposed to mimic those of (biological) neural networks. This means there are no units called 'representations' like 'hospital' or 'verb' that get handled in the course of mental processing. These are just convenient ways for us to describe and think about processing patterns but no more than that. Viewed from the perspective adopted in this book, this strictly nonmodular approach is neither what brain research suggests nor is it how psychological function can be best explained. In radical connectionism, however, neural networks are composed of simple units. Each unit has a particular activation potential. When a unit is activated it triggers activation in units that are connected to it within the network. This interactive process is called *spreading activation*. Learning amounts to changes in the system which can be accounted for by changes in activation patterns or connection strength and without recourse to symbolic representations. Later on in the following chapters the notion of spreading activation will be used but in a very different way than the one just described.

To the extent that the mind in the current framework is also based on networks and key notions such as 'competition' and 'spreading activation' it can be called 'connectionist' but certainly not in the most widely understood, radical sense described earlier. This is firstly because, unlike radical connectionist approaches, we will be dealing with *symbolic* representations as an integral feature of how the mind is organised. This is opposed to radical approaches where 'representation' is just a convenient description of clusters of elements, each of which have no intrinsic meaning and have come about to be connected to others elements without any meaning being involved as a guiding principle.

Secondly, as already mentioned, the present framework is *modular*. The interfaces linking the individual modular systems influence the way in which representations compete with one another and the way in which the activation of representations in one system is allowed to spread and trigger activation in representations elsewhere in the network. Interfaces thus facilitate cooperation between modules but do not have the effect of letting structural information flow from one to the other. This is impossible simply because structures and the organising principles within one module make structures in different modules *incompatible* with one another. Also, structures in one module cannot be transformed to make them compatible with structures elsewhere. Interfaces link structures together in chains and networks but do not translate them into a common code. Again, the details of all this will become clear in the following chapters. The best that can be said with regard to connectionism is that the framework incorporates connectionist insights, but interprets them within a modular perspective.

Emergentism

Emergentism is a term that describes the development of complex systems. New patterns emerge from old ones. The type of connectionism just referred to is a type of emergentism. These new patterns are different from the patterns from which they have emerged. The process also results in a greater number of patterns in total. At first glance, this might seem an appropriate characterisation of growth in the current framework. Could it therefore be called, in any sense, 'emergentist'? Just as there are different kinds of connectionism, there are also different kinds of emergentism. Closest of all, especially where language is concerned is the type of emergentism proposed by William O'Grady although O'Grady's approach to language is in the last analysis quite different in that he sees the principles according which language systems are constructed in the mind as entirely the same as those any other kind of cognitive system (O'Grady 2005).

Dynamic(al) Systems Theory

Dynamic(al) Systems Theory is another approach which has been applied to all sorts of problems including growth in the mind. It has been eagerly embraced in some quarters of second language acquisition and applied linguistic communities (de Bot et al. 2007). This approach emphasises the continually changing nature of the mind as everything interacts. This is in contrast to the apparently static, compartmentalised picture painted by those adopting some version of the modular mind. It is emergentist in the sense that the mind is a self-organising system in constant flux albeit with areas of relative stability. At some level, the current framework certainly has features that relate to this approach. Performance when viewed as a whole, driven as it is by the different systems within the mind interacting with each other, will inevitably have a shifting, dynamic character as indeed will growth over time. However, dynamic systems theory still seems to have difficulty explaining convincingly the fact that different mental systems obey discernible, stable principles that work for everybody and which have been described in various ways and in great detail by researchers in psychology, biology, linguistics and psychology.

To sum up, all these alternative views of the mind contain insights that are useful for building up a picture of how the mind operates but none of them offer a satisfactory account by themselves.

What Is Special about Language?

Thanks to the popular science books of Steven Pinker such as *The Language Instinct*, the Chomskyan idea that humans have from birth a special ability to acquire language has become widely known (see also e.g. Cook & Newson 2007; Maher & Groves 2007). At the same time, popular misconceptions and oversimplifications have inevitably grown up around what these claims really amount to. The framework adopted in this book supports the idea that the grammatical underpinning of any human language arises through an interaction between exposure to the language and

1. linguistic principles *not* shared by other species and which form part of our biological endowment;
2. general principles that *are* shared by other species and which also form part of our biological endowment.

For the mind to work out the way to construct and interpret grammatical utterances in a specific language, it has to be exposed to samples of the language concerned. Many features of these samples that are crucial for working out the grammar of the language are not grammatical themselves. Obvious ones include many features of the situational context which will help the listener to work out or guess the intended meaning of the utterance as whole. Understanding the meaning of at least some of the individual words involved in the utterance is also required. Learning the meaning of words also involves general principles that are not really specific to humans. Which words and which parts of words actually belong to what we think of as a 'grammatical system' and which do not has to be defined by our preferred linguistic theory. Most people, however, would accept that in 'John washed them', the pronoun 'them' is a part of the grammatical system so learning how pronouns work *does* require linguistic principles whereas the word, 'John' and, to some extent, 'washed' do not: their meaning can be learnt independently in the same way you learn what a bucket is and what it is for. In other words general learning principles are invoked. However, the 'ed' ending in 'wash*ed*', marking past tense, like the pronoun 'them', is part of the grammatical system and in order for people, especially very young children, to work out how they work along with a whole raft of linguistic elements, general principles of learning will simply not do: so goes the explanation in this framework and theories it is based on.

Finally, it should be noted that, in this book, the expert systems that handle grammar – this includes the way languages organise speech sounds – differ from the standard Chomskyan account. Rather, they follow lines suggested by one of Chomsky's most prominent students, Ray Jackendoff. Again, for those who prefer some version of the standard account, the map outlined in this book could, in principle, be adapted. Some argumentation would be required to justify the change and account in detail and in a processing explanation for how the reconfigured language module would then interact with the other systems that make up the mind.

The more important point to be made here is not so much which approach is 'right' but rather that the framework is to some extent open-ended and adaptable: many parts of it can be individually elaborated in different ways following different theoretical accounts. For the moment, a basic assumption is, that certain aspects of language are uniquely human and other aspects may differ in character and complexity from behaviour exhibited by other species but are the product of systems that are shared, in other words, are not uniquely human. Concerted attempts to teach language to great apes, chimpanzees like Washoe and Nim Chimpsky, and especially the highly talented bonobo, Kanzi, seem to bear this out although there is disagreement about how near they really got to human language ability (Savage-Rumbaugh & Lewin 1996).

Summary

The various chapters in this book will develop a view of the mind that is based on an integration of research findings across a number of disciplines. As such it should provide the reader with a general overview. At the same time, the framework to be used places special emphasis on what makes us, to use a term sometimes used to describe our species, *homo loquens*, in other words on *human language ability*. Also, since an estimated half the world's population regularly use more than one language, no privileged position is accorded here to the monolingual native speaker. In other words the characterisation of human language ability will be about the development and use of language*s*, in the plural. Part I of the book deals with the mind as a whole, Part II will focus on language.

Part I Mechanisms of the Mind

Part I deals with the basic components of the mind that are, albeit in very different ways, shared with other species. Topics will include, for instance, perceptual systems, the emotions, concepts and conscious awareness. How language fits in to all this is covered in Part II.

It is important to remember that the main focus of the framework is on processing: it is about the way that we store and use mental structures or 'representations' in real time. This means working with stretches of time that are measured in milliseconds but also, when structural change is the issue, with much longer units of time that that. The nature of the mental structures themselves is also an integral part of the story of what their properties are and how they come to be the way they are. In this book only linguistic properties will be looked at in any detail at all but even there, since this is a theoretical framework and not a fully fledged theory, much is still left for the relevant specialists to argue about and elaborate on.

To sum up, the whole idea is, then, not to focus exclusively either on knowledge structures *in abstracto*, setting aside any real-time processing considerations, nor is it to do the reverse of that, i.e. taking the abstract properties defined in some sister discipline as a given and only focus on how they are processed in real time. In other words the framework, whatever its limitations, offers a combined, *integrated* perspective in which both dimensions, knowledge and the use of knowledge, can be studied.

1   The Basic Design

In This Chapter

This chapter introduces some basic features of the framework to be used in the book. The term 'design' should be understood as a metaphor without any implication that there was a 'designer', unless nature can be given that role. As was mentioned in the introduction to the book, the framework represents an integration of theory and experimental findings taken from various different areas of cognitive science. Even those who do not fully subscribe to the underlying principles behind this design should find some value in seeing the mind connected up in an explicit manner that can be talked and argued about. As already indicated in the introduction, the mind is a *network* of collaborating 'expert systems': it is *modular*.

What are the advantages of modularity? The mind is much more efficient by virtue of the fact that these expert systems, in dealing with a complex problem, can work independently on one type of task alone while, at the same time, other expert systems are working on other tasks. This way is better, faster therefore beneficial not only in trivial ways but also for our survival. It is an optimal way of dealing with all that life throws at us every millisecond that we are alive and given the limitations we are born with. Both complexity and simplicity can be found in the system as a whole. Despite the variety of experts and the flexibility this modularity brings with it, the mind does have characteristics than could be called 'simple': all the modules have a basic design in common.

The Module or 'Processing Unit'

All the mental modules are unique, having their own exclusive area of expertise. They are also different in the ways in which they are instantiated, physically, in the brain. However, as modular 'processing units', they are all composed of

a. a store;
b. a processor.

The Store

The store is where a module's *structures* are housed. Structures were briefly discussed in the introduction to this chapter. In some contexts it is useful to think of them as individual memories, in other contexts as representations. 'Structure' is the neutral term. The precise nature of the contents of the stores will be explained shortly. The module's processor is what manipulates the structures in its particular store, activating ones that are already there or creating new ones. The principles that the processor works with to do this are not shared with other modules. They are unique as is the way in which the structures are built up and they work with a unique 'code'. This means in effect that a structure in one store is written in a code that cannot be handled by any other processor except its own.

Modules and Brain Locations

The framework, being about the mind, presents a simpler picture than the architecture of the brain. The basic *processor + store* unit is always subserved by a variety of brain systems in different locations. Unlike the mental module, the various equivalent systems in the brain can look very different from one another in the way they are organised. Take perceptual systems for example, and specifically, let us look more closely at the *auditory system* that processes sound.

Auditory structures – let's call them auditory memories here – reside in the *auditory store* along with basic elements that they are constructed from. The contents of this store may simply be referred to together as *auditory memory*. This is where the results of auditory experiences are stored after auditory processing has taken place. The *auditory processor* that does this job works exclusively with items in that memory store and has no access to anything else. This then is the mind's auditory system.

The *physical* system that supports this particular mental system and is often called by the same name, i.e. the *brain's* auditory system, comprises the peripheral areas, i.e. the *inner, middle and outer ear* and the pathways and connections spreading through the brain via the *midbrain* and the auditory division of the thalamus ending up with the *primary and secondary auditory cortex* in the *temporal lobe* on the side of the brain and also areas of the *frontal cortex*. A figure illustrating this physical support system would look much more complicated than its psychological counterpart which is structured according to the basic design as displayed in Figure 1.1.

The details of the brain areas associated with other mental modules will not be systematically listed and discussed in this book. However, the story will always be the same although the pathways and subsystems will look very different: the primary visual cortex (V1), for example, one component of the brain's visual system is an area in the occipital lobe at the back of the brain. Both auditory and visual pathways do include the thalamus but still different areas of the thalamus. These

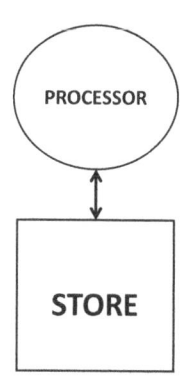

Figure 1.1 *A module or 'processing unit'.*

two examples are provided here simply to underline the differences between the *mind* and *brain* levels of description. If, by the time we get to Chapter 5, our map of the mind begins to look complicated, keep in mind the fact that the brain would require a very much more complex and detailed description. The distinction between these different levels was discussed briefly in the introduction to this chapter using the example of a subway network.

Processing Input

Our human ears respond to what they are capable of responding to – hearing ability can differ radically between individuals and across species – but the flow of perceived acoustic signals from the environment, i.e. what will become *input* into the auditory system, works in a similar way. The initial processing of acoustic input originating in patterns of sound waves triggers activity in the auditory module. The specific task for that module is then to interpret these signals. But 'interpretation' here is used in very specific sense: auditory 'interpretation' is an early stage in the process of making sense of the patterns of sound waves that have been picked up by the receptors in the ear. It does not yet involve conceptual interpretation, that is, assigning *meaning* to what you hear. At this earlier stage, it involves activating up existing structures, auditory memories, that are in its auditory store. It is as though the auditory module says to itself "here's an acoustic pattern relayed from the ears: let's see if I have something in my store that matches it". Alternatively, if it does not have anything to match it, that is, if the acoustic patterns in the input are unfamiliar, i.e. there is nothing available in the store that matches what is coming in, another type of activity is triggered to remedy the situation: the auditory processor uses its inbuilt expertise to try to build new structures on the spot to match or 'represent' the patterns of the input. If successful, these new 'structures' – we can also call them 'representations' – remain in the auditory store for future use: they become, for the time being at least, one of the mind's auditory memories. Like all other modules, the auditory module will *automatically* try to respond in these ways to any input that it receives via its interface(s).

Processing involves both activation and manipulation. Nothing happens to an item in a memory store if remains it a resting state: to be involved in processing, items have to be in an *activated* state. In fact, they have to be activated strongly enough for the appropriate processor to be able to manipulate them. Items that are highly activated are said to be in the store's *working memory*. This is the store's processing workspace where activated items can be momentarily combined in various ways and also linked via interfaces to associated items in other memory stores. Working memory will be explained more fully in Chapter 6.

In the next chapter we will deal with perceptual modules, of which the auditory expert system is one, in a little more detail. In Part II of the book, we will look at how raw acoustic input which happens to convey messages in the form of language, i.e. is speech coming from someone talking to you, is eventually processed as speech. One question that will be answered in detail later is whether the auditory system is where speech is processed *as* speech rather than as just another sound like the buzzing of a bee or whether some *separate* expert system needs to be involved to explain the special characteristics of speech sounds that buzzing does not possess.

How Many Experts?

Any modular theory of the mind has to establish *how many* modules are needed to explain human behaviour. A natural preference is to avoid proliferation of modules and limit the number as much as possible, at least as a default strategy until research prompts an increase in their number.

Decisions about the design of mental architecture will certainly be influenced by scientific progress in the various relevant research fields. This is not to say that the identification of a special area of the brain serving a specific function *necessarily* requires an analogous change in the mental architecture, only that it prompts a consideration of the possibility. To take just one example, visual perception is subserved by not one uniform visual system but by a cluster of mental modules running different aspects of visual perception. For instance, to the extent that neuroscientific research has sufficiently confirmed original claims that the *fusiform gyrus* in the *brain* houses, amongst other things, a separate, dedicated system just for face recognition[1] then it might in principle be worth including its counterpart as an additional module in our *mental* architecture (Kanwisher et al. 1997). Such a module would take visual structure as its input and assign 'face' structures to it.

The possibility of distinguishing more mental modules on the basis of neurological evidence that such small independent brain systems do exist would

---

[1] This is called the fusiform face area (FFA), although its function is still a matter of controversy.

certainly be a possibility worth considering but this does not have to be the case.[2] It may simply be the case that face-related structures can simply be treated as one type of visual structure that populate our single visual module (as currently portrayed in this book). The issue of how many modules there are might well be of interest to those who study the development of both mind and brain through the ages where increasing modularity might be treated as a cause or symptom of transition to some more advanced stage of evolution. The framework allows for both options of course and only stipulates that they follow the same basic design. As has been made clear earlier, the relationship between brain function and the framework's functional map of the mind is important but is nonetheless an indirect one. At least for the present purposes we can, where possible, try to be as parsimonious as possible and treat the further proliferation of modules as an unnecessary complication.

The Store's 'Primitives'

The contents of a store deserve further mention at this point. We never begin at zero. In other words, from the very beginning each store will contain a set of structures that are called *primitives*.[3] Think of these primitives as part of the code needed to build structures specific to a given module, for example a special 'programming language' for vision to create visual representations of visual events in the visual world outside. These are the basic elements that were referred to earlier. The organism really needs these to cope with life from the very start.

The primitives are part of what is known as our biological endowment and play a vital role in explaining the characteristic, instinctive behaviour of infants or indeed the young of any species. To put this in the context of the framework, any store, be it motor memory, auditory memory or any other memory store, consists of the primitives that are there from the start and which have evolved to enhance an organism's chance of survival. What happens thereafter may be called learning from experience. This is a process by which new structures in any of the stores are created by combining and recombining the primitives so that the store becomes steadily filled with more and more new memory structures.

---

[2] Some argue for 'massive modularity', which is really an argument against the idea there is a central system plus modular systems existing on the periphery like planets round a sun. However the lack of a non-modular central system that integrates information coming from different sources does not necessarily require an enormous proliferation of *mental* modules. Different positions are taken on this. The details need not detain us here and the simplest most parsimonious, 'non-massive' version that is reasonable will be used in this book (Cosmides & Tooby 1992; Fodor 2000; Carruthers 2006).

[3] An alternative view would be that some, or possibly all, of the primitives are in the processor and placed in the store the first time they are needed. This explanation would also have to account for the preset associations to be mentioned in the next paragraph. One way or the other, each module has its own set of primitives.

The processing of the primitive elements along with any more complex structures that are built using them is carried out according to the unique code (processing language) of that module. It should be noted that our inherited system not only contains the special principles and elements of each expert system but also *preset associations* which bind structural elements in one memory with structural elements in others. In this way we are able to respond 'instinctively' to certain harmful or beneficial things in the environment. For this to happen, we need associations between one or other of the *perceptual* stores on one hand, sensing something happening, and, on the other, the motor system that governs physical responses to those sensations: an example being a baby's 'parachute' reflex triggered when falling forward (see Chapter 6). Even though the body movement experienced by the baby is based on structures in the perceptual system called the somatosensory[4] module and is written in somatosensory code and the *physical* responses reflect structures in the motor system, written in *motor* code, the preconfigured association between the two is what underlies this particular reflex in infants. In other words, our biological inheritance does not only consist of the primitives: some preprogramming, i.e. ready-made combinations of the primitive structures and connections across different stores, is provided in advance as part of the organism's 'survival package'. A slightly misleading but popular way of seeing this is to talk of certain responses being 'hardwired' into us. Both in terms of mental connections, as illustrated here, and in terms of physical connections in the central nervous system, hardwiring does suggest systems that are there from the start and cannot be changed. In reality there is more flexibility involved that this metaphor would suggest.

Interfaces

As mentioned in the first chapter, expert systems serve no purpose at all in isolation. They must link up with other systems in some way so that they are able to collaborate so the mind can accomplish all the many tasks that make up our daily mental and physical activity. Collaboration is achieved through a matching-up process whereby structures (memory units or representations if you will) are linked and form a network of associations activated in a series of working memories (Chapter 6). This collaboration is made possible via *interfaces*.

Interfaces allow items in the stores of the different systems involved to participate in a structural *chain*. In this way, an apple is never processed simply as a visual object but as a constellation of different associated memories, for example taste, feel and smell memories as well as motor memories to do with peeling, cutting and eating apples. Figure 1.2 shows a simple example of just one

---

[4] Now considered one of the traditional five senses, the somatosensory is actually a complex of different ones including touch, sensing pain and temperature and the relative positions of different parts of the body (roughly put, 'body sense').

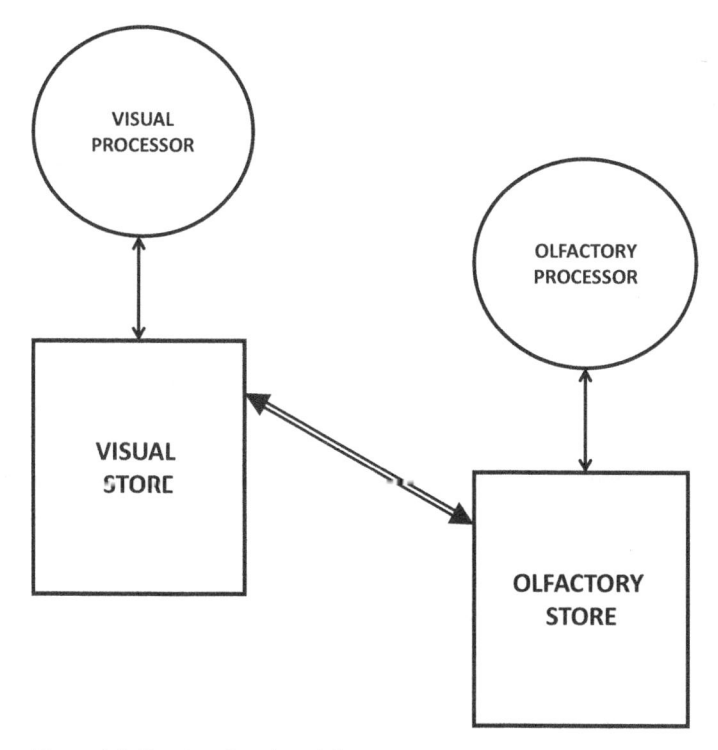

Figure 1.2 *Two interfaced modules.*

interface, in this case the one between olfactory and visual memory stores shown as a double-lined arrow. This particular interface mediates between associated items in the two memory stores and thus permits collaboration between the smell and vision systems.

The way it goes is very roughly as follows: one expert system receives input from the other and tries to come up with an appropriate matching representation from its store. If there is nothing readily available, as would be typically the case in a first encounter with the input in question, the processor will attempt, using the structures it has available, to assemble a new representation.

If you had never encountered an apple before, this is basically what would happen in any module that has been recruited for the purpose of making sense of the experience. New associations are thus formed between structures in different modules. An *index* – a kind of identity tag – is attached to each of the matched structures, marking this chain of associations. Each structure in the chain gets the selfsame identifying tag (index). Once a structure with a given index is activated in one module, the interfaces ensure that structures in any other module with the same index are also *coactivated*. All coactivated structures now form, for a brief moment, a chain in working memory, or to be absolutely precise, a chain linking structures in the working memory of each individual store involved.

In the case of the apple example, using the modules displayed in Figure 1.2, coactivation occurs between coindexed items in the visual and olfactory stores.

Assume that an individual is encountering an apple for the hundredth time, in other words he or she is quite familiar with apples. Say for example that the perception of an apple *smell* without as yet any *visual* identification of an apple has triggered an existing olfactory representation to match that olfactory input. The visual-olfactory interface (depicted in Figure 1.2 by the two-way arrow) would then trigger activity in the visual module bringing about the activation of already established, coindexed visual structures related to the visual appearance of apples.

Whether it goes, as in the preceding example, from apple smell (olfactory memory) to apple image (visual memory) or in reverse from image to smell or indeed when the apple is viewed and smelled *simultaneously*, the result is the same: a chain of representations bridging the two working memories thus: VS ⇔OfS.[5] For a brief moment the two items in quite separate working memories participate in a chain of two thanks to the operation of the interface. In reality, this chain of two structures will lead to the coactivation of not just a chain of two but a whole network of associations, i.e. involving other modules all created as a result of previous encounters with apples. A simple experience of an apple, in other words, is underpinned by a rich and complex set of associations all of them mediated by the operation of collaborating expert systems.

The role of the interface, then, is to allow structures (representations) that in other respects are incompatible with each other to, as it were, join hands and participate for a brief instant in a network of representations. Interfaces do not make the structures they are linking mutually compatible: they just make a straightforward association between some activated structure in one working memory with another activated structure in a different working memory. The way they operate is more like putting a hand into one box and catching hold of something there and putting the other hand into an adjoining box and catching hold of something there. There is no exchange of objects or moving anything from one room to another, only a linking between one object in one room and one object in the other. Only items that are currently in a state of activation can be matched up and temporarily linked together: those that are relatively inactive or not active at all never get linked. Interfaces, if they can be thought of as processors in their own right, are therefore very simple ones.

Summary

This chapter has provided a preliminary sketch of how the modular framework is organised and how it operates, i.e. its basic design. Each mental *module* or 'expert system' is equipped with a *processor* that uses its own unique *code* plus a store containing its structures also referred to as 'representations', 'memory structures' or more simply as 'items' or 'elements' in a store. Temporary

---

[5] Visual structure ⇔ Olfactory structure.

associations normally lasting milliseconds are formed by linking structures in one memory with structures in other stores. Two things happen for such a temporary *chain* to be formed. Firstly, the structures in question must enter a state of *activation*: this places them in the *working memory* of their store. Secondly, there must be an *interface* between the stores in question. The interface brings the two structures into a temporary association with each other. This association is achieved via an *index* system. In other words, while active in working memory, items that share the same tag, i.e. the same index, each participate in a processing chain. Items that have appeared in a store's working memory may then be matched with others in other stores, via the appropriate interfaces, and it is also in working memory that they can be manipulated by the processor that belongs to that same store and combined into larger structures all the time processing is ongoing.

2   Perception

In This Chapter

From now on the map of the mind will be built up from scratch using the basic design outlined in the previous chapter. Chapter 2 begins with the systems that organise our perception.[1] As the framework is gradually elaborated, it should become increasingly obvious how important the perceptual systems are. They process the mass of sensory information that originates both from outside us and from within our bodies. Even though the different senses are handled by different mental modules ('processing units'), the different perceptual systems can also be seen as a tightly knit group with a lot of crosstalk going on amongst its members. Activation levels can typically be very high. The continual efficient operation of this group is absolutely vital for the individual's chances of survival, especially during, but not only in, the waking hours. Also, as is discussed in more detail later, the operation of the perceptual systems as a group lies at the heart of how attention and conscious awareness are explained in the framework.

This chapter does not contain anything like an exhaustive description of the human perceptual systems, but it should be enough to build this particular part of the map. What happens in physical terms, in the environment and in the body, is discussed alongside the description of how the framework handles the psychological aspects of perceptual processing. The illustrations and focus of discussion in this chapter mostly concern the visual and auditory systems, as these are most important for the discussion of language in Part II.

From Sensory Experience to Representation

Imagining an Apple

If I asked you to imagine an everyday object like the apple from our previous example, you would be able to do so without difficulty in situations where there are no apples in your immediate environment. Where does your completely imagined apple come from? It comes from something that has been

---

[1] Part II discusses in detail how perceptual systems are recruited for linguistic purposes.

created by one or more of your perceptual systems and stored in memory. It is there when you are asked to *imagine* an apple, when you *think* or *dream* of apples spontaneously, when you *remember* an apple and also next time you *encounter* another apple. Once you have a representation of an object or scene, perceiving, imagining or remembering it involves activating a visual memory which has been created sometime in the past and is located in your special visual memory store, the store that belongs to your visual module. Together with that visual memory, other related stores will be accessed activating anything that has come to be associated with apples in your mind.

Perception as Transformation

As was illustrated earlier, recognising a particular apple, one that you are currently looking at, results from matching up the visual patterns projected from the apple onto your retinas with something in your visual memory. This is not a straightforward process. Now looking at it in more detail in neural terms, the way the receptors in the retina of each eye register these light wave patterns results in a *new* set of patterns. This receptor information or 'code' is passed on down the optic nerves and processed again in your visual system. This is called *transduction*, a term applied to any of the types of sensory encoding, not only what happens with visual input. In the terms of the framework, in the final processing stage in visual perception, a particular structure or combination of structures is activated in the visual store. This structure is the visual representation of the apple, written in the special visual code of the visual system. The original 'raw' visual input, in the form of electromagnetic radiation, coming from the immediate environment is quite different from the end result of processing – in terms of the framework and in neural terms as well, the process of transformation goes through two major stages thus:

> LIGHT WAVES → Process 1 in the EYE → Process 2 in the VISUAL SYSTEM

Part of this process is interpreting the different wavelengths of the light coming at us and which are registered by particular receptors in the retina of each eye. Initial processing in the retina itself and what then follows from it results in *colour perception*. It means that colours are not at all as they seem to us. That is to say, they are not the inherent property of the apple we see before us. They are constructed internally in response to something quite different, in this case in response to variation in length of the light waves emitted from the apple in the particular environmental conditions that happen to exist at that moment in time. A light wave of a particular length is not the same as a particular colour that we see. The green colour we perceive on an apple is green only in our internal representation of the apple as it is projected into our consciousness, not something 'belonging to' the apple outside us. Again, this shows how the world as we perceive it is very much the creation of our own minds.

Categorical Perception

Another aspect of the processing described here is that you immediately perceive the apple as a member of a familiar, specific *category* of objects. This enables you to distinguish apples from all other perceived objects in your field of vision. Of course, you will have other perceptual experiences of apples, and these will be processed in a similar way, allowing you to associate particular smell and touch and taste sensations with apples so that, in the end, encounters with apples will simultaneously trigger a number of different perceptual memories. These memories will allow you to see different objects as different objects and associate like objects with like objects. However, to become *meaningful*, perceptual representations need to become associated with something in the *conceptual* store. Once a link between a perceptual store (in this case, the visual one) and the conceptual store is made, then you have ways of understanding what an apple is and its relationships with other concepts. This means that, to see an apple as a variety of fruit along with oranges, bananas and so on, perception by itself is not enough. On acquiring a new perceptual structure, the conceptual system will automatically attempt to match it with a conceptual structure or create a new one if necessary. Conceptual processing is covered in the fourth chapter.

Perception as Illusion, of a Kind

Summing up so far, the organisation of perceptual systems means a number of things: **construction**, **storage** and **use**. It means the *construction* of stable ways of representing the many patterns of sensations we experience via transduction from one or other of our sense organs. In each case, construction means using the basic building blocks (primitives) supplied to us in advance. The results of this construction process are *stored* as structures in their respective perceptual memory stores. Then they can be *used*, that is, they may be activated in further encounters, as just illustrated. With every new experience they can also participate, with the primitives, in the construction of new memory structures or in the adaptation of old ones.

Considering what was said in the preceding section, we should be much more suspicious about the impression that we generally have that objects outside us are exactly as they appear to us. Seeing was taken as an example, but it would apply to any of the perceptual systems. What we *think* we see and *think* we hear (feel, smell, etc.) undergoes a major transformation before the act of perception takes place. From the raw data coming from the outside, we *create* our perceptual experiences. As was the case with the example of colour perception, what we sense is actually an amazing feat of construction that takes place inside our heads.

We also assume that what is outside us has some permanent quality, but the internal constructions that determine how we experience the world certainly differ from individual to individual, and they differ radically in the case of other species exposed to the same environment. In the case of vision, even what impacts on our eyes varies all the time. The optical illusions that psychologists intrigue us with are in fact not really so special. They are typical of everything we see. You might also turn it around and say that the visual world we see is *all* illusion. Things are brighter or darker than the way we see them. Shapes are square when we see them as rectangles. Objects are moving in one direction when we perceive them as moving in another direction. Even changes in the atmosphere change the way the light hits our retinas, creating the raw data with which our brains decode and represent inside the visual world outside, reconstructing a reality that differs in many ways from the physical reality outside as measured objectively. In other words, the signals that reach us are not even identical to those actually emitted by the objects we perceive.

Unsettling as all this may be, it underlines an important truth about the objectivity we wish to attribute to what we perceive first hand and provides a special twist to the meaning of the expression 'seeing is believing'. Perhaps it would be a little safer to say 'touching is believing' since our sense of touch places us in direct contact with physical objects, but even that sense can be fooled, as demonstrated by the Aristotle illusion.[2] To sum up, perception is not a passive, faithful recording of everything that reaches our senses but a truly creative process, organising sense impressions in particular human-specific ways to build the inner world of our experience. Since we all have more or less the same perceptual apparatus, the result is that our individual reconstructions of the world outside have much in common, so it is easy and convenient to treat our shared illusion as reality. And, in a sense, it is our 'reality', and there are no cats or dolphins or eagles around capable of arguing with us and telling us otherwise.

The Perceptual 'Group'

For us to be able to make fullest sense of the rapidly changing environment outside us, the structures or 'representations' in the various different perceptual stores (see Figure 2.1) are highly attuned to one another. Their interfaces are such that activation in one store will always cause some activation in the others. This suggests we see these richly interconnected perceptual systems as a special group.[3] Each of the members of this group takes as its input a tsunami of signals that come flowing in from the physical environment, each individual system processing just those signals that it is 'responsible' for. Each system creates, uses

---

[2] This is when you cross your fingers and, with your eyes closed, run them along your nose or touch a small object like a marble or a pea, giving you the illusion that you are touching two objects and not one.
[3] The MOGUL framework term covering all structures in the various perceptual stores is POpS, standing for 'perceptual output structures' (Sharwood Smith & Truscott 2014; Truscott 2014). 'Input' here consists of the sensory signals from the environment, and the 'output' is the set of structures that are constructed in the various perceptual memory stores in response to this input.

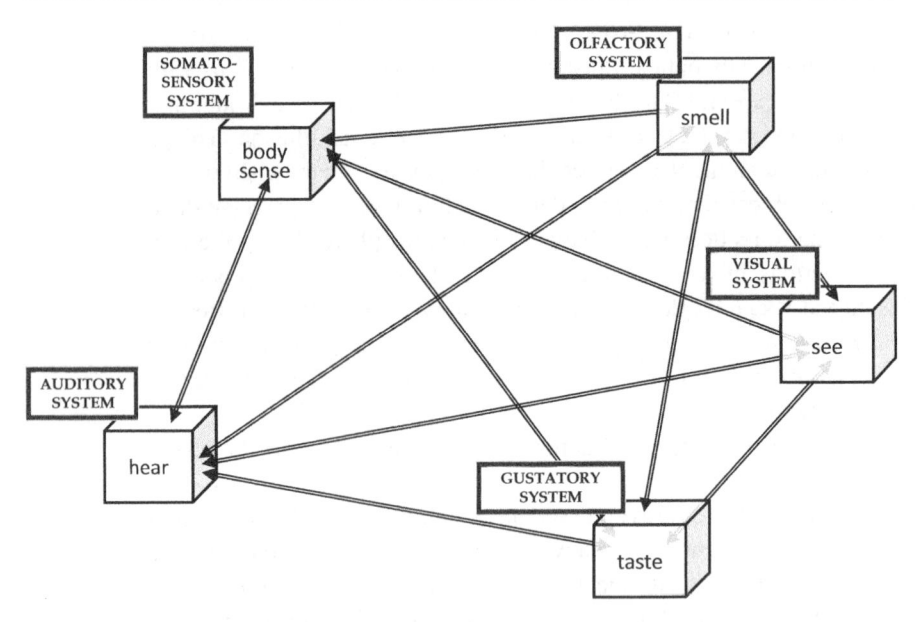

Figure 2.1 *The perceptual group.*

and manipulates the resulting perceptual structures (memories/representations) during on-line processing, but with a lot of crosstalk (coactivation) going on between other members of the perpetual group.

Synchronisation

As just suggested, any element in one perceptual store is highly likely to trigger the simultaneous activation of associated elements in other perceptual stores. More than that, this group of systems is highly synchronised so that any activation in one perceptual system will raise the activation levels generally in other systems in the group. This facilitates a continual, multisensory grasp of what is happening around us. It is, as we will see in Chapter 8, implicated in the phenomena of *attention* and *awareness*, each of which is created in response to various levels of intensity of activation in the perceptual systems. Conscious thought itself appears to be perceptual in nature, and so, not surprisingly, sensory (as well as motor) neurons are typically activated when people are given cognitive tasks to solve: the visual system is activated not only when perceiving visual objects but also when tasks require thinking and deciding about and mentally manipulating visual images (see e.g. Tucker & Ellis 1998). Indeed, such research findings have led to theories that present human cognition as entirely founded on our perceptual experience: this is called 'embodied' or 'grounded' cognition (Barsalou 2008; Lakoff & Johnson 1980; see also Morsella et al. 2015 for a related view of consciousness, including a discussion of the role of somatosensory and motor systems).

Collaboration Rather Than Complete Integration

Although there are good reasons to see the perceptual group of systems portrayed in Figure 2.1 as a single, integrated entity in its own right, it is still the case that the modules that make up the group, by following the same basic design, must have their own independent characteristics to differentiate them, one from the other. In the visual store, there will be elements that are written in visual code, as was already discussed in the introduction to this chapter, where the code was compared to the way JPG[4] files are encoded. The code in which visual structures are written will not be recognisable to any of the other systems. Mental 'JPGs' will always be distinguishable from their auditory or tactile equivalents, for example. Visual processing behaves differently from auditory or tactile processing in the mind and, indeed, engages different pathways in the brain. There are no conversion programs to rewrite one code into the format of another and the same goes for all the other stores in the framework. As discussed earlier, the interfaces that link stores together are not conversion programs. They simply pair up structures during processing to form an associative chain, as discussed in Chapter 6. This makes it more appropriate to see the kind of synchronisation that is so characteristic of the perceptual systems as a form of *intensive collaboration*.

Five Senses Extended

It should be easy to appreciate how important this perceptual group is for us. It is fundamental to our survival and in combination with the motor systems (see Chapter 3) allows us to react to whatever is happening around us. Figure 2.1 shows five individual perceptual systems and their interfaces: this is our gateway to the physical world of our immediate experience. *The exact number of senses is open to question.* Five senses have been chosen here for illustrative purposes, although it is nowadays generally assumed that there are more than five (traditionally, vision, hearing, smell, taste and touch). The group in Figure 2.1 is not exactly the one most people are most familiar with because it includes 'body sense', here called the somatosensory system of which the sense of touch is just one part (see later). This system can be seen as a complex set of senses, including those registering balance, temperature and pain. These details are not so important for our mind-based description; they will all fit in with the modular (processing unit) scheme adopted in the current framework.

Synaesthesia

The tension between close collaboration and the complete integration of members of the perceptual group becomes clear when it comes to a

---

[4] JPEG stands for Joint Photographic Experts Group.

phenomenon whereby the senses actually seem to merge and get confused. Normally, what we attend to and become aware of (the topic of Chapter 7) involves *a very high degree of activation*. The focus of attention consists in those structures whose activation has the highest level of intensity. So if we see an apple on a branch, the visual structure associated with apple should be the one that is most highly activated and receive the focus of our attention. We will have a straightforward visual 'sensation'. The same goes for the surrounding objects in the visual environment, but less so until our attention happens to turn to something else in front of us. Either way, the visual structures will predominate over all other types, with the exception of conceptual structures that give the apple meaning. When we see the apple, we do not necessarily have a taste sensation as well. When we taste an apple, we do not necessarily have a visual experience of it as well (unless we are looking at it as we taste it). The visual structure corresponding to the visual perception of an apple will also take precedence over other associated perceptual structures representing smell, texture and so on, that will also have been activated at the same time. These will often not have sufficient levels of activation to enter into any kind of awareness. However, sometimes the competition for first place that takes place between the different perceptual systems is not always resolved in the usual way. This can, for some people, result not in the selection of the most appropriate sensation but in the merging of two or more sensations at the same time: this effect is known as *synaesthesia*. For example, hearing or thinking of a word may evoke a particular taste sensation. The number 2, say, may be regularly experienced as though it were coloured red. In this case, structures from *different* perceptual stores have both been activated to an identical or similar degree of intensity, and a conscious experience of the senses merging is the result of this coactivation.

Although certain people may have these mixed sensory experiences on a regular basis, perhaps because their brains are 'wired' differently, characterising synaesthesia as unusual or abnormal may not be the right way of presenting it. A similar process, but of a more subtle kind, would seem to be happening all the time and to everyone. This emerges in studies of taste, for example. Following up previous research into the effect of different plateware, Harrar and Spence (2013) report a study in which they showed that just the cutlery, its weight, size, colour and shape, affected the perception of the saltiness and sweetness of food tasted, all of these collaborative but misleading effects of the perceptual group of systems clearly working in everyone's minds and below the level of conscious awareness. Flavour will be mentioned again in this connection, i.e. in the later section on taste and smell.

Other cases of common synaesthesia include the *bouba/kiki effect*, where people from different cultures, when asked to associate jagged and rounded shapes with invented words like 'bouba' and 'kiki', regularly associated the bouba-type word with the rounded shapes and the kiki-type with the jagged shapes, the idea being that associations are evoked between the auditory and tactile characteristics of the sound and the visual characteristics of the shape (see e.g. Gómez Milán et al. 2013; Ramachandran & Hubbard 2001).[5] Synaesthesia of this more subtle kind probably involves more than just the perceptual systems alone but also systems interfaced with and influencing them, namely those dealing with meaning as well as with value and emotion.

Perceptual Systems Are Not Equal

The members of the perceptual group are not equal in terms of their complexity and influence; such a state of imbalance is true of all species. Humans, for example, have evolved a set of senses of which some, vision, for example, are more developed than others. For example, olfaction (smell) is relatively weak in humans. In other species, this order of importance is reversed and smell becomes a much more important source of information from the outside world. The number of smell receptors in a cat vastly exceeds that in humans, and in turn, those of dogs vastly exceed those of cats. It is therefore not surprising that humans have not recruited the sense of smell for use in language but rather vision and audition (hearing).[6] Although the olfactory system delivers much more information to us than we are aware of or can identify, it still cannot compete with the other two senses.

The McGurk Effect

Seeing and hearing are of course both important to us, but they are not equal as is demonstrated by the *McGurk effect*. This is an illusion whereby you can watch someone pronouncing a particular sound but actually hear a different one. This conflict between what you see and what you hear is engineered by presenting a subject with a video that shows a person close up producing a syllable-like 'ba'. At the same time, the subject hears 'ba', as is appropriate, so the movement of the person's mouth on the screen exactly matches the sound heard. Then, in a second video, the subject is presented with the same person on the video, but this time mouthing the syllable 'va', starting with the lower lip clearly tucked behind the upper teeth. This time, a mismatch is deliberately created: the sound that is presented to the subject is identical to the one in the first sequence, i.e. 'ba'. This presents the listener/viewer with a conflict. You might imagine that listeners will not be fooled by the wrong mouth movements they see. This is not what happens. Despite what he or she hears, the subject will always hear the sound suggested by the mouth position ('va' and not 'ba').[7] Revealing the deception to

---

[5] Thanks are due to John Truscott for suggesting the inclusion of this example but who suggested a possible alternative hypothesis, that the number of receptors is adequate but the interfaces are not; we have a reasonably healthy taste (gustatory) system but cannot do much with it. This is based on evidence that humans are actually pretty good at distinguishing different smells but very poor at putting labels on what they're smelling (Truscott, pers. comm., 2015).
[6] And also touch, for Braille.
[7] Numerous examples are available on the Internet. This one was provided at https://www.youtube.com/watch?v=G-lN8vWm3m0, retrieved 1 March 2015.

the subject makes no difference. A replay of the experiment will have the same results. It turns out that the mind, faced with a conflict of this kind, resolves it by choosing the visual information over the auditory information. Apart from teaching us which perceptual system has precedence, it is also another example of how the mind experiences something different from what the outside world presents it with.

Perceptual Experience without External Cause

This closely interrelated perceptual network is something we have in common with other animals despite the many ways in which it can vary across species. It also comes into play not only in our thoughts and when we consciously attempt to imagine something but also when we dream, something animals appear to do as well. Deprived of stimulation from outside, the perceptual structures that we possess in the various memory stores (the boxes in Figure 2.1) float freely, allowing the mind to create all kinds of different life-like experiences. In certain circumstances, they also permit what we call hallucinations, waking dreams as it were, where we see, hear, smell or feel things that are not there.

The Charles Bonnet Syndrome

With the *Charles Bonnet syndrome*, failing vision due to some specific kind of degeneration in old age is accompanied by hallucinatory experiences. This includes the appearance of landscapes, pictures and people that are dramatically reduced in size but also the occurrence of quite simple visual patterns.[8] With reduced visual information originating in the immediate environment, the mind or more properly its visual processor responds with supplementary information from its visual memory store. The result mixes dreamlike experiences with the normal construction of reality that relies on input from outside.

Hallucinations do not necessarily depend on some lasting malfunction and many people experience brief moments of hallucination in their everyday life such as sounds (auditory hallucinations) or smells (olfactory hallucinations) that 'are not there'. In fact any of our perceptual systems can generate such experiences drawing on the contents of their various perceptual stores and the associations between them created and activated by their mutual interfaces.

Making Sense

Once the initial sensory signals have been 'transduced' by the appropriate receptors, they arrive at the door of the relevant perceptual module.

---

[8] TED2009, "Oliver Sacks: What hallucination reveals about our minds | Video on", http://www.ted.com, retrieved 7 March 2013. See also Sacks (2012).

The operation of that module, as it tries to 'make sense of' the signals coming in from the outside, may be labelled a first major stage in the processing of input. As discussed earlier, it involves what could be described as the *initial recognition* of patterns of stimuli by matching them to associated structures on its store. In this way the signals emitted an apple can be 'recognised' by the visual system as belonging to a visual structure that has already been created as a result of past experience.

As the individual in question interacts with the apple in other ways rather than just looking at it, a similar kind of matching process will have taken place in other perceptual modules as the smell and feel are 'recognised' by the other relevant systems. Because the systems in the perceptual group are richly interconnected, even if interaction is limited to just looking at the apple, the sight of the apple will have activated associated 'smell' and 'feel' structures at the same time even though no actual smelling and feeling may have taken place.

At this particular point, all this interpretation and coactivation of perceptual systems has not rendered the perceived apple *meaningful* yet. That is, the 'making sense' of the input thus far is only true metaphorically. The original sensory input and the outcome of its processing by one or more perceptual systems remain literally lacking in sense, i.e. everything is still *meaningless* until a second important stage in the process has been completed, namely *interpretation*, i.e. the attaching of a meaning, or in terms of the current framework, a matching *conceptual* structure. This is a more comprehensive form of recognition. At this stage, input into the conceptual system, is not the original sensory input that was processed by perceptual systems, but something different: it is the output of the recognition process in the form of perceptual structures: in this particular case – seeing an apple – the input is the *visual* structure that has been activated.

The interface linking the visual system and the conceptual system will trigger a process of finding some conceptual structure ('meaning') to associate with that visual structure. All kinds of meaning associations may be matched to the perceptual structures associated with apples. All of this adds up to that individual's concept of an apple which may well share much with other individuals who are familiar with apples but at the same will have features that are special to that person alone and the result of many prior personal experiences of apples.

It is always instructive to look at situations where something goes wrong. The recognition/interpretation process may not function properly. Patients suffering from some kind of agnosia provide examples of this dysfunction. In the case of visual *apperceptive* agnosia, for instance, patients presented with different shapes may not be able to distinguish between them and are unable to copy them. The problem arises at the first, perceptual recognition stage. Those suffering from *associative* visual agnosia can copy them, so 'recognise' them in the special sense defined previously – but have difficulty interpreting them. In other words, it is a problem arising at the interface between visual perception and meaning, that is to say, expressing this in terms of this framework, at the second major stage where the relevant visual structure is to be associated with an appropriate *conceptual* representation (Warrington & Shallice 1984). Any interpretation that takes place would have to be via another perceptual, i.e. involving a modality other than the visual one.

Adding Value

Initial recognition and interpretation are the two major stages but not, of course, the whole picture. Apart from the spreading activation to other members of the perceptual group, there is also the value or 'valence' aspect of processing, as will be further explained in Chapter 5, on *affect*. This is about the way in which a given visual experience is valued, positively or negatively. A representation may have a particular value assigned to it directly via the affect system in advance. It remains unclear, for instance, if we are genetically programmed to associate the colour red with danger. There is good evidence, for example, that a certain type of finch responds instinctively to red as a danger signal (Pryke 2009). If this is also true for humans, this would be an example of our interpretation of a particular visual experience being affected at some point by the predetermined assignment of a negative value. This could be either at the second, conceptual interpretation stage or even earlier at the first, perceptual recognition stage, in which case there would be a representation of red already present (at birth) in the visual system and already paired with a strong negative value via the affect system. Alternatively, it may be the case that we have to actually learn that red means danger when encountering a red traffic signal in which case the visual structure corresponding to the experience of red would come to be coindexed with strong negative affective structure at some point during the course of an individual's life. Many associations are indeed learned via experience and this includes the assignment of values by the affective module. For example we need to have prior experience of apples for the sight of one to evoke a pleasant memory of some person or place or simply a pleasant taste association.

The Two Basic Stages Illustrated

Figure 2.2 shows an example of the two-stage process of initial recognition and interpretation as it works with visual input. The example would work equally well if we chose to deal with any other kind of sensory input. It would just be a matter of replacing the visual system with another perceptual system.[9] The small black circles located at the top of each store and connected by interface arrows represent the two structures that have been currently activated in working memories. The one in the store on the left is the *visual* representation of an apple that has been called up in response to the sight of an apple, that is, the initial processing of the light waves that results in input to the visual system. The black

---

[9] Also, this illustration is simplified because it ignores the co-activation of other perceptual structures such as the smell and touch (see Figure 2.1).

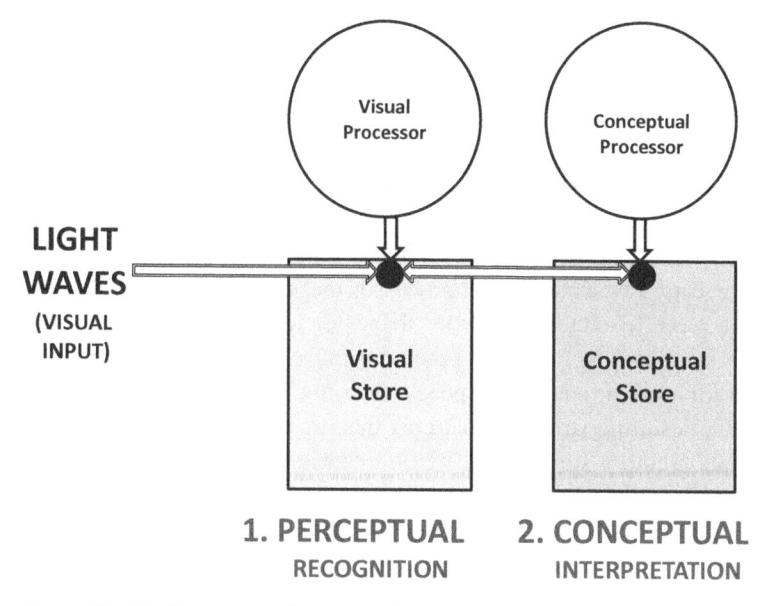

Figure 2.2 *'Making sense' of perceptual experience.*

circle in the store on the right is actually a complex *conceptual* structure representing a cluster of all the meanings that the individual associates with apples. Assigning the visually perceived, i.e. recognised 'apple' a meaning constitutes the second stage: this is assuming, for the moment, that processing goes from left to right, starting with the input from the environment (the sight of the apple) and ending with attaching a meaning to the visual representation of an apple. The two basic stages are actually virtually simultaneous in practice as is made clear in the next section.

Processing Is Bidirectional

Although initially the processing goes from the outside world inwards in a sequence, as displayed in Figure 2.2, it is best seen as a to-and-fro, bidirectional affair with interfaces across adjoining modules in our minds trying always to match up the various structures in an optimal way, finding the best fit and not necessarily succeeding at the first attempt. The Charles Bonnet syndrome referred to earlier would be an extreme example of this. Not everything we see is so instantaneously recognisable. Even though all the processing takes place in a flash and typically below the level of awareness, it is typically a case of sorting out the best overall match amongst a number of competing candidates in all the relevant stores. The details need not concern us for the time being as processing is the main topic of Chapter 6.

The Auditory System

The auditory system, like the visual system that has been referred to several times already, is important for the processing of language. In the case of audition, it is relevant for the processing of speech sounds. However, also like the visual system, its primary function is nothing to do with language specifically but with the processing of generic sound input, in this case *any kind of sound* that is picked up by the ears. Just as the visual processor makes no distinction between the shapes on a piece of clothing and the shapes of letters or any other script used in written language, the auditory processor makes no distinction between the sounds of traffic and the sounds of speech. In both cases, that is both in sound and in vision, the resulting structural patterns that are stored as representations in the appropriate memory store are written in the same 'code', i.e. visual code or auditory code[10] whether they happen to have something to do with language or not. Linguistic processing is a separate, further stage (see Chapter 10, in particular).

The input needed to create new items in the auditory store comes from the acoustic patterns, sound waves, registered in the bones and membranes of the ears. In the brain's auditory system, the encoded information from the ears goes first to the brain stem and from there on to the thalamus and from there, for central processing in the primary auditory cortex. Whether the neural coding is different at the different stages of auditory processing in the brain need not detain us here because the main focus is on the mind. The input is the sound waves registered in the ears, the output is auditory structure, housed in the auditory store. Once in the store, those auditory structures can be activated in response to new *external* input, that is, to identify the same acoustic patterns that were used to form them initially and that are encountered again in the environment outside. They can also be used in response to *internal* input, that input originating in other modules that have an interface with the auditory store. In this way the newly created auditory representation can play its part in imaginings, dreams and hallucinations where there is no external stimulus at all. As far as spoken language is concerned, we will return to the role that auditory structures play in speech processing in Part II. Suffice it to say here, that some auditory structures provide input for speech processing and are matched via an interface to structures that are specifically linguistic.

Taste and Smell

Gustation (taste) and olfaction (smell) are handled by separate mental systems following the same basic design as all the others. In the brain, they are

---

[10] In the introduction to this chapter, analogy was made between auditory code and the audio code in which MP3 digital sound files are written. MP3, somewhat misleadingly, stands for Moving Picture Experts Group.

also handled by separate systems but their internal architecture and functioning is also different.

The olfactory system is unique amongst perceptual systems in the brain in that it connects directly to the olfactory cortex in the frontal and temporal lobes whereas other sensory information is always routed through the *thalamus*.[11] However, it should perhaps be mentioned that these two (neurally very different) sensory systems cooperate in producing the sensation of flavour very effectively: this is 'normal' synaesthesia although it is not usually thought of that way.

Neither gustatory structures nor olfactory structures play any significant role in language (see Note 18). Perhaps animals that have a much more refined version of either of these two might be able to use it as a medium for language but this would be impossible without the possession of linguistic systems to be described in the second part of this book. On the other hand, olfaction, in association with affect, is regularly used as a medium of nonlinguistic communication. Many species, snakes, sharks, insects and all kinds of mammals use smell as a means of attracting and warning others of their kind, by marking territory, for example.

Body Sense

The somatosensory system is a complex one, especially at the brain level of description. It includes touch, the sensing of body position and the sense of body movement. Unlike the other sensory systems its receptors are to be found all over the body. Somatosensory processing is handled by the primary somatosensory cortex and the cerebellum. Predictably, there is a high degree of connectivity between the somatosensory system and the motor system. The coordination of somatosensory activity and motor structures, especially those that drive involuntary body movements is clearly important for survival.[12] Place your hand, or rather imagine placing your hand near a candle flame for a painful reminder of this.

If the way the somatosensory system works in the physical body including the brain is complex, at the 'mind' level of description, the story is simpler. The somatosensory module functions like all the other systems, in accordance with the framework's basic design. Apart from its primary function it also plays a part, together with the motor system, in language production, a secondary function, simply because various parts of the body are involved, in speaking and in the paralinguistic activity (gestures, facial expressions) that accompanies speech and adds on to or emphasises the meaning that is conveyed in words. It is naturally

---

[11] As regards its role in perception, the thalamus is often referred to as a kind of information hub relaying messages from the sensory systems (except the olfactory one) to the cerebral cortex (grey matter). It is composed of various subdivisions.

[12] Not surprisingly perhaps, the motor and the somatosensory systems in the brain are located right next to one another.

crucial when it comes to sign language production, where all meaning is conveyed this way, and in reading messages written in Braille.

Perceptual Structures without Meaning or Value

Finally, it is important to reiterate that perceptual structures have been discussed so far as though they were meaningless and valueless. It is true that the structures that reside in the perceptual stores do not possess any *inherent* meaning or value. As has been briefly mentioned already, meaning and value are supplied by other systems, the topic of the next two chapters. Via interfaces with the perceptual systems, perceptual representations thus become both meaningful and 'valued', that is valued in various positive and negative ways.

Summary

This chapter dealt with the expert systems involved in perception. The perceptual modules can be thought of as a highly interactive group, richly interconnected. They each take sensory information from their respective sources – receptors in the eyes in the case of vision – but this information is first converted into a particular format which is determined by the receptors and is then transmitted to the relevant perceptual system which, in response, activates perceptual structures in the particular code of that perceptual system – visual code in the case of vision – or tries to create new perceptual structures. The perceptual group as a whole plays an important part in the explanation of attention and awareness.

Perceptual systems do not straightforwardly reproduce the world outside but interpret it in particular ways. The result is not a simple straightforward recreation of objective reality but very much a creation of the mind, even before we take into account aspects that will be addressed in Chapters 4 and 5, namely the meaning and value of what we perceive.

3 Motion

In This Chapter

In physical terms, the motor system is part of the central nervous system consisting of two subsystems: the pyramidal subsystem (for voluntary movements) and extrapyramidal subsystem (for involuntary movements). It has to do with movement such as the articulation of limbs and their component parts, but it also has to do with more subtle changes in physical state. This not only includes what are obviously movement related changes like the blink reflex and changes in heart rate but also perspiration and gooseflesh (goose bumps). All these involuntary phenomena are related to the 'autonomic system'. In other words, the motor system as a whole includes both voluntary and involuntary changes of state and also movement ranging from very tiny changes to large-scale movements of the body. The motor system is one way or another connected up to all the other systems. Within the framework, however, the focus will be on voluntary motor control. Note here that 'voluntary' does not necessarily implicate conscious volition: in any kind of skilled behaviour, motor control is typically, at least for the most part, subconscious. In language, the motor system will be important for explaining the articulation of speech and sign language together with all the other body movements that accompany language performance.

Interconnectivity

The motor system happens to be important for a comprehensive account of language ability. We recruit the motor system, both voluntary and involuntary parts, when communicating with others. We articulate different parts of our body for example to manipulate objects, to attack and defend ourselves, to dance and simply to move to a different location: we also use it to produce messages. It may also be activated even during the comprehension of messages.

The affect system which governs our subconscious evaluations of what is happening around us as well as our consciously felt emotions[1] also interacts with the autonomic motor system producing bodily responses that can be measured

---

[1] This is the topic of Chapter 5.

and this too is implicated in accounts of language behaviour. In fact, the motor system is not only linked to the affective system, but also to all the other systems, that is, the perceptual systems including, most obviously, to the somatosensory system (dealing with body sensations), and to the conceptual system.

The connections between the motor system and other systems described in this book can be demonstrated in various ways. Obvious examples include movements easy to understand and connected with fight or flight reactions to stressful situations when we freeze, run away or adopt an aggressive stance to protect ourselves. Sometimes connections operate to activate fellow systems when at first glance the result might seem pointless. Take *subvocalisation* in message comprehension for example. This is when, while reading silently, i.e. without the intention to speak, the mechanisms of speech are nevertheless activated. It is quite easy to detect this, for example when experiencing difficulty in reading a text. Try reading silently a word that seems to you to be difficult to pronounce. You can then feel minute involuntary movements of your lips and tongue rehearsing as it were what you would have to do if you decided to reread the text aloud. Advice of how to read swiftly and efficiently often refer to subvocalisation as an obstacle and includes tips on how to minimise it but claims that it can be 'eliminated' should be discounted. The brain, and mind will have their way.

Mirror Neurons

It is, in the spirit of this book and the framework on which it is based, to try and continually keep 'mind' architecture more or less aligned with current 'brain' research, that is, while still seeking to keep the two levels distinct. There is neurological evidence that suggests that humans, like monkeys have special neurons that enable them to 'mirror' actions that they are observing. However, in humans at least, this is still the subject of controversy; for example, evidence that children are born with these 'mirror neurons' is not compelling (Heyes 2010, 579; see also Hickok 2014). This leaves open the possibility that human imitative behaviour, and the mirror neurons themselves are acquired by associations built up as a result of experience. Heyes (2010, 581) claims that the evidence actually supports the *associative hypothesis* which claims that mirror neurons come about from sensorimotor experience, much of which comes about through social interaction.

There is also a theory that even suggests that perceptual representations and motor representations are linked by a common code (Prinz 1997). However, the strong coupling between these systems is accounted for in the framework not by the existence of a common code but rather by the operations of the various interfaces involved, notably between the visual and somatosensory systems on one hand and the motor systems on the other. This would certainly fit in with the associative hypothesis as multiple associations between body sense, vision and the motor system would arise through the activation of chains of structure across these various systems. The structures would still be written *in different codes* according to the modular principles of the framework and they would become more readily activated with repeated stimulation. In other words collaboration between modules can, reflecting life experience, be anything between once-off, sporadic and therefore weakly established up to very frequent and deeply entrenched. The collaboration also be set up already, i.e. available from birth onwards as part of our biological starter package.

Imagined Movement

Whatever the views on mirror neurons may be, a particularly dramatic demonstration of the links between the motor system and other systems, also involving language, is demonstrated in research that seeks ways of communicating with patients with *locked-in syndrome*, in other words, who are unable to move any part of their bodies to demonstrate to others that they are conscious.

Using brain imaging (fMRI[2]), researchers were able to show that, when asked to imagine playing tennis, the motor areas of the brain associated with articulating those parts of the body used in tennis are activated even though no movement is detectable in the patient: this response also showed up when a comatose patient was asked to use imagining playing tennis as a way of answering yes to a question and to imagine moving around home as a way of producing a 'no' answer (Owen et al. 2006). There is imagined movement, in other words, confined to the part of the brain, the motor cortex, which manages voluntary movement. It is a response to the imagined experience which can only happen if the patient is able to hear and comprehend what is being suggested. This opens up a channel of communication with patients with whom communication would otherwise seem impossible.

In terms of the current framework, a verbal command is issued to the patient by the doctor. The message, when perceived (heard), activates in the patient a chain of structures, part of which will contain the meaning. Assuming of course that the doctor and patient speak the same language, this meaning will be an identical, or highly similar *conceptual* structure that the doctor has just encoded and articulated as a spoken utterance directed at the patient. It could be, for example:

'Try to Imagine Yourself Playing Tennis'

The patient, having decoded this message, can then use stored *visual* representations (visual memories) and associated *somatosensory* structures (the memories of various body movements associated with running and manipulating a tennis racket) to construct an imaginary game of tennis. As with subvocalisation, the

---

[2] fMRI (functional magnetic resonance imaging) measures brain activity as changes in blood flow.

motor structures associated with performing the actions involved in playing tennis will be activated. Unlike in the case of subvocalisation, this activation cannot in this case trigger any visible body movements precisely because of the patient's completely comatose condition. However, even though it triggers no movements at all, the activation of the motor system would still be sufficiently strong to show up as brain activity on an fMRI machine and provide evidence that the patient was conscious despite appearances to the contrary. This shows how modular systems each with quite different tasks to perform are still multiply interconnected: they collaborate sometimes in quite unexpected ways and largely, though not exclusively, below the level of conscious awareness.

The Language of Our Ancestors

Talking about the role of the motor system in language production usually involves reference to the movement of the speech organs or, in the case or writing, movement of the arms and hands to produce text. However, this is not the whole story. There is a continuing controversy concerning the origins of human language but certainly many believe that gesture played a fundamental role, perhaps before, perhaps in combination with the production of vocal sounds. Manipulating pens, pencils and keyboards, gesturing with hands and face and other body positions as well as using parts of the body that are used for swallowing, tasting, biting, chewing and breathing to communicate makes it clear how many parts of the motor system were eventually, at some point in our evolution, recruited for the purposes of language production at the same time, *or even before* speech became the primary channel of communication.

Integrating Motor Structures with the Perceptual Systems

Figure 3.1 displays the various interfaces between the perceptual group of systems and the memory store containing motor structures. So as not to complicate the figure, the circle that stands for the motor processor has been left out of the picture. Also, as a convenient set of reminders, each store has been labelled with the name of the appropriate sense rather than with the name of the structures it holds (respectively, OfS, VS, GS, AS and SomS, in clockwise direction). This labelling will be repeated at the end of the next two chapters as we add in two more systems into the same picture.

As elsewhere, the thicker two-way arrows in Figure 3.1 indicate the interfaces between the various stores. These interfaces should always be thought of as simple *processors* and not just connecting pathways. In each case, the interface attempts to match structures in one store with structures in the other using the index system to identify appropriate partners.

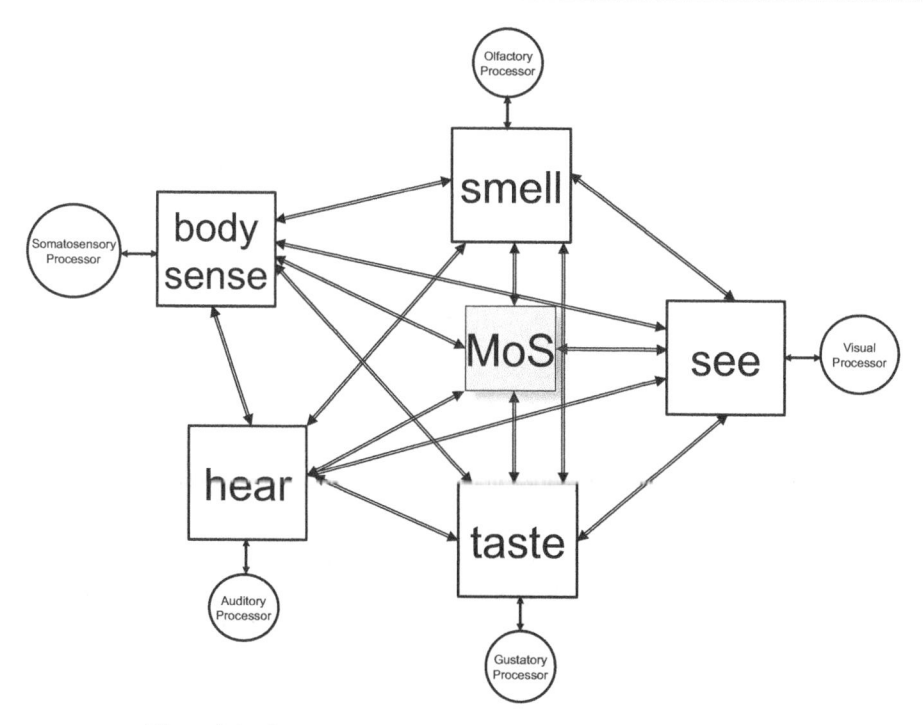

Figure 3.1 *The motor store and interfaces with the perceptual systems.*

Summary

This chapter added the motor system into the map of the mind which was initiated in the previous chapter: the motor store is connected up by interfaces to all members of the perceptual group. Even though an account of voluntary and involuntary motor systems in the body will look very different, it still remains important to explore the connections between the map of mind and physical architecture, especially that of the brain so that research at both levels can keep pace with one another and so that accounts of one type do not turn out to be difficult or impossible to relate to accounts at the other level of description. Theories about mirror neurons and neuroimaging research with comatose patients are therefore all worth discussing in the context of the mind's motor system and how it connects up with other systems in the framework. Both levels will be needed to explain motor aspects of human behaviour. Finally, since there will be little discussion of the motor system in Part II, some reference was made to the articulation of speech and writing and to interesting speculations about gesture and the origins of language.

4 Meaning

In This Chapter

The conceptual system handles meaning. It can be seen as lying at the centre of an individual's accumulated knowledge of the world. Meaning is encoded in the mind's conceptual structure. In the framework, 'meaning' is not shorthand for simple associations between objects and events. Human conceptual ability may be associated especially with the large size and complex organisation of the human frontal cortex, situated in the front of the brain (the frontal lobe). In describing animal cognition and depending upon the species in question, it may be questionable whether a separate conceptual system should be assumed at all. At any rate, as far as humans are concerned and almost certainly some other species as well,[1] the conceptual system is very much about *abstract* meaning. Abstraction involves categorisation, complex accumulations and hierarchies of meaning. So the meaning of 'apple' is not just a straightforward association you have with a particular apple at a particular moment in time but includes the generic meaning of apple as a type of fruit and associations with all things to do with fruit. An individual apple that you are familiar with will have, along with the features making up its generic meaning – the ones it shares with all other apples – also meanings associated just with that apple, all of which is expressed in the code peculiar to the conceptual system. Much conceptual structure can be linked to language forms but the conceptual system contains concepts that have no linguistic expression in those languages known to a particular individual particular but can nonetheless be grasped when explained, but also, perhaps, concepts that appear to defy any clear explanation at all such as meanings expressed in music, visual art and poetry.

Conceptual Representations

Conceptual representations, as just mentioned, supply the meaning that we associate with various types of linguistic structures, but also provide meaning for other types of structure as well. For example, a particular sound,

---

[1] See contributions to Balda et al. (1998).

```
              auditory-conceptual
                  interface

 A SOUND                              A 'MEANING
 REPRESENTATION                       REPRESENTATION
 [auditory structure]                 [conceptual structure]

     ┌──────────┐      ┌──────────┐
     │ Auditory │      │Conceptual│
     │  Memory  │      │  Memory  │
     └──────────┘      └──────────┘

       AUDITORY            CONCEPTUAL
       PROCESSOR           PROCESSOR
```

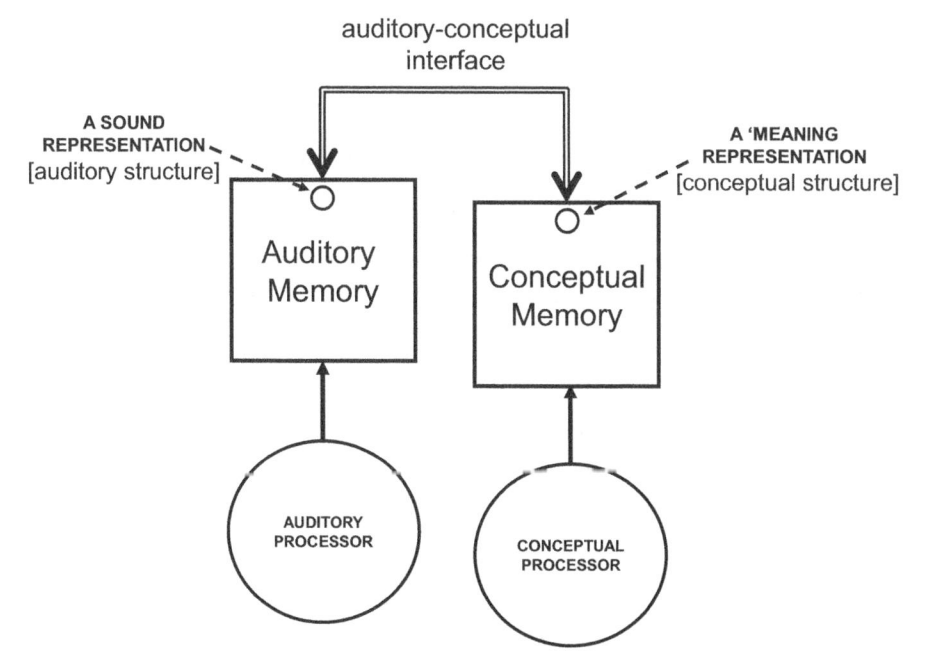

Figure 4.1 *Sound and meaning matched up.*

taste, smell or a given touch sensation may have meanings that, for any given individual, may have no linguistic expression at all.

Take the example of an alarm clock and the two systems displayed in Figure 4.1. The associations with the sound of an alarm clock will be the auditory representation of that sound paired with many other representations across the system as a whole. Figure 4.1 shows just two of them, the sound representation matched up with the conceptual representation via the auditory-conceptual interface. Although, for the sake of simplicity, the figure depicts structures as small, single circles, as in the preceding apple example, the actual representation will be a very complex one, especially the conceptual ones since alarm clocks, as with the preceding example of 'apple', will have a whole host of meanings associated with them, some of them very personal ones, so not just the generic meaning.

Any representation, wherever it is in the mind, will necessarily involve a cluster of features to distinguish it from other representations in its store. It is not necessary to detail the additional conceptual structures that would be associated with the generic 'apple' in the mind of a sophisticated apple expert to see how many such connections there must be for everyone, expert or not, within the conceptual store: this is especially true when we consider all the associations that connect them up with other modules, perceptual or otherwise to give us the combined stored memories of feeling apples in our mouths, their texture and taste as we bite them, their, smell, colours and the sensation of their weight in our hands, the individual apples and types of apple that we like and dislike and so forth.

Our current knowledge, as embodied in many complex conceptual representations in our conceptual memory store, should be seen as involving large networks with rich internal combinations *within* one module, as exemplified by the apple example, but also many connections *across* many modules. In this way, the fact that the mind is built up from separate modules that are each unique and which each possesses a great deal of independence in the way it operates should not obscure the fact that the mind is also, at the same time, characterised by massive interconnectivity.

Thinking, Imagining and Sensing

It is worth noting here that, although we cannot become directly aware either of the organisation or the contents of our conceptual system, or indeed of any of the systems described in this book for that matter, nevertheless many meanings (conceptual structures), when highly activated, may be projected into the state we call consciousness. Because thinking and imagining originates in the conceptual system. This has given rise to descriptions of conceptual structure as 'mentalese' and the 'lingua franca of the mind' (Jackendoff 1987; Pinker 1997). This does not however mean that we are conscious of our conceptual system, that is either its structures or its operations. We are only able to have some access to what lies within our conceptual memory *indirectly*, that is with help from outside. This help comes from the perceptual group of systems and is the main topic of Chapter 7.

The present chapter will look in more detail at consciousness and attention but in any case, meaning involves not only conscious reflections and imaginings: it also involves lower levels of awareness as when we are dimly aware of things going on around us without any reflection on our part until something in this peripheral area alerts us and we switch our focus of attention. Many of these vague sensations certainly have meaning for us, some highly valued ones, and will therefore have associated conceptual structures. Once we focus attention on them as when someone talking near us mentions our name, what we were thinking of at the time is abandoned as our thoughts engage with the situation that has now caught our attention.

The Conceptual System and the Brain

Whether conceptual activity in the mind is conscious or not, the richness and complexity of the human conceptual system would seem to distinguish us sharply even from our nearest cousins on the evolutionary ladder. To speculate a little about the phylogeny of our species, it may be that increasing sophistication in our mental meaning system over time was what triggered the development of human language. Alternatively, the process might have been the reverse of that. Language may have triggered development in our conceptual abilities. One way or another we can be sure they interacted with one another to promote development. Although the potential capacity of the conceptual system will remain the same during one person's lifetime, similar processes works ontogenetically, that is, as an individual matures from babyhood into and through adulthood acquiring, in principle at least, ever richer conceptual resources with increasing age. This means in effect a more or less continuous expansion of, and increased complexity in the conceptual system lasting into old age together with connections forged across the interfaces between the conceptual system and the other systems in the mind. This development will be reflected in a parallel synaptic growth, that is, the connections between cells in the central nervous system.

At a neural level, the conceptual system would seem to be most strongly associated with the development of the frontal cortex. Research certainly suggests that this, although not actually differing that much in size relative to the rest of the brain when compare to its counterpart in the brains of the great apes, nonetheless, apart from its being larger, the frontal cortex has *a different internal structure* associated with it and *more interconnectivity* with other parts of the brain (Semendeferi et al. 2002). Thanks to neuroplasticity in the human brain, changes in the brains' physical structure and functional organisation, especially in the prefrontal cortex (front part of the frontal lobe), are possible, both in the mature adult brain as well as in the child even though there are limits: some aspects of maturation come to end early on and cannot be altered. This continuing flexibility provides individuals with a *cognitive reserve* which can to some extent and given the right stimulation, compensate for degeneration in old age, even where this is accompanied by various types of age-related brain disease (Whalley et al. 2004).

Integrating Conceptual Structures with the Perceptual and Motor Systems

Figure 4.2 displays the various interfaces between the perceptual group of systems and the memory store containing conceptual structures (CS). Adding on to what was displayed in Figure 3.1 in the previous chapter, it fills in the framework map of the mind a little further. To minimise the resulting increase in complexity of this map in the middle of the figure, three simplifying adjustments have been made to the big picture. Firstly, the CS *processor* has been left out (as was the case in the previous chapter with the motor processor displayed behind it). Secondly, *all other interface connections* with other stores

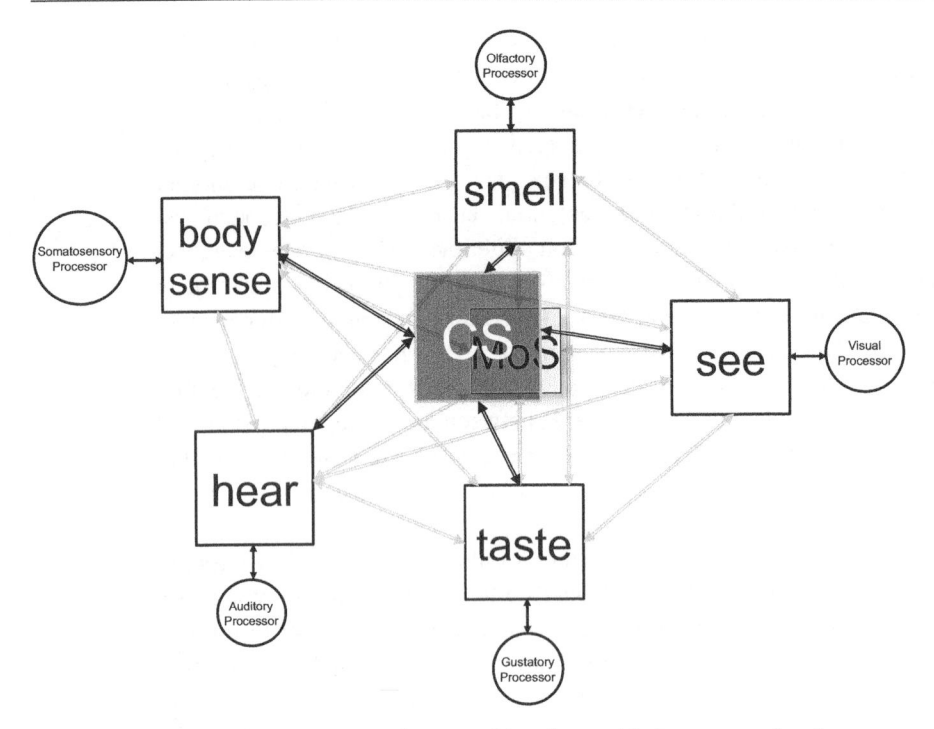

Figure 4.2 *The conceptual store and interfaces with the perceptual and motor systems.*

have been reduced from black to *grey* so that the newly added CS interface connections stand out clearly. Finally, the CS store has been partly superimposed on the MoS store. This means that the reader will have to imagine the CS/MoS interface going from behind the conceptual store stretching back to the motor store that it partly obscures.[2]

Summary

One way of distinguishing humans from their nearest relatives, the great apes, if not by reference to language, is in their phenomenal conceptual ability, enabling them, for example, to think well beyond the here and now, reflect on the past and plan for the future. In the framework, this advantage is located in the human conceptual system. This is how representations of different kinds in the other systems get their meaning whether it be the meaning of a smell, a particular tactile sensation or a line of a poem. Conceptual structures and all activity within the conceptual system must remain firmly anchored in

---

[2] The same adaptations will be applied to the figure in the next chapter, when the affect system gets included, again in the centre.

our subconscious but, thanks to the perceptual system, some of their contents can be projected into consciousness, enabling complex thought. The structure of the human brain, especially the neocortex, its internal structure and its rich connectivity with other brain areas, reflects the complexity, storage capacity and importance and computational power of the human conceptual system.

5 Affect

In This Chapter

Research into emotion has a long history back at least to Sigmund Freud and William James. Emotional responses to language have recently become an important part of language research, especially in areas to do with learning a new language and using languages in the community. Teaching methodologists have been concerned with attitudes and motivation amongst learners for a much longer time. As will soon become clear, emotions are anything but peripheral to the study of mind and that includes the more 'cognitive aspects' concerning rationality. The emotional system, whether it is manifested as consciously experienced feelings or as operating below the level of awareness lies at the heart of all mental activity and any explanation of the mind would be worth little without an account of how it works.

Affect, or rather affective science is the rubric under which such research can be grouped: the study of affect has also become a respectable part of neuroscience. Pioneering work by researchers such as Ekman, Frijda, Panksepp, Damasio, LeDoux and Zajonc amongst others has made it clear that, in any comprehensive account of mind or brain, we ignore affect at our peril. This is because affect not only supports our emotional life as we experience it *consciously*. As just implied, it also works *below the level of consciousness* and to a much greater degree than most of us realise (Öhman et al. 2000). One of the consequences of this is that affect has a powerful influence on decision making, normally thought of as a rational, cognitive process. This is why it makes sense to integrate accounts of affect with accounts of cognition. Even though affect and cognition can still be seen separate, their respective mental and neural processes are intertwined (Damasio 1999).

Evaluation

Underlying the various emotions that everyone is familiar with is something more basic namely the mind's system of *evaluation*. This is the (more or less) negative and (more or less) positive evaluations of practically everything we perceive, do and know. The terms often used for handling this evaluation, carried out by both mind and brain, is *appraisal*. Appraisal lies at the heart of affect so the *affect(ive) system* is essentially a value-processing system responsible for determining, often at a subconscious level, things that we should try to avoid and things that we are attracted to, what is often referred to as a choice between *approach* and *avoidance*. It also includes handling preconfigured values governing, for example, instinctive responses to threats to our safety and well-being. In other words, affect is constantly guiding our behaviour. In this connection, Carroll Izard has highlighted the attention-guiding function of affect and its evolutionary benefit describing how a particular emotion 'sensitizes an organism to particular features of its environment' (Izard, cited in Öhman et al. 2000, 298–299). The topic of evaluation will be returned to later in the section on valence and appraisal.

Neuroscientific Views

So what about the neural underpinning of affect? Terminology in this area inevitably differs from researcher to researcher. LeDoux, for example, talks about affect, and especially its neural basis, as the 'emotion system' with 'feelings' referring to just that part of it that we experience consciously: much of our emotional (affective) processing is in fact subconscious.[1] Traditionally such a system, in that it is responsible for the processing of emotion, is associated with the *limbic system* in the midbrain containing, for example, the *hypothalamus*, the *amygdala* in particular, and the *hippocampus*. This group of systems is not very well defined and the general consensus nowadays seems to be to treat the emotion system as including connections and locations across a much wider area of the brain (LeDoux 1996).

Somatic Markers

Antonio Damasio (1994) proposed the somatic marker hypothesis. *Somatic markers* are associations between the physiological affective states (increased heart rate for example) and the stimuli that aroused them. They can be rapidly reactivated in all kinds of situation which evoke the original stimulus, not necessarily an identical one, preparing the individual for a given type of response even before they have time to reflect. This could result in spontaneous avoidance behaviour for example in a situation perceived to be threatening (even where it turns out there is no real threat, as in a bad dream). The basic idea behind this mechanism is that this is a way of reducing a possibly large set of options that an individual is faced with every moment of the day so they have only a few ones

---

[1] Somewhat differently from LeDoux, Antonio Damasio distinguishes 'emotions', which for him refers to the physical responses of the body, and 'feelings', i.e. mental states, which *may or may not* be conscious (Damasio 1994).

to consider. In other words it facilitates decision making by narrowing the set of possibilities.

Affect and Decision Making

The somatic marker hypothesis is one way of imagining what, in Daniel Kahneman's view, underlies human decision making. Kahneman explains decision making, in simplified terms, as an interplay between two separate systems (Kahneman 2011).[2] Roughly speaking, what he calls[3] *System 1* is the *fast intuitive, typically subconscious* mode of thinking as opposed to *System 2*, which is *slow, analytic and conscious*. System 1 performs a rapid assessment and, removes a whole lot of possibilities leaving just a few for the slower system to deal with if need be. The subconscious system runs effortlessly whereas the second one is often experienced as effortful. For this reason we often leave it up to System 1 to guide us, a strategy that can sometimes work well but can also lead us into error.

Consciousness and Affect

The influence of affect on subconscious mental operations highlights one interesting aspect of current work on the neuroscience of affect, that is, this idea that emotions do not have to be at the level of awareness. This goes against a common assumption that a core part of the definition of an emotion would be that they have to be conscious. How can you feel something and not be aware of it? In contrast to this assumption is the more or less established view in affective neuroscience nowadays that, like cognition in general, affect can, just like knowledge, indeed be either subconscious or conscious (Öhman et al. 2000).[4] Indeed, it just so happens that we, as humans, are also aware of, and can talk about emotions because of our enhanced metacognitive abilities[5] and not because it is an integral part of the emotional system per se.

The classic example of the workings of subconscious affect is the organism's instinctive response to threat. Although there are different interpretations of the idea, many now accept, in broad terms, what William James maintained a long time ago, namely that the actual experience of fear *follows*, rather than precedes instinctive flight.[6] He claimed that when someone is running from a bear, they are

---

[2] This is intended as a useful abstraction so these are not separate systems in the sense of systems in the current framework.
[3] These two terms he took from Stanovich and West (2000) and are part of what are called 'dual process' theories of reasoning. Indeed these two authors prefer to talk of two 'processes' rather than two 'systems'.
[4] The terms *implicit* and *explicit* are also used for this distinction (Kihlstrom 1999, 432).
[5] Metacognition is awareness of our own knowledge, our capacity to 'think about thinking' and therefore to manipulate our knowledge in planning and imagining.
[6] This idea is known as the James-Lange Theory.

doing so not because they feel frightened. Rather, they become frightened when they are *already* running away: in other words, the fear arises as a response to their bodily state (James 1884, 1894). Instinctive responses precede and are quite separate from the conscious experience responses that inevitably follow them by virtue of the relative speed with which each type of response are processed.

LeDoux (2002) provides a graphic demonstration of this idea in his account of how his interest in motivation was sparked. This was a video of when, while a crowd was enjoying a concert in Olympic Park, Atlanta, a bomb suddenly exploded. A slow motion replay shows clearly how nearly everyone in the crowd reacts by freezing for several seconds. Only then did they start running. The initial, evolutionarily programmed response, freezing, has long been effective in keeping humans and other animals like us alive.[7] The decision taken by members of the crowd to run might just have been conscious, or partly conscious but it will have originated in a 'flight' (rather than 'fight') decision initiated in what would be Kahneman's System 1. Underlying this particular decision, there would have been both negative affect and associated involuntary responses triggered by the motor system. This would mean that people 'found themselves' in a physical state of extreme arousal, and running, as in James's bear example, and then instantly had the conscious experience of fear, possibly in that order although both responses would surely have seemed simultaneous and if they were simultaneous, in any case the flight response followed on afterwards.

'Partly aware' is certainly a possible state to be in. In other words, consciously experienced emotions or 'feelings' can have a subconscious component. An example of this in-between state is what Freud called 'free-floating anxiety' where you are aware of being anxious but have no sense of what has caused it (Zajonc 2000).[8] Zajonc and others have talked about the possibility of subconscious emotion but maintained that, although the *source* of the emotion may remain completely hidden, the resulting feeling is *always* conscious. However, Berridge and Winkielman show that affective responses can also occur when no subjective feeling *at all* is experienced. They report studies where they demonstrate entirely 'implicit' emotion affecting people's subsequent behaviour and influencing their mood without their knowledge (Berridge & Winkielman 2003). In sum, explaining emotion and awareness of emotions and the way it affects behaviour, although of great importance, involves the nature of particular connections between affect and other mental systems. There is however much more to say about the affective system than its role in the creation of conscious feelings.

---

[7] Freezing is the result of information relayed from the thalamus to the amygdala. It is the activity in different parts of the amygdala that triggers the freezing response and the immediate action taken afterwards (LeDoux 2002, 243).

[8] This is an unpleasant halfway state which is chronic in people with generalised anxiety disorder (GAD) and there is a tendency in us to resolve it by pinning the blame on something we know about but which may not necessarily be a real cause of the anxiety.

```
       ┌──────────┐
       │  Affect  │
       │ Processor│
       └────┬─────┘
            │
            ▼
       ┌──────────┐
       │  Affect  │
       │  Store   │
       │  (AfS)   │
       └──────────┘
```

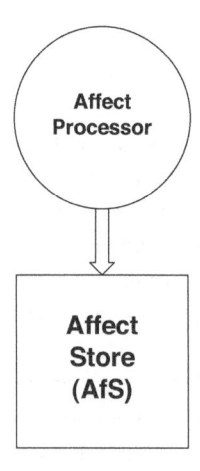

Figure 5.1 *The affect module.*

Valence and Appraisal

Affect has already been referred to as an evaluation system. The outcome of an evaluation (appraisal) by the organism is the assignment of a particular value to the structure(s) concerned; this outcome is generally referred to as *valence*, used here in its most basic sense. Valence can be positive or negative (Fridja 1986, 207).[9] Valence settings may be associated with negative emotions like sadness and anger (negative valence) and, on the positive side, happiness and admiration (positive valence). Affect, as has been described earlier, goes deeper than that. It begins with a primitive, automatic system that is shared with thousands of organisms helping them to survive both as individual members of their species and ultimately as a species in general. In other words, at the heart of affect is a basic 'approach' and 'avoid' valence system.[10]

All emotions, whatever else sets them apart have either one or the other type of valence in the form of a feature that is associated with them. In the framework, such features would be primitive **affective structures** residing in the affective store (Figure 5.1). These primitives would have preset connections with many other systems already giving affect a central role in the mind as a whole (see Figure 5.2). This role becomes even more important as new experiences are

[9] This two-way division of valence is not entirely uncontroversial as, for example, with reference to how you might classify the surprise or 'startle' response, which is generally treated as a negative response diminished in the presence of something positive and enhanced in the presence of something negative. How valence is defined naturally depends on the theory of affect that has been chosen to account for the emotional system. Valence can also be used as a way of distinguishing between different basic emotions.

[10] Truscott (2014, 83) uses *val* and *harm* respectively as labels for positive and negative valence indicating the basic opposition between things that have value and things that are harmful.

evaluated during an individual's lifetime and existing evaluations are amended. At the brain level of description, this is reflected in the extensive reach of the neural network that governs affective responses. The affect system associates positive or negative values to structures (images, sounds, tactile sensations, involuntary movements, etc.) that are stored in other expert systems. As already suggested, some of these values are already assigned *at birth* to optimise the child's chances of survival. By their involuntary responses, like sneezing and blinking babies show that they are attracted to and also seek to avoid certain things from the very beginning. However, many positive and negative values, both strong and weak, are indeed *acquired* during an individual's lifetime.

As mentioned previously, affect is also the crucial component driving consciously experienced emotions. This includes basic feelings like fear, anger and disgust but also more complex emotions like pride, shame, self-consciousness, embarrassment and guilt arising from interactions between affect and other systems like the conceptual system.

Basic Emotions

Although the idea goes back at least to Plato and Aristotle, the researcher probably most associated with the idea of basic emotions in recent times is Paul Ekman whose search to isolate basic emotions that are universal, that is, valid for all cultures and part of our biological inheritance led him to analyse many different facial expressions and other physiological responses (Ekman 1972). He has isolated the following discrete categories: *anger, disgust, fear, happiness, sadness and surprise*. Since then researchers have argued about the number of basic emotions and the overall validity of this concept but the general idea is that more complex emotions will be combinations of the basic ones. Seen from the perspective of the framework, emotions that reach the level of awareness are likely to be the outcome of collaboration between different systems including the conceptual system.

For the time being we can treat the basic emotions whatever they are and however many there are, as composed of affect structures (AfS) that are not basic but at least minimally complex since they will each include one or other of the two primitives: positive and negative valence. This would mean that *surprise*, for example, might have two manifestations depending on whether it was pleasant or unpleasant, the first being a structural combination of surprise and positive valence and the second, surprise and negative valence (but see Note 7).

A minimal definition of the affect system would be that the only structures the store ever contains are positive and negative valence. In that case, all other emotions would be explained as a more or less complex network of associations with structures in other modules, for instance, between one of the two affect options and the meaning structures in the *conceptual* system as well as *motor* and *somatosensory* structures (governing the physical responses and sensations accompanying the emotion in question).[11] To take a specific example, fear, one of the basic emotions, could simply be a primitive affective structure available from birth in the affective store along with the other basic emotions. Alternatively fear could be explained not as anything within the affective system itself but as a particular set of external connections with strong negative valence in the *affective store*, motor structures governing fight or flight responses in the *motor store*, somatosensory structures governing associated bodily responses in the *somatosensory store* and conceptual structures governing associated meanings associated with fear in the *conceptual store*. These two possibilities for representing the role of affect in the mind provides just one example of how alternative accounts can be worked out using the framework, one with and one without the idea of basic emotions.[12] Theoretical considerations would play a role but evidence coming from brain research would be an important factor as well since the two maps, that is, of *mind* and *brain*, need to be kept in some sort of coherent relationship with one another.

Another important aspect of affect, not yet mentioned, is how to account for different degrees of *intensity*. In terms of explicit emotion, what, for instance, distinguishes *mild surprise* from *astonishment* or *shock*? Within the framework, this could be handled by the degree of activation of the structures involved. Highly activated affect will trigger degrees of awareness making whatever affect is being processed an explicit emotion. Clearly anything with *negative* valence that is very strongly activated will create a strong sense of unpleasantness. This would mean that, by passing the threshold of consciousness, structures have not yet reached their maximum degree of activation and can still be differentiated between relatively mild feelings and relatively intense ones. We will return to the topic of activation in the next chapter.

Integrating Affect with Perceptual, Motor and Conceptual Systems

Finally, to bring the map of the mind almost to completion, we can now add in the affect system. To fully complete it, the core language part will be added in Part II. The map is displayed in Figure 5.2 again with all five senses chosen for this account. As before, adjustments have been made to simplify the picture and so the processors for the AfS store as well as for the CS and MoS

---

[11] For a highly readable discussion of many complex emotions that might be represented in such networks, see Tiffany Watt Smith's *The Book of Human Emotions: An Encyclopaedia of Feeling from Anger to Wanderlust*.

[12] An even more radical alternative would be to put positive and negative valence in the conceptual system, perhaps as the most primitive version of a conceptual system which has subsequently evolved into something much more complex. The framework is flexible enough to accommodate this and other options.

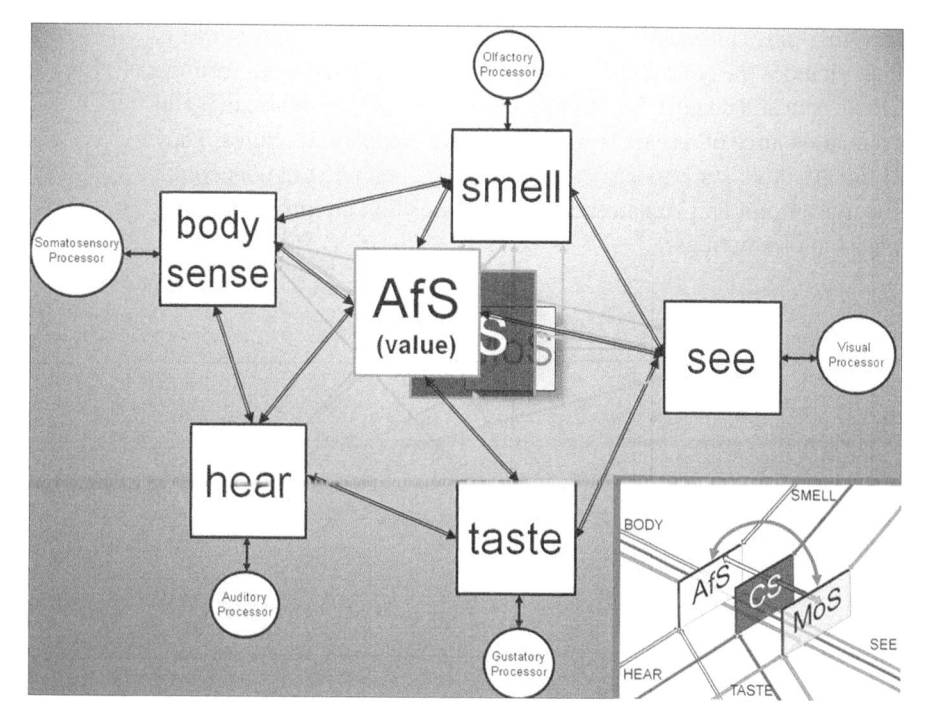

Figure 5.2 *The affect (AfS) system and its network of interfaces.*

stores have been left out in the main part of the figure. However, in the small insert (located at the bottom right corner of Figure 5.2), the three systems in the centre of the whole network have been rotated to the right and slightly downwards to show the missing interfaces connecting them up. All but the interface arrows radiating from affect to other systems have been shaded grey so that only those parts relevant to the affect system stand out. Also included are all the other radiating connections that were already displayed in the main part of the figure.

Summary

Much fascinating research into the human affective system is yet to be done both at the neural level and at the mind level which augurs well for our understanding of both dimensions of human cognition. Already we know that much goes on beyond our ken since, as with cognition in general, most mental life proceeds below the level of awareness. Apart from the affective setting that we are born with to optimise survival chances, we can assume that every experience we have is appraised and given some valence rating that will influence our behaviour on future occasions. This includes preferences and all kinds of decisions, including the ones that appear to us to be purely conscious and rational. It may be best to think of the affect system first and foremost as a system that assigns values although one of the important manifestations of this is emotion, which includes the consciously perceived emotions that we call feelings such as fear, love, hate and disgust. Basic emotions that we can recognise in facial expressions, a major source of research on emotions, are complex structures. They link items in the affective store to associated meanings, encoded in conceptual structure, as well as motor and somatosensory structures that are involved in the physical expression of emotions.

6 Memory, Processing and Activation

In This Chapter

Previous chapters have discussed many of the individual expert systems that make up the mind. Figure 5.2 at the close of the last chapter displays the framework almost in its entirety, that is, all except the core language system. This chapter will now look in more detail at the operations within and between expert systems in the framework, also with reference to the two remaining systems to be introduced in Part II. It will include an account of how memory works and the role it plays in processing in general.

Mental 'processing' refers to what takes place as the mind engages in the vast number of tasks it has to perform every minute of our lives. Sometimes the adjective 'on-line' is added to 'processing' to indicate that it refers to ongoing activity at a given moment, measured typically in milliseconds. 'Off-line' processing in the literature on processing refers to processes that are generally thought to take place over a much longer period such as the processes of learning and forgetting although, as will be explained, momentary instances of learning and forgetting actually do take place on-line.

With the ever more sophisticated brain-imaging techniques at our disposal, more and more mental activities can be identified and tracked. Although neuroscientific research is beginning to give us exciting insights into the neural underpinnings of many psychological processes we are still a very long way indeed from a full account of brain function and hence also a long way from a comprehensive matching up of mind and brain. As usual, it is all 'work in progress'.

Memory

As has been illustrated in previous chapters, mental structures ('representations') reside in special *memory stores*. Our framework incorporates a particular version of the widely held view in the psychological literature that memory is not a single system but is modular. This is implied in frequent references to notions such as 'semantic memory', 'episodic memory', 'motor memory' and 'muscle memory'. The way memory is split up in the current framework may

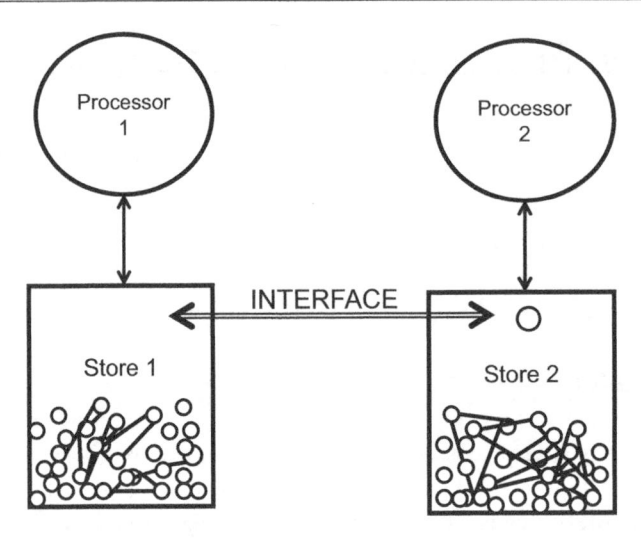

Figure 6.1 *Two interfaced memory stores.*

suggest affinities with some of these commonly used categories in the psychology literature but the framework has a particular way of dealing with memory so its terms will not have necessarily identical matches with these popular categories. Some translation may be necessary when comparing them. The approach in this book will however reflect the underlying modular principle underlying the organisation of all memory. This means that the mind does not possess just one single common memory for all purposes or even one working memory used during processing. Even in the brain, the existence of shared pathways in the building and use of memory should not be taken as evidence that all memory works in precisely the same way at the neural level either. There, indeed, memory is also modular. Auditory memory is wired differently from visual memory. Olfactory memory is organised differently from motor memory. As has already been exemplified in all of the previous chapters, the consequence of this modularity of mind is that each module not only has its own processor and set of operating principles, it also has its own memory store.

Memory stores, to reiterate what the basic design implies, are each part of one or other of the particular expert systems or mental modules. Any of these will always contain a *processor* that works with the items in its store and is equipped with *interfaces* that connect up items in its memory store and memories in stores belonging to other modules (see Figure 6.1).

Each store, according to the framework, contains various items – both the basic building blocks, i.e. the *primitive structures*, and various combinations, i.e. *complex structures*. If we can imagine the primitive items as memory 'atoms' then the combinations, the complex memories, are 'molecular' in design. It is not just primitives by themselves that are provided in advance: a number of associations across interfaces, that is, associations between structures in one module and structures in other modules will also be part of our biological 'starter package'.

In this way, several systems can be activated simultaneously as in a baby's response to something dangerous or to something rewarding. For example, if a baby suddenly feels itself tipping forward it will spread out its arms instinctively. This is the 'parachute reflex' referred to in chapter one and is triggered by a cluster of predetermined associations between affect (in this case strong negative value) and structures in the somatosensory and motor systems. Such connections therefore do not need to be formed during our lifetime. They are there from the start. However, a new face, sensation or place, say, will normally trigger the construction of new memory structures. These will be stored in the memory stores of the appropriate modules along with associations in the form of given interface connections; they will remain, at least for a short while, depending on how useful they turn out to be. These constructed memories, formed as a result of life experience, represent the *vast majority* of what each store contains. The construction of new memory structures is at the heart of developing new knowledge and ability, which is the topic of Chapter 8.

The 'molecular' complex structures (see the smaller, joined-up circles in Figure 6.1) are assembled on-line using a selection from

1. the primitives (the single circles);
2. other preexisting complex items (combinations of joined-up circles) that have been previously assembled as a result of the individual's personal life experience.

Construction of new memory structures can happen any time as a part of regular processing activity. This chapter will now go through the basic concepts required for a basic understanding of how memory works.

Communication between Modules

As just mentioned, the memory stores contain items that are there from the start but these may be combined and recombined to form new items during the individual's lifetime, all of which serve the purpose of that particular expert system. For example, as a result of the ever-changing visual world experienced by a given individual, new *visual representations* are formed in *visual memory*. Figure 6.2, in which the larger single circles inside the stores represent both primitive as well as complex structures, shows the visual memory store on the left and its interface with the auditory memory store on the right. Two separate memory items have been activated, one from each store, and their connection via the visual-auditory interface has been temporarily activated. In this way, a particular event can bring about the activation of, say, a visual representation which, in turn, triggers the activation of an associated auditory representation. This can happen the other way around when you hear something and an associated visual memory is activated. For example you might hear an alarm go off and immediately the image of whatever sounded the alarm might pop into your mind.

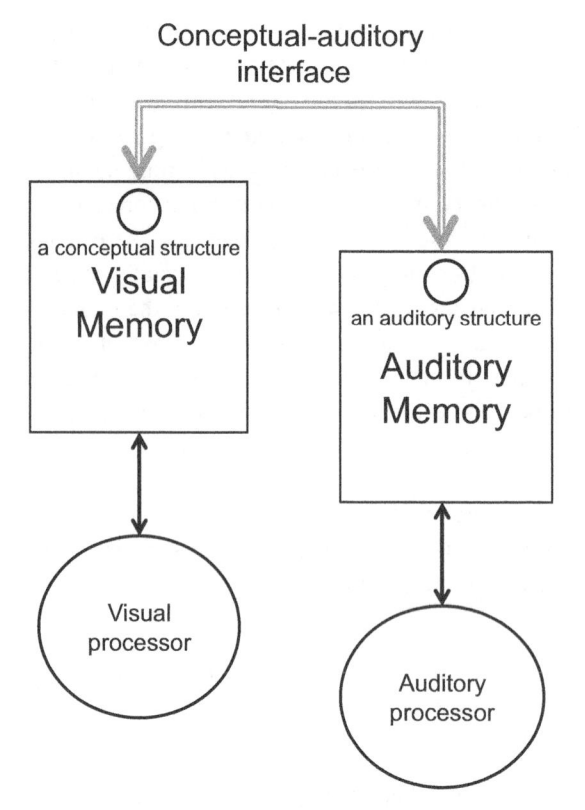

Figure 6.2 *Two working memories with an interface connection.*

The communication between these two associated structures, the visual and the auditory one, takes place once they have appeared in *working memory*, or more precisely in the two working memories of the respective modules when the activation of one has led to the visual-auditory interface triggering the activation of the other. In the framework, by convention, working memory is represented as the *upper part* of any memory store as will be explained in the next section.

Working and Long-Term Memory

It is usual to distinguish between *long-term memory* (LTM) and temporary memory which is used purely during processing to store items that are currently being used in some way, in other words working memory.[1] Some models of memory treat these two types of memories as quite distinct, a classic

---

[1] 'Short-term memory' (STM) is sometimes used as a synonym for working memory and sometimes not. STM will not be used in this framework (see a useful explanation of these confused terms in Cowan 2008).

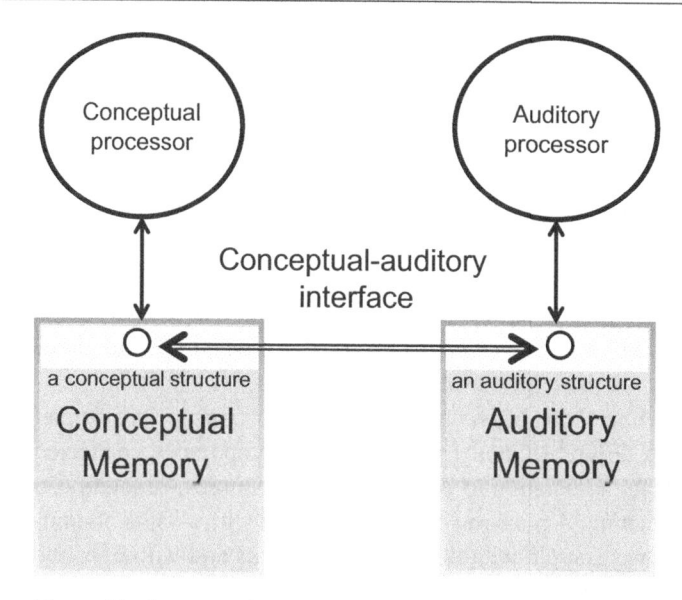

Figure 6.3 *Coactivated structures in two working memories.*

example being Baddeley and Hitch (1974), but in the current framework, working memory and LTM are seen as different *states* within a single memory store (see contributions to Miyake & Shah 1999a). The two basic states are *resting* and *activated*. In this perspective, then, LTM and WTM refer to different states of activation and not separate systems. An item in is in a *resting* state unless it is part of current working memory in which case it is in an *activated* state. The latter basic state is actually a matter of degree and varies from weaker to stronger. Activation could be visualised as an item becoming excited in some way, hotter or brighter or louder. As already indicated in the previous figure, in the framework used in this book the preferred way of visualising levels of activation places a given item in memory on a vertical plane. This metaphor works well in diagrams as long as one realises the hot/cold metaphor, involving no movement through space, would really be just as appropriate. Whether currently activated or simply resting, i.e. inactive, structures/representations can be found 'higher up' or 'lower down' in their particular store. The uppermost level is the working memory space, represented in Figure 6.3 as the unshaded area.

What elsewhere is called 'long-term' memory simply refers here to those items that remain in the memory store, activated or inactivated, in other words do not fade rapidly away.[2] As indicated earlier, primitive items in a given memory store will normally remain there even when not used at all so it is the *combinations* (complex structures) that are created as a result of life experience structures that

---

[2] We leave aside the question of whether, once formed in memory, some trace always remains or, alternatively, whether complete forgetting as opposed to long-term or even permanent 'inaccessibility' is always possible.

may have only a fleeting existence or, alternatively remain in memory for a longer time should they prove useful.

The idea that frequent use not only ensures the continuous existence of a complex memory structure but gives it a higher resting state relative to those that are less frequently used will be crucial in the way learning and forgetting will be explained. Activated items, normally resting at some position below, may rise up for a brief moment into this uppermost, working area of memory.[3] There they take part in on-line processing activity. This working memory area, in other words, is the 'workbench' on which the processor can combine or manipulate in other ways the items in its store. This area is also the place where the linking of items in *different* stores via the relevant interface takes place.

As just mentioned, interfaces between expert systems open up a channel through which items in different memory stores can be temporarily connected up. This allows an instant association to be made across modules. A sound can be associated with a meaning. A meaning can be associated with a value or emotion, and so on and, as we grapple with the reality around us and within us, the associations typically involve not two but many interfaces, all at once.

Interfaces are not just pathways between two modules: they can be best thought of as *very simple processors* whose job it is to match up items across different stores so that chains or whole networks of activated representations are formed to cope with some current task. Figure 6.3 shows two structures, each in the store belonging to a different module, in this case the conceptual and auditory module respectively and linked via an interface. This process is called coactivation. In this particular example a particular auditory representation is paired with a particular meaning (conceptual representation). For instance, the meaning 'burglar alarm' is coactivated with an auditory memory originally created in response to the sound of a burglar alarm. One triggers the activation of the other so that both can appear in the working memory area of their respective stores and temporarily form a chain. In the framework this would be a CS⇔AS chain linking a conceptual representation (CS) with a sound representation (AS).

Items in working memory, it should be emphasised are only there for a brief moment, after which they gradually resume their resting state. This means they 'fall back' into a position somewhere below, that is, at or near the position they were in before. Their fallback position or *resting level* can change. The general idea is that, once they have been activated in working memory, they experience some gain in their resting level however minimal that might be. In other words their new position will be at least fractionally higher than it was. By the same token, if they are not activated for a long time, their resting level will tend to gradually decline. This would be an example of an 'off-line' process. The consequences of this for an individual's knowledge and performance will be elaborated in Chapter 8.

---

[3] The image often used for this temporary workspace is of a 'blackboard' on which representations are written.

To sum up so far, items in memory can be either in a state of activation or resting. Activation is not a simple on-off process but a matter of degree. Any item (structure, representation) at rest, i.e. not currently in working memory, is in a 'long-term memory' state. This is because both working memory and LTM are not thought of as independent systems but as different states within the same memory store. This is an implementation, within the current framework, of Nelson Cowan's view of memory rather than those associated with the work of Alan Baddeley (Baddeley & Hitch 1974; Baddeley 2012; Cowan 1993, 2005). The state approach appears now to be the preferred one in psychology (Miyake & Shah 1999b, 443–445, 450; D'Esposito & Postle 2015).

Indexing

So far the matching of items across memory stores has not been explained. How does an interface between two stores identify which item in the one store corresponds with an item in another, adjoining one? The mechanism driving this process of matching items across an interface is a tagging system called coindexing. Associating the one item (structure/representation) with the other has the effect of giving each the same index. For convenience, we can imagine these indices as numbers so the visual representation of an alarm clock can be paired, i.e. coindexed with the auditory representation of the sound it makes in the following manner (choosing an arbitrary number, in this case 124):

[visual representation of alarm clock] $_{124}$ ←→ [auditory representation of alarm clock] $_{124}$

This means that whenever one of these activated items pops up into their respective working memory area (using the preferred 'vertical movement' metaphor for the process), the interface locates any item in the associated store that has the same index. That item is then activated and rises into its own working memory and the matching illustrated earlier takes place. Typically any structure in a memory store will have or will acquire a number of indices. In other words, a given structure such as the one representing the meaning ALARM CLOCK, may have many potential associations so each one would have the same index (124). The activation of one structure will therefore trigger the activation of the others and each could be in a different memory store. This would result in all the structures marked with the index 124 being associated across the various working memories, temporarily activating a '124' network of associations during a particular moment of mental processing.

The neural equivalent of an index might be, but not necessarily, a single neuron, like the one unique cell that fires only when we perceive or think of, for instance, a particular person, or place (Dehaene 2014, 145). There should be at least one or otherwise a particular ensemble of neurons that have the unique identifying function of an index so that the appropriate coactivation can take place.

The process whereby the activation of one item in working memory in one store triggers activation with items in other stores that share the *same index* is called spreading activation creating whole *networks of association* across the memory stores of various different modules. In psychology, spreading activation is used in both modular and nonmodular approaches. In nonmodular approaches, spreading activation is unconstrained. In modular approaches, such as the current framework, activation spreads across the system as a whole only where there is coindexing. There will be some coindexing that has taken place in advance as part of the survival package at birth. Apart from that, indices have to be formed across systems via the interfaces and within systems according to different sets of principles, the principles of the individual modules. Life experience drives the creation of new networks of connections that carry this spreading activation but the rich internal structure of the mind determines when and how that might happen. We will return to this subject again in the chapter on development to explain how the indices first get assigned.

Competition

So far a simple, straightforward account has been given of a single structure being activated in a memory store leading to another single structure being activated in another and spreading further in the same manner. In actual fact it is a lot messier than that. In trying to establish, in the milliseconds that fly by, the associations that represent the current 'best fit' for making sense of whatever it is that the mind is dealing with, there is normally a tussle between rivals going on. In other words, there is *competition* between *candidate structures* both or all of which might get to participate in a current chain of structures across different stores. At any given moment, the strongest one will win, in other words the one most strongly activated is the one which participates in the ultimate chain. Using the term 'selection' for this participation is possible but misleading in a way because it suggests a decision by a higher authority[4] rather than the natural outcome of competition; it can be used here with the proviso that the decision is just a shorthand way of referring to the best match between all structures in the chain/network at the time.

Mostly unbeknownst to us, this competitive activity is taking place in our heads all the time. Language performance provides clear examples of this. We can get a sense of it when we find ourselves uttering a spoonerism like 'not in the sleast'. Here the competition between two rival candidates, *not in the least* and *not in the slightest* fails to be resolved before we open our mouths to utter the expression. The competition itself takes place below the level of conscious awareness and so

---

[4] The same danger surrounds the use of the term 'executive function' and similar ones with the words 'control' or 'supervisory'. These should not be seen to imply a single, orderly command-and-control centre in the mind, much as this idea might reassure us, but rather a number of different coordinating systems not necessarily linked by a single chain of command and not necessarily there from birth onwards.

we can only become aware of the result. It happens all the time. If you recognise an object in front of you, its recognition will normally seem spontaneous: the fact that you have successfully identified something after an internal struggle between rival interpretations will not attract your attention at all. The struggle is often an unequal one.

Sometimes awareness can arise as we become conscious of the fact that the result of an initial decision is problematic, in other words ill-fitting and unsatisfactory in some way: people who speak more than one language will be very familiar with trying to choose a word in one language that they definitely know but nevertheless find that, perversely, the wrong word, its equivalent in another language, pops up instead, suppressing the one that they intended to use. This can also occur, even within one language, when we temporarily forget the right word for something. The same thing happens when we start searching for an item in one drawer, the one we are used to finding it in, when we have recently moved it to another drawer. Old habits die hard, as they say. The dominant candidate is no longer the right one. In our heads, the more firmly established knowledge of the old location temporarily outcompetes its replacement, i.e. our relevant but still weakly established knowledge of the new location. The old chain of associations is overcome when it turns out not to be the best fit in the circumstances but the error may still persist for a while. In other words the resting levels of the 'erroneous' chain will continue to make it a winner on some occasions until the activation of the new chain is strong enough to outcompete it on every occasion. The odd moment when we become aware of the results of this competition process should not obscure the fact that competition between items itself is a regular feature of all mental processing and takes place below the level of awareness.

The example in Figure 6.2 showed a single visual representation matched up with a single auditory representation in their respective working memories. It should now be clear that the normal situation is different: there will be a number of rival candidates jostling for a prominent position in working memory. Imagine a situation where you are in a room and an alarm goes off. You know that there are several possible sources of that sound in the room as you scan the area. You have three possible sources, electronic devices that make similar beeping noises. Figure 6.2 displays a particular instant in time when, for example, a *visual* representation, say of a particular alarm clock, is paired in your mind with an *auditory* representation of a sound that that alarm clock makes. Several candidate visual representations, representing other electronic devices nearby will all have been activated and have been in competition with each other for a period of milliseconds before the right one, say that of an alarm clock, by virtue of its stronger level of activation, beats off its rivals and takes part in a wider network of representations that underlies your ultimate interpretation of the sound. In the activity surrounding this event, the activated networks will of course include at the very least the conceptual structure ALARM CLOCK[5] and the motor structures guiding your movements involved in, say, switching off the alarm.

---

[5] The convention in the framework is to represent conceptual structure labels in block capitals.

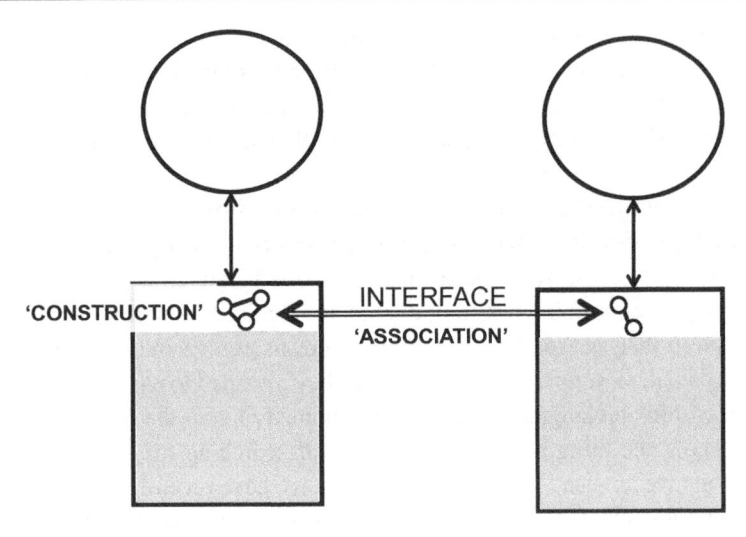

Figure 6.4 *Constructing and associating.*

'Construction' versus 'Association'

Reference has already been made on numerous occasions to items being 'constructed', 'combined' or 'assembled' and also being 'associated', 'linked' or 'matched up' with each other. Some further clarification may be necessary at this point. There is one basic distinction that is relevant here and that is between operations that link elements *within* a memory store (to be referred to as **construction**) and the interface operations that link elements temporarily *across* stores. Those processes taking place within a memory store are the unique responsibility of the processor in that module (see the complex memory item constructed in the store on the left displayed in Figure 6.4). That is all it can do. It cannot combine into a new structure something from its own module with that of another. The reason is that the encoding in each module follows the unique principles of that module. A visual processor cannot handle anything in the auditory memory store simply because it is encoded differently. It is, as it were, written in a language it does not understand. It is like a processor that can only process JPG (image) files and crashes when it is asked to deal with a MP3 (sound) file. Another way of looking at it is that each processor deals with a different jigsaw puzzle. Giving it a piece from a *different* jigsaw puzzle will not work because the piece is shaped so that it will not fit anywhere except in its *own* puzzle and is therefore useless when applied to another puzzle.

This construction process in working memory within a module shows how sophisticated processing there contrasts with the simple processing operation of an interface. What can an interface do? It can only form a temporary *chain* between two structures, a chain that may also be part of a wider network. If this association 'works'[6] on a particular occasion it will give them an identical index

---

[6] In other words, it works if all the currently linked items in the various memory stores turn out to be the best fit for the current target. This is discussed in the chapter on development (Chapter 8).

so that the next time around, activating one will automatically cause the other one to be activated.

The interface process of 'association' is, then, a simple one and therefore quite unlike the often complex building operations that are performed by a given processor on items in its working memory. The processor combines and creates structures that may last for some time, certainly longer than the brief moment when two items are briefly linked across stores during on-line processing. Just think of the visual processor creating a visual representation of 'apple' with all the various colour, shape and texture features that this will involve. These features will be combined together, in visual code, to form a complex item in visual memory. The resulting complex memory structure may then be coindexed with a similarly complex structure in the olfactory store, for example, associating the visual appearance of an apple with its smell.

Processing Goes Both Ways and at the Same Time

Processing, which is extremely rapid, does not normally operate purely as a sequence of operations, one after the other, but works in parallel as different mental systems simultaneously handle just the input that they are designed to handle. In other words, processing is both *parallel* and *bidirectional*.

Initially spreading activation will proceed in one direction incrementally, that is, building up a chain of representations in a linear fashion in response to an initial trigger but the chain construction process will soon change into one that is not a simple one-way process.

In the solving of a current task, whatever it might be, the business of on-line construction and association of memory structures will yield a rapid first attempt at building an appropriate structural chain or network which may or may or may not work out. You hear something, say. For an instant, you interpret it as a knock at the front door. That is your mind's first attempt. The first attempt may not turn out to be optimal so the flow also goes backwards and forwards to seek matching items in different stores that form an optimal response to the current input. The initial input may be from outside, from the environment. It may be from inside, when you start searching for something in your mind or when you want to express a thought. In other words, in the milliseconds that follow, our minds go on processing, building up a network of associations until they have achieved the best fit. You recognise the sound as the radiator pipes knocking. You may not even have been aware of your first incorrect interpretation of the knocking.

Activated, competing structures that have *failed* to participate initially in building a chain of structures may still get selected[7] in the end because the 'victory' of originally selected structure may turn out to be transitory if it then turns out not to fit the overall interpretation of the event once a wider network of representations has been activated. You might interpret a word at the beginning of a spoken

---

[7] That is, 'selected' in the cautious way in which we are using this term now (see earlier discussion).

utterance in one way but then have to immediately reinterpret it when you had heard more of the utterance or after the utterance had been completed because the original interpretation of that word made no sense in the light of what followed. For example the utterance might go like this:

> "I watched the branch break [interpretation 'branch' as 'branch of a tree'] one of its main promises to its customers [abandon first interpretation and reinterpret 'branch': 'branch of a bank' or 'store']" etc.

Another example of this reinterpretation process would be when, for example, you see a friend coming towards you and your first attempt at interpretation identifies him or her as 'unknown' but a second later you recognise that person. This may happen relatively slowly so you become conscious of the delayed recognition of your friend but, again, it could equally well happen so rapidly you are not aware of the initial lack of recognition. This portrayal of parallel, bidirectional and incremental processing is in general agreement with many current approaches within cognitive science.

Every Module Is Both Expert and Stupid

It is important always to keep in mind that each processing unit has its own unique operating principles, that is, its own ways of assembling and combining items in its memory store. Its processor can only access and manipulate items in its own memory store, i.e. it cannot handle items in other processing units. A processor deals only with activated items in its own store, that is, in its working memory. The interfaces permit associations between structures of different types, i.e. the formation of chains of representations. At the same time the structures remain distinct. Auditory representations remain auditory, that is, structured in auditory code, and, by the same token, visual representations which have been linked with them during processing remain formulated in visual code. In other words the auditory system is expert in matters auditory and 'stupid' as regards any other type of structure. This principle will be further illustrated in Part II when talking about language.

Summary

This chapter began with defining what memory is. There is no common store. Each expert system has its own memory. The only sense that there is anything like a shared memory is when different memories are activated together and cooperate in some complex mental task.

Activating an item in memory places it in a state that is referred to as working memory. Some items are more easily put into this state, or to use the standard analogy in the framework, can more easily 'rise' into the working memory area, pictured as the upper level of the store. This relative accessibility is because the item in question has a higher resting level in the store, so it does not have far to go to enter the upper area, again using the analogy of height.

Items in memory, i.e. structures, often referred to also as representations, include the primitive elements supplied in advance as part of our biological representations. These give us the basics for handling the very first sensations we experience and are the result of evolution. Life experience allows us, or rather the various expert systems we possess, to build complex structures out of these simple ones. In this way our memory stores fill up with items in response to our personal experience but still constrained by the construction principles of each particular processor. Consequently our visual store will never build an auditory structure.

Since making sense of our experience entails a collaboration between many expert systems, the modules, that constitute the resources at our disposal, there has to be a way of associating items in one store with items in another. This is the job of the interfaces that link them. To be matched, an item must be given indices, an index being a kind of identification tag. The interfaces between stores, given one item activated in one working memory, will trigger the activation of items with the same index in other stores thus forming a chain or network of matched items across the stores in question.

In coping with a particular task, the various processors involved will typically have to sort through a number of options to arrive at the best fit across the network as a whole. Processing therefore tends to race back and forth across the individual working memories involving various candidate items each activated in their particular working memory. This results in competing sets of structures in the various working memories. Usually in an instant, this search will resolve itself and a best-fit chain will be selected. All of this is concluded in milliseconds and beneath the level of awareness. There is no supervisory system making decisions. Selection is the outcome of a collaboration between modules to resolve the competition.

7 Consciousness and Attention

In This Chapter

Despite the fact that most of what happens in the mind is subconscious, our awareness of what is going on around us, our conscious attempts to solve problems and to increase our knowledge are vital for any explanation concerning any aspect of human cognition. As already suggested and in tune with various approaches to consciousness within cognitive science, the perceptual system in the current framework also plays a key role in generating the experience we call conscious awareness. Even though a complete understanding of what consciousness is may always elude us, it is certainly possible without going into too much philosophical detail to have an explanation of what it involves within the current framework. At least it will provide an explanation that has some degree of plausibility given current thinking in this area.

Included in the (inevitably modest) explanation of the phenomenon of consciousness will be an account of how conscious awareness differs from attention, a major topic in psychological research, and to what extent (and how) either of these two concepts is involved in learning. The relevance of consciousness and attention to language will largely be left out of this discussion since it will come into focus in Chapters 11 and 12, in Part II.

Activation-Based Explanations of Consciousness

While a comprehensive account of consciousness has so far eluded everybody, and some people say that goal is impossible, a great deal has been written about the possible mechanisms that give rise to it. The framework as currently implemented adheres to an activation theory of consciousness, which bears some relationship to the Global Workspace model proposed by Bernard Baars (see Baars 1988; Baars & Franklin 2007; Truscott 2014). In the current framework, the activation theory is interpreted as follows: the experience of consciousness is the immediate result of very high activation levels within the perceptual systems as was outlined in Chapter 3. Especially in the case of coherent thought, this also involves very high activation within the conceptual system.

Activation-Based Explanations of Consciousness 79

This intense activation characteristic is compatible with recent neuroscientific research linking conscious states with specific neural firing patterns following on from Crick's well-known hypothesis that associates consciousness with the synchronised firing of relevant neurons at a frequency of about 40Hz (Crick 1994; Crick & Koch 2007). Also, subconscious responses to the same perceptual content may vary with each encounter. By contrast, conscious responses registered as activation patterns in the brain seem to be reproducible giving another way of distinguishing between the two (Schurger et al. 2010).

Affect has an important role to play in an account of whatever rises into conscious awareness. The awareness of affect itself came up for discussion in Chapter 5. Although affective structures themselves are inaccessible, affective states can certainly be recognised consciously and many can also be described. This is true whether or not we treat basic emotions like fear, anger and disgust as directly reflecting primitive affective structures or whether they rely instead on the activation of a positive or negative value in a simpler affective module but in combination with structures from other modules, together making up one or other of these basic emotions.

More generally, the different value structures in the affective system are very active in all kinds of processing as is the case with structures in the perceptual group with which the affective system interacts all the time. Highly valued representations in the normal course of processing will have high resting levels of activation and so remain very accessible: they 'matter' more and are thereby more likely to participate in conscious experience. At lower levels of activation we may attend to something but not be aware of it. This is the case with *blindsight* where subjects with this condition (a brain lesion in the primary visual cortex) actually do respond to visual stimuli in a way that shows that they have actually seen something, in some sense of 'seen' but, at the same time, they will report (misleadingly) that they haven't seen anything. The mind has registered something but the resulting percept – the weakly activated visual representation – has not acquired the level of activation required for it to reach awareness and hence be reportable by the patient. Apart from anything else it is a graphic illustration of how input from outside involves various stages handled each by different systems. In this case, a particular brain deficit has disrupted the normal process whereby a normally highly active perceptual system will ensure a degree of accompanying awareness in such a situation.

Conscious awareness involving what we choose to call 'knowledge' and 'thinking' derives from collaboration between perceptual structures and other mental systems. In particular, conceptual structure ('meaning') plays a crucial role because it is here that we build up a complex representation of the world. Knowledge of, say, the geography of Peru or the way the local transport system works is encoded in conceptual structure. Using this knowledge consciously involves a projection of the relevant conceptual structures into the perceptual system, that is, not literally the structures themselves in all their fine detail for these remain inaccessible but their *contents*. This is an example of coindexed structures being coactivated across interfaces between the conceptual system and various perceptual systems. In other words whereas the fine detail of conceptual structure remains completely inaccessible to us, the meanings as given shape within the perceptual systems are very accessible. While easy to grasp when talking about concrete objects like laptops, hats and trees, it might be more difficult when it comes to abstract notions which by definition have no physical form. Nevertheless they too are projected in consciousness by the perceptual system: in this way, notions like 'beauty', 'inequality', 'subtraction' and 'distance' are 'objectified', recast in perceptual clothing by their associations with concrete objects as well as the visual appearance of the written words and numbers and associated auditory structures.

Thinking Consciously Works Slowly and Sequentially

One generally agreed characteristic of such conscious thought is that it operates sequentially. This is Kahneman's System 2 at work (Kahneman 2011). We cannot think of two things in parallel, i.e. simultaneously. If there are two things that currently occupy our thoughts we have to switch back and forth to keep them in our thoughts. The high levels of activation required and the synchronisation[1] of structures across many modular systems allow for only one thing to be held in the spotlight at one time. Lower levels of activation and a reduced use of the system as a whole which is characteristic of the vast amount of mental activity going on beneath the accessible levels of conscious awareness allows many things to be done swiftly and in parallel. Mental arithmetic is a good way of demonstrating to oneself both accessible and inaccessible activity. This requires a bit of careful introspection. If one pays close attention while doing some challenging mental calculation, it is possible to distinguish the conscious mental processes engaged in the task from those moments where the required numbers simply pop into our heads as if called up on a mental computer screen. How the numbers got there is a mystery but it was from somewhere our conscious minds cannot reach. In sum, most of our mental activity, the subconscious part that is, involves parallel processing (as opposed to serial processing) so many things can be done at the same time making the system enormously more efficient and effective.

Attention, Awareness and Activation

If once projected into consciousness, thoughts and ideas cannot be entertained simultaneously so what then, is the difference between conscious *awareness* and *attention*? Thoughts have to happen one by one. As far as unfocussed sensory awareness is concerned, the vague awareness, for example, of

---

[1] For a fuller explanation concerning the role of synchronisation here, see Truscott (2014, 120–123).

your visual surroundings when you are focussing on something else, a worrying problem at work, for example, it may seem that you *can* be, albeit dimly, aware of different sensations at the same time: you can be focusing on one thing but can switch to some detail in your surroundings if it suddenly, as we say, 'claims your attention'. In other words, it looks as though awareness can be spread out into an area that is in focus and one that is out of focus. If that is true, it is still the case that just the area in focus admits of the kind of resource-intensive higher level processing involved in thinking. If thoughts are to be directed towards something in the vague *unfocussed* area, that area now jumps into focus and excludes the former object of your focussed awareness: Bernard Baars in outlining his Global Workspace theory uses a theatre metaphor, comparing consciousness to a stage with the spotlight as the area in focus (Baars 1988, 1997).

The study of, and theorising about attention has a long history (Styles 1997, 2005). A simpler account of attention than many is provided in the framework integrating attention into the explanation of conscious awareness, in other words it is about the generation of various levels of activation.[2] In most accounts, attention is seen as a different phenomenon: in one sense it is the gateway to awareness: you cannot become aware of something without attending to it. It is also the case that passing a certain threshold of activation will result in what might be called attentional processing but not necessarily producing awareness. Attention seems to be used as a cover term for different processes some of which involve conscious awareness whereas others do not (see discussion in Lamme 2003; Posner & Rothbart 2007, 2012; Van Boxtel et al. 2010).

The role of affect is important in accounts of consciousness and attention. A boost in activation levels may be caused by the introduction into a currently active network of a structure that is *highly valued* (either positively or negatively). In other words, a match has been made between a currently activated structure and an affective structure and this has the effect of bringing about a general increase in activation across the network. For example, say something has suddenly been perceived which happens to be coindexed with a very negative or very positive value, effectively making it into a threat or something very attractive. The threat or attractiveness becomes strong enough to boost the activation sufficiently to cross the threshold of awareness and causes the individual to focus on whatever it is.

An entertaining example of how affect might influence what becomes conscious is the invisible gorilla illusion which is a demonstration of **inattentional blindness** (not to be confused with blindsight mentioned earlier). Here, participants are asked to watch a video clip[3] of two teams, each composed of three basketball players. One team is wearing white T-shirts, the other black ones. The instruction given in advance is to count how many times the 'white' team pass the ball. At least half of the viewers, watching this for the first time do not spot

---

[2] For a more detailed account of this, see Sharwood Smith and Truscott (2014, 272–277) and Truscott (2014, 67).
[3] A video of this may be available at https://www.youtube.com/watch?v=f94o3B3csYI.

a woman dressed as a gorilla walk through the players right across the screen from right to left. If they did notice the gorilla they probably failed to notice either the curtain at the back changing colour or one player leaving the game. As a result of the instruction given to the participants before the clip was played, attention is focused on the passing of the ball. In other words, the effect of the instruction is to place a particularly high value on this aspect of the visual scene to be presented and boost the activation of structures related to that task. This results in the viewer being aware of the players and their ball passing precisely because activation levels of these particular features in the visual field have been boosted enough to pass the threshold of awareness and into the spotlight. At the same time, other activated features, have not received, in at least half the first time viewers, sufficiently high boosting to pass the awareness threshold: these viewers will not notice the gorilla. For these participants, the threat level of what they may well have perceived and perhaps even formed some meaning association with, was not given a sufficiently high affective boost to overcome the effect of the highly charged competing structures as influenced by the instructions. The account of attention and awareness here would mean that if the gorilla ran towards the camera baring its teeth, everyone doing this task would notice the gorilla the first time around. This at least would be what the framework suggests and further empirical investigations with the appropriate techniques would be needed to test this out.

Things that have received our attention but not enough for us to be aware of them may still have some impact as is evidenced in various *priming* studies.[4] If, for example, a word is flashed on a screen for a period too short for the participant to notice it (consciously), the resulting rise in activation level of the unnoticed word can still bias ('prime') the participant's response to a following stimulus. If the prime is 'tan', for example, and the subject is then instructed to supply the missing letter in 't-n', there would be increased likelihood of that participant filling 'a' to produce the primed word 'tan' rather than other possible responses such as 'tin' and 'ten'.

To sum up, whereas things that we are consciously aware of can only be experienced in a slow, sequential manner, as discussed earlier, things that are not sufficiently activated to trigger slow sequential processing, i.e. enter into awareness, can be processed much faster.

Perception as the Engine of Consciousness

The philosopher, Ned Block makes a distinction, which has provoked quite a lot of controversy, between what he calls 'P-consciousness', i.e. *phenomenal* consciousness, and 'A-consciousness', i.e. *access* consciousness (Block

---

[4] It is appropriate to point out that priming studies may also include primes of which participants have been made aware.

1995). Roughly speaking P-consciousness is immediate, raw experience, sensations of all kinds and emotions. A-consciousness, on the other hand involves rational thinking, reporting, planning and controlling. We may imagine that we share A-consciousness with many other animals but not P-consciousness.

In terms of the framework, where ultimately all consciousness in perceptual, Block's P-consciousness necessarily involves the conceptual system, which in humans is particularly complex. While some conscious visual or tactile experience, say, may yet be meaningless, i.e. have next to nothing in the conceptual system associated with it, abstract thought cannot but be meaningful in some way. The point about perception being the engine of consciousness is rather than abstract concepts by themselves cannot become conscious without being embedded in some perceptual clothing. It is not that notions like *beauty* and *truth* and *trickery*, for example, must have a straightforward connection to some specific, recurring perceptual experience. I don't need to have, say, a visual image of Plato in my mind every time I think of truth or some famous actor whenever I think of beauty. Nevertheless when first grappling with the particular abstract idea in question, I need to invoke aspects of the perceptual world that contains examples like this. Initially, maybe, when the still unfamiliar abstract concepts are invoked, I may well have a reoccurrence of fleeting perceptual experiences that I originally associated with it, not necessarily busts of Plato or memories of some glamorous actor but perhaps short scenes are played out in my head which illustrate the idea. In time, once that abstract concept has become familiar any associated perpetual structures used while learning them will have ceased to be activated sufficiently to appear in my conscious thoughts at the same time. In the same way, the pedestrian manner in which I first learned to do arithmetical sums, visualising the whole process of counting items, adding them and subtracting them and seeing what is left at the end will be reduced to a brief visualisation of the numbers to be manipulated and the solution popping up without any sense at all of the intervening calculations.

Awareness of Emotion

Emotions were covered in Chapter 5, where 'emotion' was presented as another concept that covered both conscious and subconscious states (LeDoux 1996; Damasio 1999). The term 'feeling' is favoured for emotional states than involve consciousness. Affective processing can occur without an individual becoming aware of it. Awareness of emotion involves awareness of the physical states that accompany positive and negative feelings. Assuming for the moment that basic emotions are affective structures (see Chapter 5 for a fuller discussion), then, depending on the nature of the affective structure that has been activated, certain *motor* responses may also be triggered such as frowning, the tensing of various muscles and so on. This also involves the *somatosensory* structures that have been coactivated intensely enough for the individual to become aware of them. Feelings are also very likely to have meanings in the form of associated conceptual structures, particularly in humans. *Conceptual* activation can vary enormously in complexity and will be closely related to the individual's past experience and also to linguistic knowledge. That individual will have various ways of categorising various feelings and giving them linguistic expression along with the related conceptual structures that have been developed during the acquisition of language giving them very specific meanings. Their intense coactivation will also bring these conceptual structures into the domain of awareness. In this way although the perceptual system is the engine of consciousness what drives it is complex processing in a variety of modules, all contributing to the feelings that are being experienced.

Summary

Much of our mental life occurs beneath the level of consciousness. This even includes some perceptual experience as in the case of blindsight and inattentional blindness. As far as describing that part which we do have conscious access to is concerned, the two dominant ideas are activation and perception. An account was given of how conscious experience is created as a result of the very high level of activation of structures in working memory. A related concept is attention which has long been the focus of interest in psychology, that is, long before the scientific study of consciousness became respectable. An important feature of conscious thought is that it is relatively slow and sequential: two conscious thoughts cannot occur in parallel. By way of contrast, decision making occurring beneath the level of consciousness, often described as intuitive, is not limited in this way: processes discussed in the literature on attention include those operating below the level of consciousness. The richly interconnected set of perceptual systems is the engine that generates the experience of consciousness but this is also accompanied by the activation is other systems working below the level of consciousness notably the affective, motor and conceptual systems.

8 Developing Knowledge and Ability

In This Chapter

This final chapter of Part I looks at structural change, how an individual's knowledge changes as a result of processing activity. This covers learning or forgetting a new physical skill like football. It also covers acquiring, and forgetting more purely abstract knowledge and skills, for instance mathematical knowledge or knowledge of the London Underground system, knowledge of your family tree, knowledge of Chinese history, knowledge of the layout of a building and so on. In Part II we will return to this topic but there we will focus on changes in an individual's linguistic knowledge and ability. The current chapter sets out the general principles by which we can explain changes in knowledge and ability of any sort. At the same time, in line with the principles of the framework, any kind of mental development must be understood in the context of its modular nature: changes in one system should be explained separately from any impact those changes might or might not have had on other systems in the mind although the interaction between modules is an important part of the story as well.

Knowledge and Ability Combined

Development involves structural changes in an individual's current knowledge and ability. Although they can still be distinguished, knowledge and ability are treated as different aspects of the same process in this framework. Ability or skill is a term used for that part of knowledge that is frequently and appropriately manifested in an individual's observable performance. It is associated with the relative *accessibility* of the relevant structures in the relevant stores. This has to do both with the availability of the right interface connections and the ease and rapidity with which the various memory structures can be deployed in working memory. There is no 'special ability mechanism' involved. Knowledge is a wider term and covers situations where an individual has not yet achieved high enough resting levels of activation in the modules concerned and is therefore not 'skilled' with regard to the given type of task. Appropriate structures and connections may be in place but they are not easily accessible.

More established structures and connections can outcompete them and as a result performance is still relatively hesitant and inaccurate.

Knowledge as Relative

It was already established in the introduction to this chapter that, psychologically speaking, 'knowledge' in this framework can also be seen as a relative concept. If you are in the middle of learning something, whatever changes have taken place in your mind (and brain) represent your current 'knowledge' even though it can still be judged according to external norms as 'wrong', 'imperfect', 'incorrect' or 'incomplete'. This relative, 'psychological' sense of knowledge may seem unorthodox and difficult to accept since normally we think of knowing as the endpoint of learning: anything else is judged as imperfect and wrong. The point behind the psychological view is, however, important: the individual mind's representation of the world can be accepted and studied just as it is *without any value judgment*. In this regard, it is useful to remember that we judge the world literally as we see it and, as was made clear in the discussion on perception, how we see the world is definitely not how it is insofar as science can tell us about the nature of 'objective reality' around us.

To avoid confusion it is perhaps best to retain the term 'knowledge' in its standard everyday sense so not only referring to a particular network of mental representations possessed by an individual but to one that is highly valued. That is to say, it is accepted, at least by that individual and usually by others, as reflecting 'the true state of affairs'. The many philosophical ramifications of this need not detain us here.

Knowledge and Ability Distinguished

Knowledge and ability seem to be related concepts but somehow, at the same time, different. If you ask someone if they 'know how to', for example, 'play' football, it seems different from asking them if they know any Peruvian history. If you have what is judged to be a 'poor' ability at a sport, you may, as mentioned previously, possess more 'knowledge' residing in the various modules implicated in that skill than you are actually able to manifest in your spontaneous performance because that knowledge is not easily accessible. Particularly in the case of physical skills, this includes structures in the motor system. Such structures will obviously play a central role unless the knowledge of the sport remains purely theoretical or 'academic' and especially where the individual has only the bare minimum of the required knowledge of how the sport should be played.

The distinction between knowing and being skilful is often explained using the notions *declarative* knowledge or 'knowledge that', on one hand, and, on the other, *procedural* knowledge or 'knowledge how'. However, the framework permits a unitary account of both of these aspects of knowledge/ability together, one that does not require a such a fundamental separation of the two concepts: the declarative/procedural distinction remains useful as long as it is understood as not referring to two separate systems (see also discussion in Sharwood Smith and Truscott 2014, 162–165). Ability is measured in terms of how you perform and can often be an imperfect mirror of what you actually know, especially in the case of fast, spontaneous performance. It has to do with the *implementation* of those current structures you happen to have in place and their various connections across modules irrespective of their accessibility and whether you are using them or not. All things considered then, knowledge and ability can be seen as are part of the same phenomenon: the currently available structures (representations), their connections, their particular resting levels of activation and hence their current potential for being deployed in both mental and physical tasks. If your knowledge, as judged by the relevant expert from your performance, is founded on an appropriate set of structures with appropriate resting levels and connections ranging across all the appropriate modules, then that expert will assess you as both knowledgeable and skilful.

There is certainly one way in which we can talk of different types of knowledge in the framework and that is a direct consequence of its modular architecture. This allows us to distinguish the combined representations that are present in one module from those in all the others. In other words, we can talk of *visual knowledge, olfactory knowledge, auditory knowledge, perceptual knowledge* in general if you take that whole group of modules together, *conceptual* knowledge and so on.

Finally, there is an extensive literature in *explicit* and *implicit* knowledge, the latter type being strictly limited to the inaccessible, subconscious level. The notion of explicit knowledge and its related concept declarative (or 'propositional') knowledge involves conscious use and conscious learning. In many but not all cases it refers to knowledge that can be reported and pondered on. In the framework, what is elsewhere called declarative knowledge consists of knowledge formatted in conceptual code, in other words, conceptual representations and specifically those conceptual representations that that can be projected into an individual's consciousness. Knowledge about Peruvian history would be an example of such knowledge. We will return to this topic in Chapter 12 when discussing knowledge about language.

APT and Bidirectional Development

Development is used here as change that can work in two directions. It covers both *growth* in the sense of an *increase* in structures and connections between structures as well as in the sense of growth that manifests itself in behaviour in ways that we would be more likely to describe as a *decline* in knowledge and ability or 'forgetting'. In both cases, the basic principle, in the framework, is covered by Acquisition by Processing Theory (APT). 'Acquisition' here is just another word for structural development somewhere in the mind, a process that can be labelled as growth but APT also covers structural change that is labelled reduction, *attrition* or loss so the 'A' in APT can stand for attrition as well.

Simply put, development, one way or the other occurs as a *result of processing* or, in cases of attrition, as a result of infrequent, or lengthy *absence of processing*. It is not typically marked by dramatic jumps although this can occur. Rather, change typically occurs gradually. When, in the act of making sense of something unfamiliar, there is nothing suitable that is currently available in a memory store, the relevant processor will create a new structure on-line. The resulting new structure will then linger on for a time. Normally it will start off with a low resting level of activation. This means when activated it will not, all other things being equal, be able to make its presence known in working memory, enough, that is, to compete properly with any other candidate structures for participation in any current on-line chains. In other words, strongly established rivals with higher resting levels of activation will outcompete it. Left alone and inactive, its level will decline further and potentially fade away altogether.[1] Further activation in future encounters will ensure it remains longer and becomes gradually more firmly established: as a result it will then be more likely to participate in an individual's observable behaviour. Lack of activation will lead to its decline. This is the 'use it or lose it' idea of learning.

The APT principle refers to processing history *within a given module* and not to frequency of events taking place in the outside world and potentially impacting upon the individual. In other words, we may be frequently exposed to stimuli that should *in principle* trigger activation and therefore keep our knowledge or ability up to scratch or strengthen weakly established knowledge or indeed create new knowledge on the basis of that evidence. *In practice*, growth, in the acquisition sense, may not take place at all. If for some reason we do not process it in all the right places, this evidence that we have been exposed to will have little or no impact. Exposure to technical literature on boiler installation will not of itself entail the gradual growth of knowledge in that area. Continuous exposure to broadcasts in a language we do not understand will not of itself cause the growth of the relevant grammatical and vocabulary knowledge. Explaining a rule of grammar to someone, as will be discussed in Part II, may not have any impact upon the system that determines syntactic growth. More dramatically, the explanation of an optical illusion will not make the illusion go away. Growth happens within the different systems in the mind only when the stream of information needed to make them grow actually knocks on their doors and is let in so that processing can proceed.

---

[1] As mentioned earlier, the idea that memory, in healthy individuals, is never completely extinguished is kept open as a theoretical possibility here. In any case, a memory still existing but remaining stuck at a very low resting level is unlikely ever to appear in an individual's performance in which case it may be treated in practice as fully forgotten.

[Figure: diagram showing Processor connected to Working Memory Store with Structures A, B, C at different resting levels]

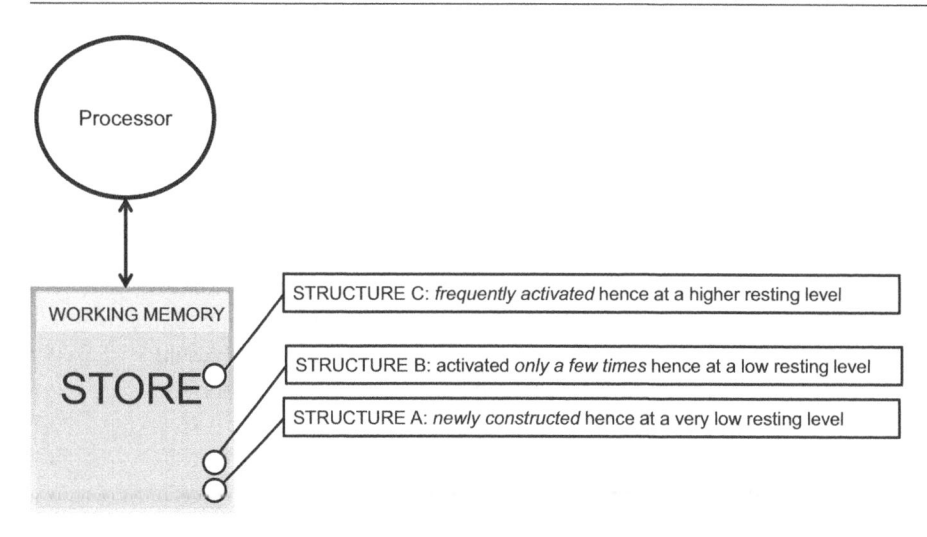

Figure 8.1 *Different resting levels of activation.*

Development means changes in resting levels of activation. Processing involves the activation of structures and connections between structures in memory stores. Any structure (representation) in a store has a resting level of activation which determines how accessible it is, that is, how swiftly and easily it can be raised into working memory. A newly formed structure typically gets a low resting level, i.e. is not easily accessed. Unless it just happens to be the current focus of processing and therefore temporarily raised up into working memory, that low level is where it will fall back to and where it will stay for the time being. The important idea behind APT is that each time a structure is activated, it will acquire, however minimal it may be, a gain in its resting level. This gain makes it more accessible in future processing events. Using the idea of a store as a box which has working memory at its upper surface, the gain in resting level brings the structure in question nearer to the top and hence gives it a shorter distance to travel up into working memory. The longer a structure residing in memory remains inactivated, the more likely it is to undergo a reduction in its resting level and hence reducing its availability during processing. It sinks, as it were, towards the bottom of the store and is therefore handicapped in any race to the top (see Figure 8.1). Rival candidates will beat it every time in the competition unless something happens to raise it to a more competitive level.

Note that it is not inevitably the case that a newly formed representation will start at the bottom since it may have been immediately associated with a strong affective valence as in so-called flashbulb memory (Brown & Kulik 1977). In the framework this means its resting level of activation is accordingly boosted to a higher, much more accessible position. For example a single event that makes a vivid impression, positive or negative, may be remembered easily for a long time to come.

It is also the case, when a structure has only just been acquired it may, at least initially, have a higher resting level because of a recency effect: it gets a boost from the affective system giving it the status of a 'valued' structure. Later on, where its resting activation level has sunk down to a typical low 'starting position', it may receive boosts during on-line processing. This will be when the particular circumstances favour its use over more strongly established rivals. This will take the form of support coming from the value (affective) system in combination with contextual clues in the environment that are associated with the use of that particular structure. Amongst the systems processing these contextual clues, the conceptual system will play an important role. A little more will be said about this when we come to the concept of conceptual triggering in Chapter 15.

Resting Level as a Relative Concept

Since our minds are in a state of constant activity with processing going on in various parts of the system as a whole pretty well all of the time, the notion of a 'resting' level of activation, taken literally, is open to question. Even during sleep, the mind is active. This means that resting levels are continually being revised up or down. In other words, 'resting' has to be understood as a relative concept. Any particular mental structure may have a 'reasonably stable' resting level for a time but typically not for long and sometimes hardly ever. In this very restrictive sense, it is a dynamic system.[2] The basic principle that governs it is APT.

Growth and Affect

Learning can be enjoyable or boring and this seems to influence the rate in which something is learnt or forgotten. In most if not all systems other than the affective system itself, there will be an interface through which structures are associated with, at the very least, some sort of valence, be it positive or negative. As just mentioned in connection with so-called flashbulb memories, this will have an effect on the structure's resting level.

The standard APT (Acquisition/Attrition by Processing Theory) account, as has been presented thus far, is that growth occurs as the lingering effect of processing and that a newly formed structure will begin its life in memory with a low resting level. This low level will be raised every time that structure participates in processing. This will make it more accessible and increase the probability of it participating in on-line processing in future. However, progress will typically be slow because that structure will be handicapped by its relative lack of accessibility. The 'old habits die hard' effect renders it vulnerable to

---

[2] See the brief discussion of dynamic systems theory in the book's introduction.

competition by more strongly established structures with higher resting levels. We go first to the drawer where the cutlery has always been, until last week. At the beginning of January, we find ourselves filling in the date with the number of the old year instead of the new one. The new structure's fortunes will improve whenever the older options prove unsatisfactory and the new structure is accessed in its place: it will be 'rewarded' with a gain in its resting level as a result. The use in processing that boosts its resting level is also aided and abetted by features in the current situation that serve to promote it use over other, stronger candidates, that is, provided those features are also perceived and processed by the appropriate modules.

Summary

This chapter discussed knowledge and ability as aspects of the same process. It allowed for the relative view of knowledge if external, conscious evaluations of objective reality are discounted. Without the mark of approval as a result of conscious evaluation by the individual and often other respected individuals as well, 'true' and 'false' knowledge are otherwise indistinguishable as far as the mind is concerned. If there is a distinction to be made between knowledge and ability, then it is essentially in terms of accessibility: this is a matter of resting levels of activation. Ability implies high activation levels and therefore readily accessible knowledge. Normally, growth or 'development', is thought of as going in the direction that we call learning or acquisition but it also includes change in the other direction, the one that we think of as forgetting or attrition. Increasing levels of activation makes structures inside a memory store and those associated with them outside more accessible and therefore better able to compete for participation in any chains being formed on-line during the handling of some given processing task. A simple way of thinking of resting levels is in terms of two possible states, either as resting, i.e. 'inactive' or otherwise as 'active'. More realistically, activation is a matter of degree. Activation often spreads from one module to another. Activation levels are typically in flux all the time with consequent minute changes taking place continually. In other words, they could be described as some sort of dynamic system. Another qualification to the simple characterisations of growth is the role of affect which can affect the initial resting levels of activation as well, the most striking illustration being the case of flashbulb memories.

Part II Language(s) in the Mind

Part II deals with how language is incorporated into the general framework elaborated in the preceding chapters. It will explain how language, taken in its broadest sense, engages the mental systems as described in Part I. Two modular systems are specific to language and were left out of the picture that was developed in Part I: they explain how babies and toddlers learn to communicate with us in a way that is so very different from other species. They form the core of human language ability. However, defining language as this core alone would be a great mistake: a great deal of language in the mind lies outside it and is processed by systems whose primary purpose is often understood to be nonlinguistic but which are nevertheless recruited for linguistic purposes. This larger domain of language in the mind, outside the core, is no mere periphery. It shows language engaging multiple systems in ways no other species can manage and is vital for our understanding of how the mind works in general.

The chapters in Part II will present the individual language user in a way that minimises the differences between so-called monolinguals and those that possess some degree of ability in other languages ranging from 'absolutely native' to a 'smattering'. The same set of systems governs all types of language acquisition and use. This holds despite the fact that the external social context, including social norms and attitudes contributes to all kinds of distinctions and value judgements that make us look and feel different about our language abilities.

9 Defining Language

In This Chapter

This chapter will elaborate, in terms of the framework, the narrow and the broad view of what language is. In its basic design, the framework is close, though not identical to the architecture that has been proposed by Ray Jackendoff for the language faculty (e.g. Jackendoff 2002). This architecture has been extrapolated in various ways to account for perceptual, motor and affective systems as well as the thorny issue of consciousness (discussed in Chapters 2 and 8).

The Broad and Narrow Definitions of Language

Apart from the two core modules that will be described shortly, language processing involves a range of processing units (modules). The most important ones are (a) the *auditory* system where all sound is processed including sounds that may be processed further as *speech* and (b) the *conceptual* system where meaning is processed including *semantic* and *pragmatic* meanings associated with language, and finally (c) the *motor* system, used for the articulation of speech, writing, signing and other modes of linguistic communication such as Braille. As is the case for all other modules, associations with affective structure are also important; in fact, all of Chapter 13 will be devoted to the relationship between language and affect.

The systems (a), (b) and (c) mentioned earlier all serve other purposes as well, i.e. not just linguistic ones. In fact their use in the production and comprehension of language is generally regarded as a secondary function. The lungs, tongue, teeth, lips and the soft palate, for example, are not there primarily to produce speech. The conceptual system contains meaning that has no expression in language. Although the contributing systems outside the core language system form a necessary part of what we understand language to be, they only figure in the *broad* definition of language.

The *narrow* definition of language involves the two systems that are unique to human beings and whose only function is linguistic. The two modules will be referred to together as the *core (language) system*. This consists of the *phonological* and *syntactic* systems. Here, respectively, phonological (speech) structures are constructed, stored and processed according to phonological principles and syntactic structures are constructed, stored and processed according to (morpho)syntactic principles.

Organising Speech Sounds

The module responsible for processing speech sounds handles phonological structures (PS) in the phonological store including those that have been matched with generic sounds in the form of auditory structures. Put another way, the phonology module receives input from the auditory module and, where it is able to, it matches the auditory structure (AS) in auditory working memory with structures from its store, it will. Not all sound admits of processing in this way so not all sounds will get processed phonologically. Speech sounds are therefore structured in a different way from auditory structures involving primitives that are irrelevant for many kinds of sound that meet our ears, the characterisation of primitives like *phoneme* and *syllable*, *accent* and so forth, again depending very much on the preferred theory.

In this way, the phonological system takes as its input (1) sound structures that are constructed in the auditory system, in other words structures that use the same code to represent the sound of a chain saw, the sound of a reggae band, tinkling glass, rustling leaves, snoring and a speech by Winston Churchill, and (2) the structures that are built by the syntactic system. The results are chains of different representations which match up auditory representations with phonological structures and syntactic structures. In comparison with sound structures built in the auditory system, the phonological system builds and encodes representations which have the special characteristics of all human speech and follow the universal principles that are the focus of phonological research.

Following the basic design of any module in the framework, phonology, so to speak, picks and chooses from among the auditory structures that are currently in the working memory of the auditory system just those ones with which it can match speech structures from its own repertoire. It may have some suitable candidates handy. If not it will build new ones but, as often as not it will not be able to produce a match for the currently activated auditory structures. As a result a snore or a snatch of reggae will not be interpreted as language and more will be said about this in the next chapter.

Organising Words and Parts of Words

The syntactic module is responsible for the way words and parts of words are formed and combined into larger units such as phrases, and sentences

Syntactic primitives like *N*(oun), *V*(verb), *Det*(erminer) and *T*(ense) are used in various combinations: depending upon the input they receive from the phonological modules and ultimately from a particular speaker, various constructions, i.e. syntactic structures (SS) are assembled in response to that input. Note that a structure like *Det* may either be paired to the phonological structure of a *whole* word as in English 'the' in 'the house' or it may be paired with the phonological structure of *part* of a word as in the Swedish equivalent '-et' as in the last part of the word in 'hus*et*' ('the house').

Together these two modules provide representations to match either input originating in the outside environment, i.e. samples of perceived language, or, in the other direction, when a message is being put together, conceptual structures (CS) that represent the meaning that the individual intends to convey. Both options are covered by the following bidirectional set of processing stages:

$$\text{SPEECH} \Leftrightarrow \text{AS} \Leftrightarrow \text{PS} \Leftrightarrow \text{SS} \Leftrightarrow \text{CS (MESSAGE)}$$

The syntactic system mediates between speech structures and the conceptual system that supplies, apart from structures that do not have any linguistic expression for the individual concerned, those meaning representations that *are* associated with language. Here structures are encoded according to universal principles that are peculiar to human language syntax.

As speech structures appear in the working memory of the phonological system, the syntactic system will attempt to build in its working memory a matching set of syntactic structures. If it goes the other way, starting with an intention to express a message in the form of speech, the input this time will appear in the form of a string of activated meanings (conceptual structures) created in the conceptual system, i.e. outside the core but with an interface with syntax. This will result in a matching set of speech representations (phonological structures) which in turn will trigger structures outside the core (in the auditory and motor systems) all ending up as audible speech. Again, more will be said about this in the next chapter.

The UG-Controlled Zone

The core language system is referred to generally in the linguistic literature as 'the language module' although the framework in use in this book, as shown earlier, treats it as containing two independent albeit richly interconnected modules. Whatever format is attributed to this central core of language in the mind, it follows principles that are best known as the principles of *universal grammar* (UG), the precise nature of which can take different forms according to what theoretical position is adopted, a subject of intense debate in the linguistic literature since the 1960s (see e.g. Chomsky 1980; Hauser et al. 2002; Jackendoff 2002; Jackendoff & Pinker 2005). In any case, UG is not to be thought of in the normal sense of 'a grammar' but rather as two separate sets of primitive elements

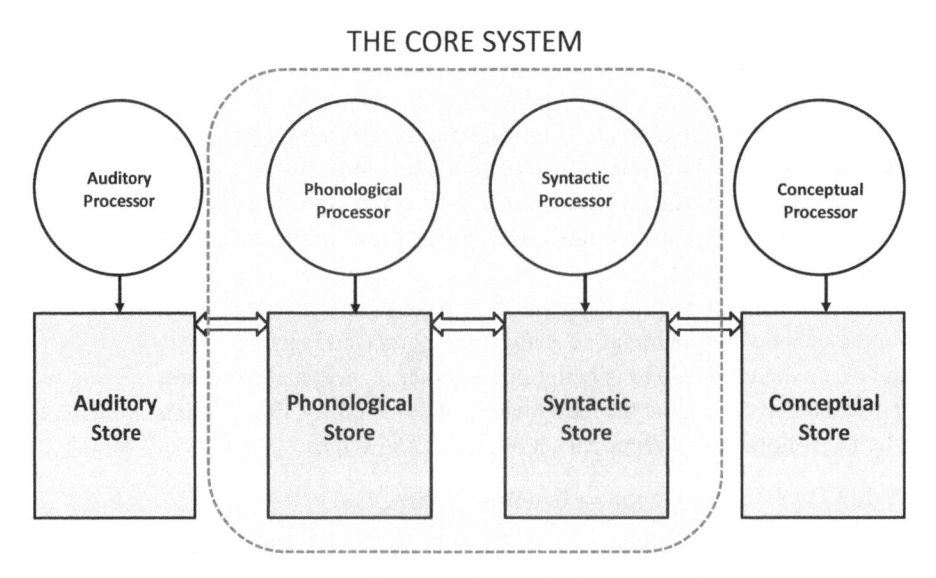

Figure 9.1 *Language: the core system and adjacent modules.*

that any language system draws from and also specific design principles that any particular mental *grammar* (not 'language') must conform to. This both closely limits the way in which a grammar can be (re)constructed using the particular input coming from a particular learner's environment but also still permits a great deal of variation between one language and another (Chomsky 1965, 2004).

Figure 9.1 shows the two modules that are part of the narrow definition of language, covering phonology and syntax plus, outside the core, two of the other modules covering sound and meaning that are needed for the broad definition of language. As mentioned earlier, the systems *outside* the core not only serve purposes other than linguistic ones but do not sharply distinguish humans from other species in quite the same way as, the two systems *inside* the core. The core, a zone controlled by the principles of UG, guarantees that humans will develop particular forms of communication[1] that are uniquely human. Not only will sounds be constructed in ways quite different from patterns observed in, say, birdsong, but the way the sounds cluster into larger units and are combined and ordered will be beyond the capabilities (or interest) of even the smartest bonobo ape.

Producing and Interpreting Utterances

Producing and comprehending actual utterances, be they spoken or in the form of text, certainly involves language in the narrow sense, in other words

---

[1] To define language as a system of communication is a simplification since we use it to think and dream in without any intention to communicate.

the two core modules. Even if the syntactic system does not contribute much, as would be the case for a learner of a first or second language in the very early stages listening to a spoken utterance, the phonological system will give shape to individual words. The auditory input will trigger some sort of response from the phonological processor calling up what it has in its store to give some shape to a word like 'dog', 'mama' or 'taxi'. Language in the broader sense has also contributed in its deployment of the auditory system supplying the auditory input. And, if the learner attempts to produce a word, this will trigger relevant structures in the motor system, also falling within the broader definition of language. In other words, along with the conceptual system supplying meanings, even a minimal use of language involves a number of modules outside the core system.

Summary

The mind as a whole has been presented as a system of systems. Even language is a system of systems, not all of which are specific to language itself. There is the core language system, which *is* specific to language and to humans. This is language in the narrowest sense. Language in the broader sense encompasses much more than that and recruits many systems none of which have only a language function but which, in fact, have a primary function that is nothing to do with language. The tongue is primarily there for tasting substances and for manipulating food. Its secondary, language function, is of course as an organ of speech controlling the flow of air, for example, and, when articulated together with other parts of the mouth, producing different vowel sounds but also making consonant sounds.

10 The Core System

In This Chapter

The core language system, elsewhere referred to as the language module, is that part of the network of systems supporting human language ability that is truly unique to humans. The ongoing debate concerning this claim will be left aside for the purposes of this discussion. In this processing-based framework, the *core language system* actually consists of not one but two independent modules following Ray Jackendoff's version so, in other words, 'language module' in the singular should be taken only as an umbrella term that covers all approaches that assume some sort of special expert system that constrains how the grammars of languages are built (Jackendoff 2002).

This chapter and the chapters that follow should not be taken as a proper introduction to linguistics although a certain amount of technical vocabulary will be used in the examples and illustrations and there will be some explanations of terms, mostly in footnotes, for the nonlinguists amongst you. Elsewhere traditional linguistic terms will be used without elaborating how these work in this particular framework (see Sharwood Smith & Truscott 2014 for a much more detailed account). Readers who are less interested in more technical linguistic detail may prefer to skip the sections on phonological and syntactic structure. Those who actually wish to know much more about how the framework handles these aspects are referred to Sharwood Smith and Truscott (2014).

What's Special about Language and What Isn't

Since recent research on the intelligence of apes such as the bonobo is having the effect of blurring the boundaries between *homo sapiens* and our nearest cousins, the great apes, it might be more appropriate to relabel our current evolutionary status as humans *homo loquens* – 'speaking man' – following, amongst others, the linguist John Lyons (Lyons 1968, 1991, 197).[1] In actual

---

[1] One might make a similar claim with respect to other aspects of human ability, musical ability, for instance. Interestingly, the generative linguist Ray Jackendoff, also a musician, has written a book with the musical theorist Fred Lehrdahl on what they call a 'generative theory of tonal music' (Lehrdahl & Jackendoff 1983). Also human conceptual ability might be a defining characteristic of 'humanness' although, in the framework, it is presented as a system that has its (much less complex) equivalents in other species.

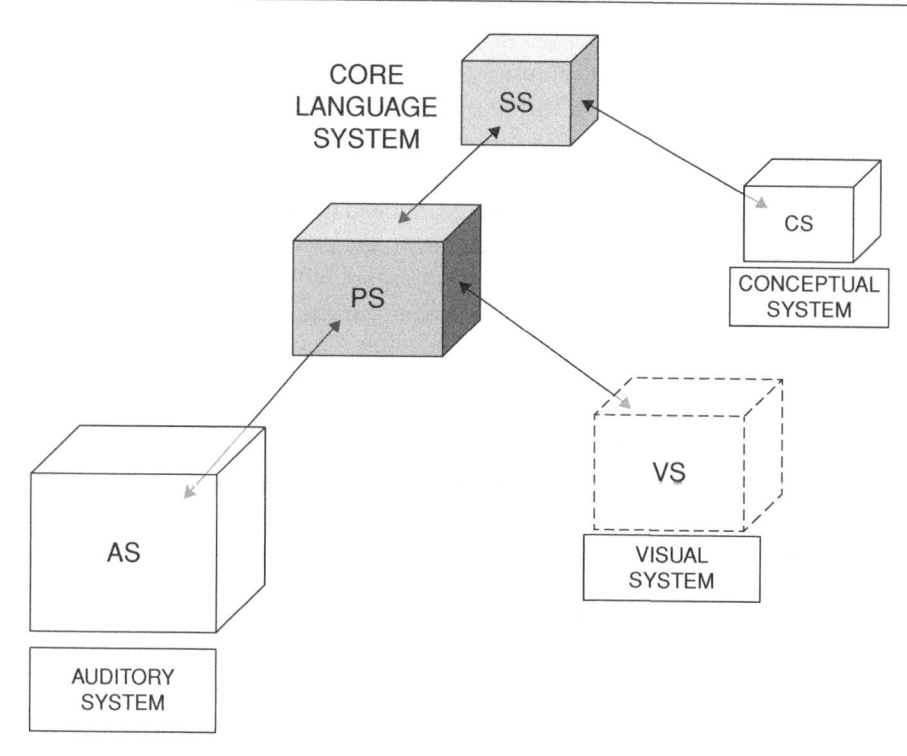

Figure 10.1 *The core language system connections.*

fact the speaking part is a collaboration between the phonology module, part of the core system, and two systems outside the core, namely the auditory system, the module that processes all perceived sound, and the motor system that runs all the physical activity involved in spoken communication (see Figure 10.1). This account leaves out input processing where no linguistic encoding takes place, namely the processing of the acoustic input that comes in via the ears that supplies the auditory system. Up to the point where auditory structures are produced and stored, nothing has happened that can be called truly linguistic as far as mental processing is concerned. This holds even where the processing of auditory input contains what are actually patterns of speech. These are not treated as such until the phonological and syntactic systems, where linguistically encoded structures are activated, constructed and stored, have been engaged.

The Two Core Modules

As mentioned earlier, the core language system specific to humans is a *dual* system, dealing in two types of linguistic code, and consists of the **phonological module** and the **syntactic module**. From the perspective of utterance interpretation, auditory representations (general sound structures) get matched with phonological ones, and phonological ones get matched with syntactic ones and finally syntactic representations that build phrases, clauses, and sentences as well as smaller parts of words[2] get matched with conceptual ones. Depending upon whether we are talking about utterance *interpretation* or utterance *production*, the initial direction of processing will be one way or the other: AS⇔PS⇔SS⇔CS or the reverse: CS⇔SS⇔PS⇔AS⇔MoS. A message initiated in the conceptual system will look for, and trigger appropriate syntactic structures which in turn will look for appropriate phonological structures which in turn will continue on via the auditory and motor system until a chain of matching structures is formed that results in the articulation of a written or spoken utterance.[3] Before that final result there will be split second, to-and-fro activity to get the best overall fit.

The contents of the two linguistic memory stores which, together with their respective processors and interfaces, form the core language system, fall into two categories. This follows the pattern for all mental modules as described earlier. Firstly, there are the representations known as primitives. As mentioned earlier, these primitives are structures that not only are unique as far as their particular processing unit is concerned but are also provided in advance, in other words are *innate* mental properties. In generative linguistics they are commonly referred to as properties of universal grammar (UG), 'grammar' here not referring to a particular grammatical system but rather a toolbox available for use when the mind is constructing a grammar of (any) language it is exposed to.[4] Note that working out the way in which *all* of a particular language system works is of course a much larger operation and follows principles that include those that have *nothing to do with UG*. This, incidentally, is not a controversial claim for any of those that support the UG perspective on language. UG principles are limited in this framework, to phonology and syntax.

Figure 10.1 displays, in three dimensions, the core language system with its direct connections to related modules outside it, i.e. the auditory, visual and conceptual systems: both core modules (shaded dark grey), are constrained by universal principles specific to human language (however, these happen to be formulated in the preferred current theory of UG).

The interface with the vision module is added here (in dotted lines) as a reminder that phonology does not interact exclusively with the auditory system[5]

---

[2] Linguistically knowledgeable readers will recognise that 'syntax' here also includes grammatical morphology manifested in words and parts of words that reflect tense, number or gender, for example. Depending on your theory, the processing of morphology and syntax may be viewed as involving one *integrated* system or two *separate* ones.

[3] The working hypothesis here is that speech production can proceed directly and only from the auditory structure, the one that has been matched with a given phonological structure. In other words our articulatory mechanisms are tuned to reproduce the *auditory* representation, not the phonological one. If that is correct, then learning to produce a word in a language is the same process as learning to imitate some non-linguistic sound.

[4] See also the first footnote in Chapter 9.

[5] In Sharwood-Smith and Truscott (2014, 23), in contradistinction to Jackendoff's preference for phonology being interfaced with the conceptual system, that is, to cover the meanings of certain speech patterns including variations in pitch that bear no relation to the syntactic structure of what

since language is expressed in the form of speech *and* writing but also *signing*: this then reflects what many sign language researchers assume, namely that signs have a phonology (even though the term 'phonology'[6] reflects its traditional function as part of the organisation of speech sound). To help the graphic display, this extra connection with the phonology module will not always be repeated in later figures as the map gets increasingly more complex so, in those cases, it should simply be understood. The next two sections cover in a little more detail the organisation and contents of the two core modules.

Phonological Structure (PS)

Phonological primitives will fall into categories that are determined by a given, preferred **phonological theory**. In terms of this framework, this theory would be responsible for specifying in detail the properties of the phonological code. PSs may involve items like, for example, distinctive features [**+voiced**] or units like **syllable, coda, vowel (V)** and **consonant (C)**. Stress, rhythm and intonation patterns are also accounted for there. These linguistic elements, whose precise nature[7] need not detain us here, will not be found in the auditory system although there will be auditory structures which will trigger them. Auditory structures (**ASs**) reflecting patterns of rhythm, and rising and falling pitch patterns do not of course need to be language-related. They might be matched up with a musical structure and not speech. The auditory system has no way of distinguishing what are musical patterns and what are language (intonation) patterns. In the same way on hearing a click sound, the auditory system has no way of distinguishing nonlinguistic clicks, say the click of a light switch, and linguistic clicks as used in the South African language Xhosa. This decision is taken later during phonological processing.

For those less familiar with linguistics, it is important to point out that phonological code is conventionally written between slashes, thus the sound uttered when a person says "dog" (in British Received Pronunciation) triggers the activation of an *auditory* representation of this sound and this in turns triggers the *phonological* structure /dɒg/. The phonological system provides no directions as regards how to move the lips, tongue and lungs in order to produce speech: so this example of phonological transcription between slashes is not intended to tell you how to *pronounce* the word 'dog'.

In this simple example, the phonological representation is a sequence of three phonological structures each of which will have a number of different auditory structures associated with it: this is because since the word 'dog' is never pronounced in exactly the same way yet it must somehow always be recognised as

---

is being uttered, the framework treats these issues being resolved via the *auditory*-conceptual interface.

[6] Φωνή (*phōnē*) is Ancient Greek for sound.
[7] See e.g. Hayes (2008) for an introduction to phonology.

'dog'. Also, each of the individual phonological structures /d/, /ɒ/ and /g/ will be associated with a set of different auditory structures depending on the context in which they appear. In English, for example, the /g/ as used in the phonological representation (PS) of 'doggy' (/dɒgi/) is associated with a *fully voiced* sound[8] whereas the identical PS in the word 'dog' coming as it does in word-final position and followed by a silence has a different auditory structure associated with it: when pronounced in relaxed, spontaneous speech, this word-final 'g' is only partially voiced and sometimes completely devoiced. In other words phonological representations are *abstract* and *fixed* whereas the associated sounds and hence their auditory representation can show a great deal of variety and this will be reflected in the differences in the auditory (phonetic) symbols used. PS /d/ in German, for example, may be associated with AS [t] as in the word 'Hand' meaning 'hand' when the word is followed by a silence or an unvoiced consonant like [p], [t] or [k].

Another example of the difference between auditory and phonological systems is the auditory equivalent of a *syllable* in phonology. Take the word 'allergy', for example. It has three syllables (all-er-gy). The analysis to establish the fact that the sound of 'allergy' is organised into three syllables is carried out by the phonological system. It is part of a wider analysis of speech sound that includes the assignment of word and sentence stress both of which have wider implications for, for instance, the cutting up of the speech stream into units that will need to be identified by syntax as nouns or verbs, etc. The mind does not categorise all sound in these specifically linguistic terms but, as is clear from our ability to recognise someone's special knock on a front door, the auditory system must be able to identify sequences of sounds that might in principle get analysed as speech by the phonological system. Three knocks on the door would, of course, not normally elicit a chain of structures forming via the core language system and triggering a given meaning thus: AS⇔PS⇔SS⇔CS. Instead, the representation of the knocking sound is more likely to link *directly* up to the conceptual system (AS⇔CS) eliciting a response like: "ah, I recognise that knock: it must be Sue at the door".

There will always be attempts on the part of the core language system to interpret any auditory input as language. It is on duty all the time. Phonological sequences of syllables along with the phonological structures they each contain may be matched up via the *phonological-syntactic* interface with categories in the *syntactic* store. For example, as has been indicated previously, the sound a speaker of English hears when a word like 'dog' is spoken is initially just that, a 'sound'. When it reaches the auditory system, it triggers an auditory representation (AS) from the store which contains many other representations

---

[8] Voicing (a sound made by air passing through the larynx where the vocal cords are brought together in close proximity causing vibration) is easily illustrated by placing the hand on the top of the head and producing a long "sssss" (not voiced) and then its exact voiced equivalent "zzzzz". The vibrations transmitted round the skull and produced by the vocal cords demonstrate an effect of voicing.

such as the one representing the sound of a glass breaking or a buzz saw or indeed a knock on the door. The *auditory-phonological* interface will trigger a match with a corresponding phonological structure. If there is no matching PS, as would be the case if the speaker were not a sufficiently experienced speaker of English, the phonological processor will then attempt to *construct* one based on the properties of the input and using its own special code and construction principles. Given that the auditory input is, in our 'dog' example, recognisable as language, some kind of phonological structure will be found for it. However, the phonological representation that is created in the learner's mind will not be nativelike. It may be the closest available equivalent belonging to the individual's native language, which will have a set of phonological structures associated with it. With a native speaker[9] of English, on the other hand, it will be processed in a way that is, by definition, compatible with being a native speaker and the result will be judged as 'nativelike', i.e. 'correct'. Alternatively if the word 'dog' is alien to the individual nonspeaker of English and is not like anything the speaker knows from another language and it is not guessable from the context, it might as well be a nonlinguistic sound like knock on the door. It will not get anything approaching a successful response from the core language system.

Syntactic Structure (SS)

Syntactic primitives will probably include categories like *Noun* (N), *Verb* (V) and *Determiner*[10] (Det) as well as syntactic features such as *tense, aspect, number, person* and *gender* which in many languages will manifest themselves as '*bound morphemes*' as well as independent words.[11] Morphemes are the building blocks of words. Some morphemes are there purely to make the syntax work. As was demonstrated with the English/Swedish 'house' example in the previous chapter, morphemes may be whole words or they may be parts of a word (as in Swedish 'huset'). The morpheme '-et' in Swedish which is equivalent to the definite article ' the' in English is an example of a bound morpheme because 'et' can never stand alone in any context as a separate word. Examples in English include *-ed* in the word 'jumped' signalling past tense. The first morpheme in that same word, '*jump*', is *not* bound but 'free' because it can stand on its own as a word in its own right as in 'let's jump'. Note that, strictly within the syntactic module, all the forms have absolutely no meaning. The syntactic processor only knows how to manipulate morphemes like *jump* and *-ed* to produce permissible syntactic structure as far as the principles of syntax (in any language) are concerned. In terms of this module all these structures are meaningless.

---

[9] The topic of what exactly a native speaker is will be returned to in chapters discussing various forms of bi- and multilingualism.
[10] This technical linguistic term covers articles like English *the* and *a(n)* but also forms like the possessive *my* and *many*.
[11] See e.g. Tallerman (2015) for an introduction to syntax.

Note that sometimes a syntactic structure may have no matching representation in phonology or in the auditory system. It will be there only implicitly like the number feature in *sheep* which distinguishes singular from plural where the shape of the word itself is the same in either case ('one sheep', 'two sheep'). Phonologically speaking, plural 'sheep' is identical to its singular counterpart and there is no audible difference between the two.

These primitive syntactic features that sometimes have a physical manifestation and sometimes not (as in plural 'sheep') are part of the language system's so-called *functional morphology*. Depending on the language, this will include not only whole words but word endings (suffixes) like the plural 's' ending in English as well as prefixes in front of words and also infixes, which are inserted into the middle of a word. In some languages morphological features like *number*, for example, even though they not manifested in sound, may be manifested in written text, as in French 'maisons', where the 's' is not pronounced.

Absence in speech or writing should not be seen to indicate these forms are redundant. This is by no means the case. The number feature, as illustrated in the preceding examples may be invisible or inaudible but its (hidden) presence is still needed in the syntactic module to trigger plural forms of associated verbs, for example, as in '(many) sheep are...', as opposed to '(a) sheep is...'. In the first case, the SS to fit the PS for 'sheep', i.e. /ʃip/, would be something like N(oun) + plural. The presence of the syntactic (number) representation marking plural, even though it is 'silent', that is to say, does not get given any phonological or auditory shape at all, will trigger, in the syntactic structure of the following verb 'to be', the selfsame plural representation to be attached to it, underlying 'are' as opposed to 'is'. A matching of /ʃip/ with the SS: N(oun) + singular would not have that effect. The following verb would of course be 'is', hence the following two alternative PS/SS chains:[12]

1.   ('... sheep are...') **PS**: /ʃip/+/ar/ ⇔ **SS**: N+plural + V+plural
2.   ('... sheep is...') **PS**: /ʃip/+/iz/ ⇔ **SS**: N+singular + V+singular

Complex Linguistic Structures

In addition to the phonological and syntactic primitives in the stores, available for activating in working memory, there are also more complex representations. These are formed by combining primitives in different ways according to the principles of, respectively phonology and syntax. As was evident in the preceding examples, the complex phonological representation of "sheep" (/ʃip/) will trigger a syntactic structure like N. This primitive (N) will be built by the syntactic processor into a complex syntactic structure with SSs like singular or

---

[12] Linguists will recognise that the notation used here is fairly informal.

plural,[13] the ultimate choice depending on how the word "sheep" fits into the wider context. As words develop into phrases and sentences and longer pieces of text, the matching process goes on and on with the processors in each module doing the building work using the simple and complex structures already available in their working memory and building them into longer and longer chunks.

Our framework does not include a specific theory of phonology or syntax as such and the definition as to what constitutes the principles and contents of the two relevant stores will be determined by an appropriate linguistic theory of one kind or another as long as it is broadly compatible with the proposed mental architecture as a whole. In any case, here, whatever pops up into phonological working memory, the interface between phonology and syntax will trigger activity in the syntax module and so an attempt will be made to match up phonological structures currently in phonological working memory with some structure or set of structures in the syntactic store. As always there will almost always be competing structures involved in this matching process and a successful match may not always be achieved.

The presence of a phonological structure in the working memory of the phonological system will have as its immediate consequence, a response from the phonology-syntax interface hence triggering activity in the *syntax* module. Candidate structures will appear in syntactic working memory to match it. One will be found and thereafter, ultimately, repeating the same procedure again, via the *syntactic-conceptual interface*, a matching *conceptual* structure will be found, activated in *conceptual* working memory, a CS representing the meaning of dog. At this point, the word 'dog' is, for a brief moment, *all of these aforementioned structures at once, connected up in a chain*. In other words, it is a structural chain activated temporarily in a series of working memories. In this way, the resulting chain of representations matches up, across four separate working memories, an auditory, a phonological, a syntactic and a conceptual structure with the following components:

1. a structure representing the 'dog' sound (AS);
2. a particular sequence of vowel and consonant categories making up a syllable (PS);
3. a singular noun (SS);
4. the meaning of dog (CS).

Rewritten, more succinctly, this 'word' chain would go as follows:

$$AS \Leftrightarrow PS \Leftrightarrow SS \Leftrightarrow CS$$

This is what a word is, not a single unit as such but rather a series of units chained temporarily together across a sequence of working memories. During the milliseconds that whip by some of the members of the chain may be replaced

---

[13] If the language in question requires gender with nouns then the appropriate primitives will be called upon and gender structures ('features') will be attached to N like masculine or feminine.

until the best possible fit is found and this will be the ultimate representation for the word in question, i.e. "dog". Although it is convenient to think of a word as a single indivisible unit, in actual fact, at least as far as the mind is concerned, it is a *chain composed of different structures, each encoded in a different way.* Also, although the chain is active only temporarily, it remains a chain in the sense that, even when inactive, the separate items in the chain retain their shared index and will be activated together on future occasions.

Processing in Parallel, Bidirectionally and Not Always Successfully

Once presented with input, as mentioned earlier, linguistic processing begins *automatically*. The core language system like other systems will always attempt to make sense of what is presented to it. Like other systems, it may often fail to match incoming input with structures at its disposal, that is, in its memory stores. The example in Chapter 9 was 'dog' for a speaker who knows no English. Another example would be a *non*-Hausa speaker exposed to the Hausa[14] word 'gida' (which happens to mean 'house') without any context to indicate what it means: this should still normally result in an auditory representation of some sort. Thus far 'gida' is only a sound so not in any sense a linguistic 'word'. The phonological system (processing unit) may nevertheless manage to match it with an available phonological structure since the phonology of Hausa may in this case just happen to be close to the phonology of the hearer's own language(s). If so, this might result in a two-syllable structure of some kind that is activated in the listener's phonological working memory. But what about its *syntactic* status? This is a task for the phonology/syntax interface and consequently for the syntactic processor. The interface looks for a matching item to be activated in the syntactic store. Is the phonological structure activated for 'gida' to be matched with, say, a noun, a verb or an adjective? The syntactic processor may not currently be able to match it with an appropriate category in its store or it may give it some sort of default analysis like noun + singular: for the moment, coindexing these with the phonological input structures will just have to do until more relevant information comes along. One thing that would help would be some conceptual input resulting from the listener's guess at what 'gida' might refer to but in this particular example, we have assumed there is no available clue as what 'gida' means. Consequently, the linguistic processing of the auditory input in this case is only partially successful. Where no matching conceptual structure can be found – not unlikely if you are listening to a string of sentences of Hausa with no knowledge of the language – there will be no interpretation of

---

[14] Hausa is a West African language spoken in the north of Nigeria and neighbouring regions in other countries.

the meaning of 'gida'. The listener will get only so far in making linguistic sense of the sound and not have enough to proceed further.

The important points here are the following. Firstly, there are the tireless attempts of the various processors to assemble a meaningful chain in response to input. And, although the input in the earlier 'gida' example is assumed to be that input originating in the ambient environment, that is, what is going on *outside*, this incremental, building-up process is equally true for the creation of messages, i.e. in utterance *production*. Here, the source of the input into the core system is coming from the *inside*, that is, in the form of conceptual structure where meanings to be communicated are being assembled and where the ultimate output is an utterance using some mode of linguistic communication (speech, writing, sign language or Braille). Secondly, the building of chains of structure both in utterance comprehension and in utterance production always proceeds back and forth, in two directions, in the search for the optimal chain of representations all the time the utterance is developing and expanding. Processing is, in other words both a bidirectional and incremental affair.

Summary

This chapter has provided a short account of what the core language system is and some idea of how it connects up with two other modules in the mind. In the next chapter we shall deal with language beyond the core. The core language system will always attempt to make linguistic sense of anything that comes its way but it will not always be able to come up with suitable phonological and syntactic structures to match the input either because the input has nothing to do with language, as is the case with a sound like a door slamming, or because it is an unfamiliar language and there is not enough context to work out what it means. In the latter case some fragmentary linguistic structures may be found but without any satisfactory result for the listener.

11 Language beyond the Core

In This Chapter

From what has been said in earlier chapters, it should by now be quite clear that language is not just syntax, phonology (and lots of words). It is therefore not *just* something that is governed by special principles that severely limit possible variation and that make it easier for the young child to work out the system of any particular language it is exposed to.

The 'language-specific systems' within the core that are only part of the language system as a whole, cannot possibly manage the enormously complicated mental business of listening, reading, speaking, writing and thinking in language.[1] Again, a comparison between different languages each taken in their totality reveals both many basic similarities but also much complexity and variation. Finding out how languages work could pose an enormous challenge for young two-year-old minds were it not for the fact that the mind, as a system of systems, 'grows' languages in different ways, one core component of which has evolved to make decoding grammatical aspects of the input straightforward even if other aspects may take much longer to acquire. This core part of it can handle any language system it is exposed to in essentially the same way. All that is required is frequent input over a period of about a year for the basics to be in place. Other systems take care of other aspects of language: *there is no single expert charged with the task of decoding everything.*

This chapter will deal with just those systems that are implicated in language use and acquisition which lie beyond the core. This will also involve the interfaces that mediate between the various systems involved ensuring the right associations are established.

Language Sounds outside the Core

It should already be clear how the generic sound processing system, as opposed to that which specialises in *speech* sounds, lies outside the core language

---

[1] Note that generative linguists, who focus on what is here called the core language system (⇔PS⇔ SS⇔), have, despite claims to the contrary, never denied this.

system, When there is acoustic input coming from the immediate environment, the auditory system is the processing 'first port of call'. At the same time, the auditory store will include structures that, although formed in auditory code, owe their existence to an interaction between the auditory and phonological system during the individual's lifetime.

The auditory structures that are created in the course of language processing are important elements in the study of **phonetics**, now usually referred to as *speech science.*[2] Although speech-related auditory structures are basically no different from other auditory structures, it is convenient, when identifying them, to use conventional phonetic transcription, that is, symbols from the International Phonetic Alphabet using square brackets. Phonetic script may be more or less complicated depending on how much detailed information about the sound you wish to convey. For example "bad" in English can be written simply, using minimal detail, as: [bæd].[3] This, apart from the square brackets, happens to look exactly the same as the abstract *phonological* representation of "bad", this time using slanting brackets, namely/bæd/. However, only in the case of auditory (phonetic) script, details about devoicing, lip rounding, aspiration and so forth can also be included. In the following example, one extra piece of information on the last segment is added: [bæd̞] showing that it is pronounced 'weakly', with less voicing. This detail is irrelevant as its phonological partner is concerned since, roughly stated, /b/ simply stands for a particular phonological category and does not indicate how it should be *pronounced.*

Naturally those many auditory structures (AS) that are *not* linguistic such as, for instance, representations of the sound of wind rustling in the leaves cannot be written using phonetic transcription, which is designed to be used with the representation of speech sounds, or, in terms of the framework, with the representation of generic sound that 'just happens' to be speech. In the framework, the square brackets used in phonetics are conventionally retained as a way of marking all auditory as opposed to phonological structures as demonstrated in the AS: [sound of wind rustling through leaves].

Language Meanings outside the Core

Language in the broader sense, following the framework scheme of things (and Jackendoff's) includes the meanings to be associated with given core (phonological-syntactic) chains. Meaning is handled by the conceptual system which, exactly like the auditory system, is not part of the core language system while still being a crucial component of language in the broader sense.

---

[2] Although in the past there was a great deal of research interest in speech production (articulatory phonetics), currently the major concern has shifted to speech perception.
[3] Unless indicated otherwise, British Received Pronunciation will be assumed.

Linguistic meaning, as opposed to any kind of meaning, is the object of study in the branch of linguistics called semantics (or 'conceptual semantics' following Jackendoff 1990). Like any other nonlinguistic meaning, it is encoded as conceptual structure (CS). This means it uses the primitives available in the conceptual store (Jackendoff 1990, 9).

In the framework, the convention is to write CS using block capitals, thus (very informally), for the CS representing the meaning of 'hippopotamus': LARGE AMPHIBIAN THICK-SKINNED MAMMAL LIVING IN AFRICA.[4] Since conceptual representations can get very complicated and vary from individual to individual only relatively simple versions will be used in this chapter without specifying their precise structure or, indeed, noting any perceptual structures with which they will mostly be associated.

Is There a Basic Difference between Linguistic and Nonlinguistic Meaning?

Many linguists may prefer to make a clear categorical distinction between language meaning and 'other' meanings such as, for instance, concepts of time and space that the young, prelinguistic infant grapples with during its early years. In the framework, this is all handled by the conceptual system.

The conceptual structures that are coindexed with syntactic ones across the CS/SS interface may well have a special character by virtue of the fact they have been shaped in collaboration with a core language system. They will still be written in the same conceptual code. One must assume that a large number of the conceptual structures in a given individual's conceptual store are ones that will indeed have some association with the core language system, and therefore some linguistic means of expressing them. This may of course depend on what language the individual knows since not all languages encode meaning in precisely the same way and some languages have words for concepts which are not available as single words in another language. For example, the English word 'wall' covers much more meaning that the French word 'mur' which is generally made of masonry and French 'paroi' and 'cloison' are walls that divide spaces but are also not identical in meaning.

Language out of Context

'Semantic' meaning is usually understood to be limited to basic definitions out of context. Of course the same phonological-syntactic chain can

---

[4] This rough-and-ready example is more like a dictionary definition. It is presented as a relatively simple CS. In reality it will be a complex of many conceptual features *within* the conceptual system. It will also have various associated visual and other representations existing *outside* the conceptual system.

be associated with more than one basic conceptual structure depending on the context. For example, 'bank' meaning the side of a river and 'bank' meaning a financial institution are two different meanings that happen to be associated with the same chain consisting of a bit of phonology, /bank/ and a bit of syntax, *Noun$_{singular}$* chained, leaving out the details, as in the following two representational PS ⇔ SS ⇔ CS chains:

a.   **PS** /bank/ ⇔ **SS** *Noun* ⇔ **CS** SIDE OF A RIVER
b.   **PS** /bank/ ⇔ **SS** *Noun* ⇔ **CS** FINANCIAL INSTITUTION

On hearing the word 'bank', in other words, both (a) and (b) chains will be activated except that one of them has to dominate in the competition and win as soon as the best match with the current input is found. The surrounding context usually has the effect of handicapping one SS/CS chain by boosting the other's level of activation. In hearing a sentence out of context like 'I was close to the bank', the competition will be much more equal although perfect equality is rare to achieve unless the two meanings in question are of equal frequency in the individual's personal experience as reflected in their respective (identical) resting levels of activation.

The bias effect, whereby one interpretation becomes more likely than another, can be manipulated experimentally in which case it is referred to as *priming*. This is where the experimental participant is presented with some information in advance which has the effect of raising the activation level of (priming) one of the options. The priming effect should last long enough for one interpretation of the target sentence, when elicited by the experimenter, to be much more likely even though the sentence itself is entirely ambiguous as in the 'I was close to the bank' example.

It is worth mentioning that in the preceding example, both (a) and (b) are presented in the *written* form so we need to remember that the PS /bank/ is associated both with the chunk of *auditory* structure (the word as a 'sound'), which is not included in the preceding chains, and with a chunk of *visual* structure (the orthographic version of the word), which has also been left out. Also excluded are the *indices* so let us include these in an alternative representation of the same set of two choices. Again the chosen index numbers, 20 and 57, are arbitrary. If you match up the '20' indices you get the (a) result and if you take the other route and match the '57' indices you get the (b) result, as follows:

a.   ⇔ **SIDE OF A RIVER**$_{20}$

               /bank/$_{20,57}$ ⇔ *Noun*$_{20,57}$

b.   ⇔ **FINANCIAL INSTITUTION**$_{57}$

To sum up, whenever you hear or read the word 'bank' with no explanatory context, the 20/57 indexing as illustrated earlier will ensure that *both* meanings will be activated and compete on equal terms in working memory until something happens to favour one CS more than the other and boost its current activation level. Context is often crucial.

Language in Context

If, in conceptual structure, semantic meaning is, roughly speaking, the 'basic' meaning taken *out of* context, what about the meanings *in* context, that is to say, what about meanings that accrue to words and longer stretches of language in different situations of use? These have the effect of *adding on to*, *subtracting from* or otherwise *changing* this basic meaning. So, included in the general account of language-related conceptual structure must be what, in linguistics, is covered by the term **pragmatics**, covering language use in context.

Note that pragmatic meaning can often, but does not always add on extra layers of meaning or can change the meaning completely. Sometimes the effect can be to actually *narrow* the semantic meaning as in "I am giving up drinking" where "drinking" refers specifically to alcoholic drinks and not any drinkable liquid (Wilson & Carston 2007). However, in all cases, the interpretation of **pragmatic meaning** during actual processing has to involve a particular relevant context so that the appropriate CS can be selected in the current formation of chains in working memory. The various conceptual structures that are activated there will include those that *include* the concept of any liquid as well as the one which specifies *only* alcoholic drinks. The more inclusive one will perhaps be stronger, i.e. have higher resting level of activation, so an acquired association between "drinking" with "giving up" will be required to raise the activation level of the 'only alcoholic' CS above the other one so that the appropriate CS takes part in the chain.

Is There a Basic Difference between Semantic and Pragmatic Meaning?

These two areas are, in some theoretical perspectives, thought to be quite distinct. Nevertheless, from the framework perspective, whether semantic meaning or pragmatic meaning is involved, both will be expressed in *the same conceptual code*. What then would be the distinction between the two? It basically boils down to a difference in complexity.

Pragmatic aspects of linguistic meaning involve more complex CS chains than would be otherwise the case if each word, that is to say, each PS/SS chain, were associated with a single, unique, uniform meaning that did not change according to context.[5] Even single words, whether or not they have one or more meanings have a range of associated conceptual structures which are coactivated with it.

---

[5] Pragmatic meaning and *discourse* meaning, both having to do with the wider context, are related terms, the study of discourse focusing on the organisation of language beyond the single sentence.

The structural chain underlying the word 'bank' meaning a particular type of financial institution will have a conceptual structure that is associated with other meanings (CSs) that have to do with banking and finance in general. These associated structures will be coactivated with bank along with the PS/SS chains that are associated with them, i.e. along with other words like 'cash' and 'loan'.[6] However, the mere presence of other semantically related words in text does not *force* the choice of bank in this sense, only make it relatively more probable. Some might argue that sensitivity to the presence of these other words already counts as pragmatic processing. It will certainly favour the choice of the most likely PS/SS/CS chain. In any case, pragmatic choice does depend on the processing of a particular context, whether it is linguistic (in the surrounding text itself) or not in the text but situational, that is, specific aspects of the current circumstances in which the word or longer piece of text is used: choosing a particular meaning over other competing meanings enables the listener (or reader) to determine what must be the intended one. For example, in 'They waited anxiously for permission and were delighted when he finally gave them the green light', the green light can only be interpreted only as meaning permission and nothing to do with a particular light that is green.

When someone responds, 'I'm so sorry' on hearing of someone else's misfortune, the listener in principle has a choice between interpreting this as an expression of sympathy or as implying an admission of personal responsibility for that misfortune. In practice, the proper interpretation of 'sorry' will be straightforward given the circumstances, or rather the listener's rapid processing of the circumstances, that is, of a very complex network of conceptual structures and their various associations to work out whether or not the speaker can in anyway be held responsible. It is not surprising that people coming for languages and cultures where the equivalent to 'sorry' can *only* mean an admission of responsibility may find the use of 'sorry' bizarre since the coactivation of the equivalent in their language including the strong coactivation of just one candidate conceptual structure (the wrong one in this case) might obscure the ambiguity of 'sorry' in English. In effect, they still have to acquire the pragmatics of the word 'sorry' which will require them to initiate more complex conceptual processing when interpreting the word.

Although the pragmatic examples provided earlier relate to *lexical* meaning, i.e. meaning associated with single words or short phrases like "drink" and 'green light', meaning-in-context can involve long phrases, clauses, sentences and stretches of language much longer than that. Although space precludes going into the differences between beyond-the-sentence language patterns covered by terms like pragmatics, discourse and text, the basic principle always holds: meaning is

---

Different views on the differences between semantics, pragmatic and discourse meaning will be set aside here.

[6] Where there is an increased likelihood of such words co-occurring in a spoken or written utterance, the co-occurrence referred to as *collocation*.

encoded in CS. The complexity and size of the CS involved in both semantic and pragmatic meaning is considerable although pragmatic processing necessarily invoked the most complex networks of structure.

Language Articulation

Finally, to complete the picture of what lies outside the core, the production of utterances in the spoken mode relies on auditory structures, recruited for linguistic purposes, and their interface with the **motor** system containing motor structures (MoS) that drive the speech organs and any other part of the body used during speaking.[7] The auditory system is used for its output to the motor system engaging all parts of the body to be mobilised to *produce* the target sounds. The original trigger is of course the message, the content of what the speaker intends to say. This is encoded in conceptual structure. This creates a wave of activity through a whole group of experts systems that must cooperate to get the message converted into sound waves, i.e. audible speech thus:

$$\text{MESSAGE (CS)} \Leftrightarrow \text{CORE SYSTEM (SS \& PS)} \Leftrightarrow \text{AS} \Leftrightarrow \text{ARTICULATION (MoS)}$$

The sound produced by this processing is then fed back in the other direction so that the speaker is able to monitor (consciously or subconsciously) the utterance just produced making him or her a listener and producer at the same time. A very similar process takes place in writing except that the articulation is obviously different and all the feedback comes via the *visual* system. In the case of sign language production, the feedback will be partly visual and partly *somatosensory* as the signer senses his or her body gestures. Some visual and somatosensory feedback might be also be involved in speech, that is feedback from the supporting gestures that accompanying speaking.

The auditory system is also used during speech production for processing feedback. This is input from the sound that the individual has just produced and at the same time *perceived*. This feedback is required to monitor one's speech production, a vital function without which as tests can demonstrate, speech becomes impossible. In such tests, participants' speech is disrupted while they have headphones on and the signals from either or both sides can be manipulated by the experimenter. If the sound coming via the headphones is kept the same on both sides but manipulated in another way, the effect can be quite unexpected. When, using the dichotic test format, the speaker is asked to read a text out loud, the sound of his or her voice is played back via the headphones and

---

[7] The working assumption is still that the motor system is interfaced only with the *auditory* system in and that there no direct connections with the phonological one. In other words we aim to reproduce the generic sound that is triggered by phonological input, not the phonological structures (PSs) themselves.

progressively delayed. When the delay between the speech produced by the participant, and the artificially delayed feedback reaches a certain level beyond a slight echo, speakers, often to their great surprise, become unable to read aloud any further. This shows that we constantly monitor our own speech and how vital that is.

Production where *writing* and *sign language* are concerned involves the visual system in collaboration with the motor system. Here the mind has to somehow link up the output of the phonological system with those motor structures that direct the body to make the appropriate physical movements that guide arm and hand movements and also, in the case of sign language, special movements of the head and facial muscles.

Language Perception

The two systems mainly involved in language perception are the auditory system and the visual one. As already discussed elsewhere, audition is a transition stage between (a) the transduction of speech signals originating in the ear and (b) the system handling phonological structure, each step signalling a change of code. The chain is set out, in the reverse order as compared with the previous one, thus:

audible speech > transduction of physical responses in the ear > **AS $\Leftrightarrow$ PS $\Leftrightarrow$ SS $\Leftrightarrow$ CS**

This is, of course, identical to the chain formation involved in the feedback of speech to the speaker as described earlier.

Language perceived in the visual mode involves visual patterns that impact on the retinas. This input to the eyes is processed further, resulting in the activation of representations in the **visual** memory store. These representations, visual structures (VS), share space in that store with other visual structures that have nothing directly to do with language. Those VS that are related to language will, in many individuals, reflect the processing of (a) language in its written form, whatever writing system is used, but also for some individuals, (b) the gestures and facial expressions of signed language. Language may also originate in the *tactile* patterns used in Braille, implicating the perceptual system which contains *somatosensory* structures (SomS). In all these cases the perceptual structures (VS or SomS) must connect up somehow with the PS and SS stores to be processed as language.

Writing

Language writing systems exhibit a great deal of variety. Apart from alphabetic systems, there are mixed systems like Japanese and like the hieroglyphic system used once in Egypt. Chinese uses ideograms rather than an alphabet.[8] As the name suggests, Chinese writing reflects 'ideas', that is conceptual structures, since a Chinese character will give little (or no) information about pronunciation but is basically an expression of meaning. In this way, language systems like Mandarin or Cantonese which mostly share the same characters and indeed are often grouped together as a single language (Chinese), are nevertheless different enough for some to claim they should be regarded as separate languages since they are not mutually intelligible. In the case of Chinese and Japanese, however, there is no dispute about them being very different languages but they do make use of the same characters. 誠 for example is 'chéng' in Mandarin Chinese but 'makoto' or 'sei' in Japanese. This is a much more striking difference than for example different pronunciations of words spelled the same in alphabetic systems such as 'Paris', ([pærɪs] in English and [pari] in French). Such systems also exhibit a wide variety as demonstrated by Arabic, Cyrillic, Greek and Latin alphabets. There is nevertheless one obvious characteristic that unites all these writing systems mentioned earlier, namely that they are *visible marks*.[9] This means that, after the process of transduction of the patterns registered on the retina of each eye has taken place, they are initially encoded as *visual* structures (VS) along with all other such patterns perceived in the immediate, i.e. visible environment. Just as the auditory structures that are created for language use can also be called 'phonetic', so the visual structures that are created for language use are normally referred to by using terms such as 'spelling' and 'orthography'. Nonetheless, all written text, along with other visual patterns that have nothing to do with language, will always be *initially* processed as generic visual structure which makes the visual processing of the written letter 'a' no different in kind than the processing of the shape of a streetlamp or an emoticon.

What options are available for representing writing in the current framework? The most obvious and interesting question is this: are the visual structures that represent visible *language*-related patterns, like their equivalents in the auditory system, connected *directly* to the phonological system, thus VS⇔PS, like AS⇔PS?

Writing is thought to be a system that developed after spoken language and to be parasitic on it. Alphabetic systems are the clearest example of this dependency because, to greater or lesser extent, they seek to 'mimic' speech. If we take the ideographic system exemplified by Chinese, it is very clear that whatever else there may be, there will be a direct connection between the visual structure of a character like 誠, and a conceptual structure, representing a meaning ('sincerity'), thus VS⇔CS. This establishes a direct meaning with another structure outside the core language system.

---

[8] There has admittedly been, since 1982, an official pronunciation-based system which was developed in China in the 1950s called 'pinyin'. In fact, there have been other such systems for Chinese, some much older than pinyin. The Wade-Giles and Yale systems are well-known ones.
[9] Tactile marks should really be included as in the case of Braille.

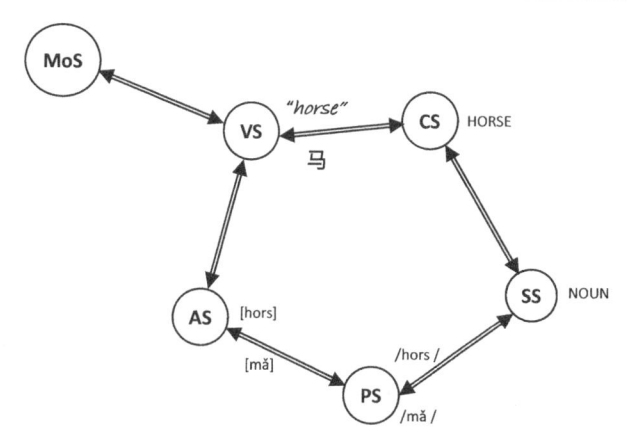

Figure 11.1 *A visible language network (writing).*

As will be illustrated in a following section, basic communication is possible without implicating the phonological and syntactic systems. Nevertheless, the CS triggered by the VS corresponding to the Chinese character in the preceding 'chéng' example will normally trigger a chain of structures representing the word, that is, including an SS, a PS and an AS. In other words, the direct VS⇔CS link ensures spreading activation round to the auditory system and then through the language core as is shown in Figure 11.1. In this way, the minds of Chinese speakers, when they see ('read') 誠, will activate a network of representations, virtually simultaneously, and this network will include every structure associated with that character.

A moment's thought will establish that this indirect connection with the core language system is also perfectly plausible even with alphabetic systems. The visual structure (VS) that is triggered in response to the sight of a Chinese character for 'horse', as illustrated in Figure 11.1, or indeed in response to, say, the sequence of four letters of the alphabet: d, o, k and i, which spell 'doki' (horse in Hausa), will both trigger the *meaning* – the CS HORSE – as well as the *sound* – the auditory structure that is associated with that CS, thus AS⇔ VS⇔CS. But the CS will also co-activate the PS-SS chain at the same time adding it to the previous chain to form a network of structures as in Figure 11.2.

Sign Language

The case of sign language is an interesting one. In principle, removing the connections with auditory structure does not have to change the way signs (as opposed to orthographic patterns) are interpreted. Figure 11.2 displays the possible ways of representing the processing chain. Links with AS are displayed as arrows with interrupted lines simply because regular users of sign languages may also have a given degree of hearing ability (required for new auditory

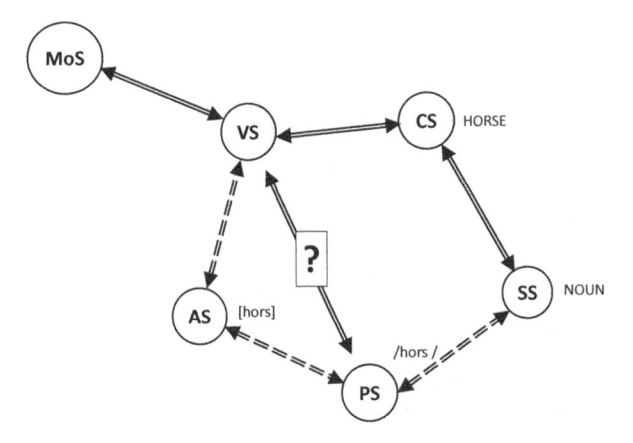

Figure 11.2 *A visible language network (sign language).*

structures to be developed) ranging from 0 to 100. However, the more important arrow is the direct one with a question mark attached to it connecting VS and PS which is an interface absent from the previous figure (Figure 11.1). Even though sign languages involve the visual mode and not the auditory mode, sign language researchers have long been at pains to point out the fact that sign languages do have a system that is equivalent to phonology as generally understood and which they also call sign language 'phonology'.[10] That is to say, the ways that signs and gestures are structured mark sign languages out as languages like any other with a phonology and a syntax that in the framework implicates the core language system. This allows for the possibility that the phonological system as described thus far could also serve sign languages. This would suggest including in our map of the mind a direct interface link between VS and PS. The detailed explanation of the relationships between visual structures in the VS store and phonological properties in the PS store is left for researchers in (sign language and non–sign language) phonology to determine.[11]

The 'Colonising' Core

As mentioned earlier, linguistics includes the study of speech sounds, called phonetics, or more commonly nowadays 'speech science'.[12] It also includes the study of various aspects of language meaning, i.e. semantics and pragmatics. Those structures, AS, CS and, if we include articulation, MoS (motor structures)

---

[10] The long series of edited volumes on theoretical issues in sign language beginning with Sipler and Fischer (1990) bear witness to the amount of work already done in this area.
[11] This would not be the case for finger spelling and signed versions of spoken languages such as Signed English where the network in Figure 11.2. would apply. On the other hand, British Sign Language (BSL), for example, despite the name, is a separate language from English.
[12] This covers many aspects, including the physiological and psychological aspects of speech production and speech reception, but generally excluding phonological theory.

```
                THE CORE LANGUAGE SYSTEM
                   (Phonology & Syntax)
```

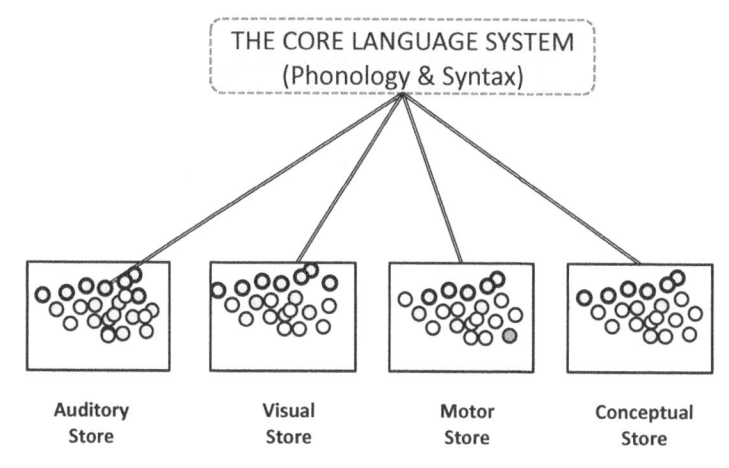

| Auditory | Visual | Motor | Conceptual |
| Store | Store | Store | Store |

Figure 11.3 *The colonising core.*

are all linguistic 'by proxy' (see Figure 11.3). They have been created through an interaction between, on one hand, systems that are specific to human language, i.e. the core system and, on the other, older systems whose primary purpose is not linguistic.

The net result of the interaction between the core language system and the modules with which it is interfaced is two-fold. Firstly, interaction with the core system may well give any of these particular structures in the three systems just mentioned a special character: for example the motor structures that control tongue movement for pronouncing 'l' sounds, even though they written in the same code as any other MoS, may differ from anything used to, say, manipulate food in the mouth. Secondly, because the noncore structures are 'linguistic' in the sense that are deployed in the use of language albeit formatted in a nonlinguistic code, there is therefore a great deal of linguistic behaviour that can be accounted for without implicating any innate linguistic universals, any 'universal 'grammar'. This simply means that the *totality* of human language behaviour cannot be explained without those universals: a great deal of it does not require any direct involvement of UG.[13]

One way of looking at the way the core system recruits these other systems is to say that it has 'colonised' them creating within their stores a host of structures (the grey circles in Figure 11.3) for its personal use. This would include the motor structures (MoS) created to manipulate the tongue during speech (or fingers in sign language production), visual structures (VS) that link the linguistic visual signs of various sorts including letters and Chinese ideographs as well as sign

---

[13] Note that the idea that *all* of language is governed by, and acquired through the application of universal grammatical (UG) principles has never been maintained in *any* version of generative linguistic theory.

language gestures with the phonological system, as well the auditory structures and conceptual structures (AS and CS) that have already been mentioned.[14]

Communicating *without* Using the Core System

The conclusion drawn in the framework used in this book is that language-like behaviour is possible to some limited extent without involving the core language system. For example, it may be possible to make a simpler, direct connection between the sound (auditory representation) and the meaning (conceptual representation) of Hausa 'doki' from the general situational context. This will still not allow the user to integrate 'doki ' into complex linguistic utterances since 'doki' will not yet have any phonological or syntactic representation that it can be associated with: only syntactic and phonological representations can be manipulated in the creation of complex linguistic constructions. We will return to the 'doki' example when discussing how learners build structure from language input in Chapter 14.

Although we have to be careful not to succumb to the temptation to ascribe human characteristics to pets, it does seem that some animals react to words and show by their behaviour to 'know' what they mean, in some sense. An animal like a dog can acquire the meaning of sounds like 'doki' or 'horse'. If we allow for the possibility that dogs may have some sort of system for representing abstract meaning, i.e. a (relatively) primitive conceptual system, then the ability in both humans and other species to link the sound of a spoken word to a meaning may work in a way illustrated in Figure 11.4. Here, the shared route forming an inverted triangle, has an interface connecting AS (the sound of the word 'horse') directly with CS (the meaning, HORSE) is possible for both dogs, say, and humans. It is highly likely that the visual representation of a horse (VS) will also be triggered at the same time, especially if there is a horse present and in view extending the AS/CS chain into a network as marked in thick black lines in the figure. What dogs and even the cleverer great apes *cannot* do, is create a language out of speech sounds however frequently they are exposed to the 'right' input. They can however amass an impressive vocabulary of sound meaning pairings of the type depicted in the figure. They may even be able to make some simple associations between two of such 'vocabulary items' in their repertoire but for the (evolutionary) time being, there it stops. A core language system is needed to take this kind of communication up another level.

In the previous chapter, a word was presented as a chain of different structures, some of which were inside the core (PS and SS) and some outside (AS and CS).

---

[14] The MOGUL glossary (http://www.mogulframework.com/mogul-glossary), in the entry on MOGUL conventions, places a lowercase L against this type of structure recruited for use with language, that is in conjunction with the core language system, thus MoSL VSL, ASL and CSL. The four systems, of course, make no such special distinction. The lowercase L is just there for convenience, as a reminder.

CORE LANGUAGE SYSTEM

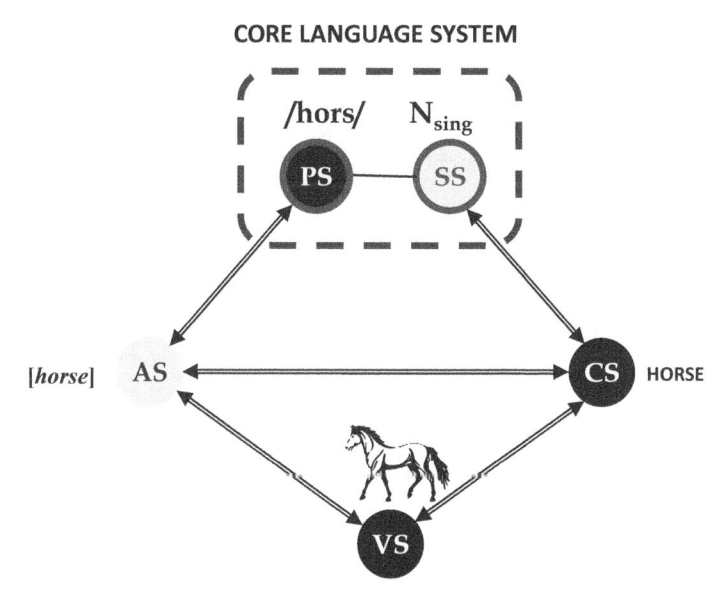

Figure 11.4 *Two ways to understand 'horse'.*

The 'doki' example shows that it is sufficient to make an AS/CS chain to make a kind of word chunk with a meaning and then use this to communicate. This will always be accompanied by attempts to come up with a matching PS for any AS that is presented to it. Still, using just the simple sound/meaning chain, (AS plus CS) some kind of simple message can be conveyed and understood. Communication using stretches of more than one of these 'words' together but still without using syntax is also possible.

The framing of utterances without properly engaging the syntax system within the core will come into the discussion of language development in the individual, in Chapter 14. This will involve using conceptual notions such as 'action 'and 'agent' ('doer' of an action) as the basis for ordering individual words, rather than syntactic notions like subject and verb.

Summary

This chapter has looked at the aspects of language that are not governed by PS or SS principles residing in the core language modules. These aspects of linguistic structure broadly defined have been the basis for some, cognitive linguists for example, to claim no language core is necessary. Much of the research carried out by those espousing this particular perspective on language is therefore of relevance to the framework, especially in working out the nature of all the complexities of conceptual structure involved in semantic and pragmatic meaning. By extending the study of language beyond the core, it becomes clear that the whole of the mind, including those parts controlling the body in language production and language perception is involved. Finally by assessing how much communication can in fact take place without having much if any knowledge of the phonological and syntactic nature of the language being used, it is possible to work out more precisely the special contribution of the two core systems that only humans possess.

12 Two Ways of Knowing a Language

In This Chapter

In Chapter 7, a distinction was made between conceptually structured knowledge as projected into conscious awareness on one hand and, on the other, the underlying conceptual structures themselves. Conceptual structures like any other structures and like the processing activity involved in activating and manipulating them, remain mercifully inaccessible to awareness. Imagine the complete confusion that would result if we were aware of every detail of what lies and what takes place in our minds, millisecond by millisecond. At the same time, as already discussed in Chapter 4, we do obviously have the possibility of somehow accessing and consciously manipulating concepts even though we cannot actually access the structure and operations of the conceptual system *directly*.

This accessibility to awareness is made possible through the activity of the perceptual systems: this is where the experience of consciousness is actually created. This 'perceptual projection principle' says that conceptually constructed knowledge can participate in our conscious thoughts and imaginings via an *indirect* route. This allows us to develop consciously accessible knowledge of all kinds and it certainly includes knowledge about what *language* is, how it might work and the kinds of things that are involved in language like speaking and listening, reading and writing including creative activities such as writing articles, novels and poems and performing stand-up comedy. At primary school we already learn about what a 'word' is. We can, perhaps, tell a teacher how many 'syllables' there are in a given word and whether two words rhyme. Later on we might learn grammatical concepts such as 'clause', 'noun' and 'verb' although many such concepts are often lost or become fuzzy memories, like much we learn at school wherever we later feel no need for that knowledge.

This chapter deals with the implications of consciously accessible language knowledge and how it relates to the inaccessible systems that drive our acquisition of first or other languages and also our spontaneous performance as we think in a language and use it to communicate with others without devoting a single second to what prepositions we are using or whether we have used the right tense.

Conceptual Knowledge of Grammar

Given the limitation on conscious thoughts that was discussed in earlier chapters, that they have to be entertained one after the other and with nothing like the rapidity of the fast parallel computations that typify subconscious processing, we can still clearly reflect on an enormous variety of topics, on how to cook vegetables, on the life cycle of the ant-lion, on the history of Egypt, on our troubled relations with the neighbours, and so on and so forth. Included in this enormous repertoire at our disposal are reflections on *language* and this naturally includes one important aspect of language, namely grammar.

When adults start learning a new language, unlike little children they are often interested in how it works. They may even regard this knowledge as essential: depending upon their beliefs about how best to learn languages, they will be more or less eager to find out about grammatical rules in the target language. Everyone accepts that learning a rule of grammar will not enable you to use it straightaway in fluent spontaneous speech and perform as a native speaker would (assuming it is a correct and reliable rule). However, if you adhere to some version of skill acquisition theory, you may well believe that this grammatical rule that you have learnt will, by dint of frequent practice, become somehow 'automatised' and can then, as a result, be used with ease and without conscious reflection (see e.g. Anderson 1982; Ullman 2001).

The popular example of the idea that conscious practice makes perfect[1] is learning to drive where everything at the beginning is laboured and conscious. It is laboured because you can't think of two or more things at the same time – checking in the side and rear view mirrors, turning the driving wheel, controlling the speed, etc. – all of which doesn't make for smooth driving. However, because they have automatised many of the tasks involved in driving, more experienced drivers can perform these tasks in parallel and, at the same time, focus their attention on something quite different like talking with a fellow passenger about a topic which has nothing to do with driving the car.

The fact that slow laborious conscious driving is followed in time by spontaneous unreflecting driving still does not lead straightforwardly to the conclusion that smooth driving is actually *caused* by the automatisation of consciously learned rules. This remains a theoretical possibility but other options are also possible, for example the possibility that the unreflecting ability to drive of an expert driver has been acquired *in a different way* with the conscious thoughts of the driver playing only an auxiliary role in the process. In other words the early stages of driving are simply the only way you have of operating the car at the time. This remains the case until quite different *sub*concious processes have been sufficiently developed for the slow laborious, conscious ways to be dispensed with. Something of this type of argument was developed in the seventies, notably

---

[1] The key term here is *conscious* since practice can occur without conscious reflection and some would argue that this is often the best strategy.

by Stephen Krashen, when he tried to account for second language learning, in particular the learning of grammar (Krashen 1981).[2]

As far as the framework is concerned, the essence of what people mean by 'grammar' has to do with phonological and syntactic representations, encoded as PS and SS and stored in their respective memories. Knowledge written in these particular codes can *never* become conscious. There is of course meaning, which is handled by the conceptual system. A full explanation of the difference between 'she runs' and 'she ran' has to involve links with conceptual structure. Through the mediation of the perceptual systems, some of what is in conceptual structure is immediately available to conscious awareness. When we hear 'she runs', the meaning is clear: we are aware straightaway that this is most probably about the present or is generally true or is about some current habitual activity and so not about some specific running event in the past. This instant awareness of the meaning is not the same as thinking *about* what signals the meaning, i.e. the form of the verb 'run'. 'Thinking about' has to do with analytic thought allowing us to reflect on the difference in usage between the two forms 'runs' and 'ran' and this requires a different kind of support from the conceptual system than simply what generates the instantly available awareness of the meaning of 'runs'.

The distinction between grammar-in-the-core (PS and SS) and conscious thoughts-about-grammar means that grammatical knowledge can be built up in two ways. The first is simply by processing language and letting the core language system work on it and the second by consciously studying the way the grammar works, giving you what the linguist and language teaching pioneer Harold Palmer, foreshadowing Krashen's distinction, called 'studial capacity' (Palmer 1921; Cook 2013, 40). The way this might work in the framework will be elaborated in Chapter 14, on language development. What we have here in any case is a clear distinction between, on one hand, grammatical knowledge that is a combination of phonological and syntactic structure and located in the core language modules and, on the other hand, *conceptual grammatical knowledge* encoded in CS and therefore, by the indirect route sketched out previously, available for conscious inspection.

One way of capturing this difference is by distinguishing knowledge *of* grammar from knowledge *about* grammar (see Figure 12.1). What has been called 'conscious grammatical knowledge', i.e. knowledge 'about', could, in the framework, equally be called *conceptual* grammatical, knowledge. So, to sum up, in the conceptual system there are, within the conceptual store

1. internal networks of CS that represent all the individual's accumulated knowledge about the organisation of language and languages, including knowledge about grammar alongside it.
2. all kinds of other CSs, including those representing the meanings of individual words and phrases, as discussed in Chapter 11.

---

[2] In fact, Krashen used the term 'learning' exclusively for the conscious learning reserving the term 'acquisition' for subconscious development (Krashen 1976).

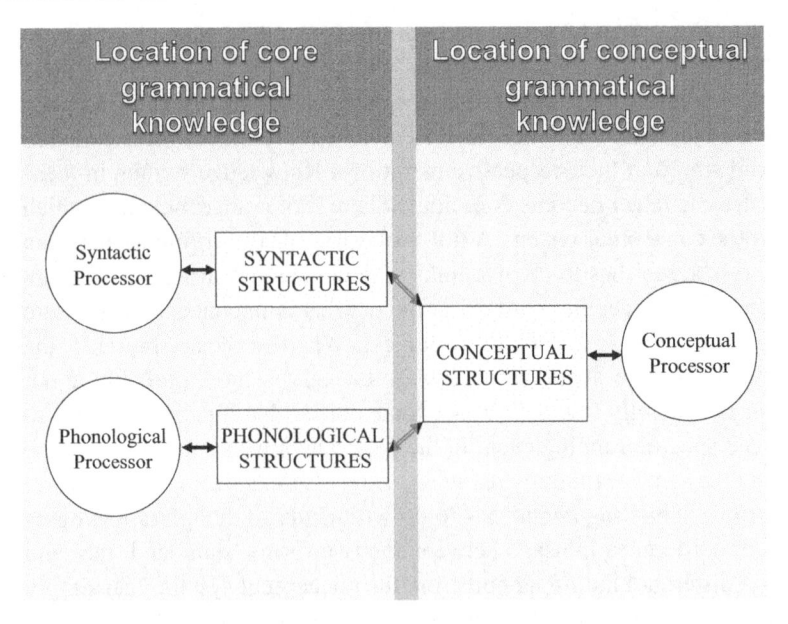

Figure 12.1 *Two ways of knowing grammar.*

All of this is potentially accessible to conscious awareness and conscious manipulation. None of it has any direct bearing on the grammar that is reflected in everyday spontaneous use of language which is governed by systems on the left of Figure 12.1.

To take a concrete example, imagine someone told you 'adjectives in French usually come after the noun'. What does that statement give you? Assuming that you actually know what an adjective and a noun is and assuming you retain this information about adjective-noun word order over a reasonable period of time, you might imagine that it is going to influence your future performance in French. One reason why it might do that in principle is that the information directly affects the relevant parts of the core language system, in particular the syntactic system. This is where, in speaking French, the sequence of adjective and noun will be determined. If before you, or your mind (the distinction may be important here), were always producing French utterances with nonnativelike SSs that followed the Adj+Noun order rather than the Noun+Adj order (e.g. 'rouge moulin' rather than the 'moulin rouge' for 'the red windmill'), your expectation might be that, as a result of the information you have been given and learned by heart, that the SS Noun+Adj will now produce the nativelike French order more often than not.

Consider now how your mind actually processed the original information given to you about French adjectives to judge where exactly that information ends up. 'Adjectives in French usually come after the noun' would, like any other sentence, trigger a set of auditory structures representing the sound of the sentence. As a fluent speaker (or 'understander' in this case) of English, the sequence of ASs will be coindexed with a string of corresponding syntactic structures. These SSs in turn will activate the appropriate meaning structures (CSs) in your conceptual system. Notice that the information about French grammar contained in the statement that you have processed *only appears in the conceptual system*, including the meaning of the words 'noun' and adjective and 'after'. *None of this information about French has registered with either phonology or syntax in the core language system*. Their job is just to handle the phonological and syntactic structure of whatever comes their way, and not to actually interpret it. That's the job of the conceptual module.

In sum, what you have gained from hearing and memorising the statement 'adjectives in French usually come after the noun' is knowledge *about* French grammar. Your French syntax, encoded in the form of syntactic structures (SSs) in your syntactic system, remains unaffected. However, this new conceptual grammatical knowledge about adjectives may still have some use. For example, you will be able to spot errors that you have made and correct them. *It will not stop you making them in the first place* unless you have time to think consciously about what you are about to say. If those conditions obtain, then you do have a chance of not actually producing the error in the first place but it will take up a lot of thinking space and may seem laborious as all conscious thought is relatively slow. What you actually want presumably is to be able to come up with 'moulin rouge' and 'nez rouge' and 'soleil rouge',[3] etc., spontaneously, without conscious reflection and buried in longer French utterances. For this you need to follow another path, the subject of Chapter 14.

Conceptually encoded grammatical knowledge is first acquired as a result of schooling and only gets to be really complex in individuals who happen to study grammar because they are curious about it or because it is important for their profession, especially language teachers and academic linguists. You might say it is virtually irrelevant as far as normal everyday language performance is concerned. We have all that we need in the subconscious parts of our mind to be able to manage without any reflections on word order, present and past tense usage or the like. Any spare conscious attention in the normal course of events is best reserved for any unexpected problem in finding the most suitable word or expression in the circumstances to express your intended meaning.

Metacognition

The previous section focussed on a very specific type of what is often referred to as **metalinguistic knowledge**,[4] namely the consciously accessible knowledge about grammar. The meanings of particular word forms was also mentioned. Conceptual knowledge of language extends to anything which is encoded in CS, i.e. the meaning of words, phrases, idioms and much larger

---

[3] Respectively, these mean 'red windmill', 'red nose' and 'red sun'.
[4] Other terms are in use such as 'explicit' knowledge of language.

stretches of discourse as well as contextual and situational meanings, in other words lexical semantic and pragmatic knowledge of language. The distinction between what is metalinguistic and what is just meaning that we are fleetingly aware of is important. All these aspects of meaning can be projected instantly into consciousness to allow us to think, speak, write, read and listen meaningfully but they can also be thought and talked *about*, i.e. metalinguistically. In other words, metalinguistic knowledge can include phonological and syntactic knowledge but also *semantic* and *pragmatic* knowledge. Basically, any time we talk about language, be it the meaning of a single word, language of poetry, literary prose, political propaganda, the language used by a particular group or generation, or the finer points of linguistic structure, we are deploying our metalinguistic ability. This we do by consciously accessing a wealth of acquired conceptual structure that is just a part of an even larger body of ideas and beliefs that we have acquired about other aspects of life. Taken together, we can refer to our use of all these consciously accessible resources as our **metacognitive** ability of which metalinguistic knowledge is just a part.

Metalinguistic Ability and the Perceptual System

Aside from the vital role of the perceptual system in creating the experience of consciousness, it has a specifically linguistic role to play, particularly the visual and auditory systems and their respective memory stores. Speech sounds and written text consist of sounds and visual patterns projected instantly into consciousness but spoken, written and signed language can also be the object of *conscious, analytic inspection*: they can be talked about and analysed and this book has already provided plenty of examples.

Discussions about whether to pronounce a given word one way or another or about different forms of writing, for instance, invoke the participants' perceptually based metalinguistic knowledge. This knowledge may be patchy, inaccurate or sophisticated and well informed but it is all built up in conceptual code, in CS, and matched up with the relevant visual or auditory representations. As before, it is important to keep two things quite distinct: on one hand there is the immediate response, measurable in milliseconds, to a familiar sequence of sounds or letters that occurs when listening to speech or reading text (or sequences of signed language). This makes us fleetingly aware of visual patterns on paper and screen or of the sounds of speech while concentrating on the *meaning* of what is being produced. On the other hand, there is the metalinguistic knowledge built up in the conceptual system enabling us to engage in discussions about the auditory and visual patterns and where conscious awareness can be anything but fleeting.

Here we focus our attention, along with the meanings which the perceptual patterns invoke, very much on the perceptual patterns themselves. In the A examples that follow, there is no metalinguistic activity involved. In the B examples, there is:

> **A.**
> *Statement*
> **Speaker 1**. "I was in town yesterday".
>
> *Sample responses*
> **Speaker 2**. "Oh, did you see the new supermarket?"
> **Speaker 3**. "Me too. When were you there?"
>
> **B.**
> *Statement*
> **Speaker 1**. "I was in town yesterday".
>
> *Sample responses*
> **Speaker 2**. "'Town'? I wouldn't have called it a 'town'. People round here call it a 'village'".
> **Speaker 3**. "You are not from here, are you? Your accent is unfamiliar".

In A, Speakers 2 and 3 will be fleetingly aware of the sound of Speaker 1's voice but will have really attended only to the meaning. In B, on the other hand, something more happens. Analytic comments are made about the word 'town' and about Speaker 1's pronunciation. Specifically, Speaker 2's response involves an awareness and a conscious reflection on semantic aspects of what was said. Speaker 3's response focuses on an awareness and a conscious reflection on phonetic aspects of what was said. Both responses in B imply the use of conceptual knowledge about language, i.e. *metalinguistic* knowledge of some kind.

Summary

Using the framework, two types of linguistic knowledge were distinguished. The first type is based on representations in the core language system and constitutes a person's intuitive grammatical knowledge; hence 'grammar' here is limited to what resides in phonological and syntactic systems. The second kind of linguistic knowledge is developed elsewhere, in the form of conceptual structures in the conceptual system. As such, it may be projected into consciousness. Conceptual linguistic knowledge includes the meanings associated with linguistic constructions ranging from single words to much larger stretches of text. Conscious access can involve more than the fleeting awareness of meaning, sound and appearance. When utterances, written or spoken, become the object of reflection and analysis, the knowledge that facilitates this is termed 'metalinguistic' knowledge. Metalinguistic knowledge is part of metacognition in general so the conscious accessible knowledge about the grammar of a particular language is no different in kind from knowledge about any other aspect of the world. Both are encoded in conceptual structure and are quite different from what is contained in the memory stores of the core language system.

13 Language and Affect

In This Chapter

Chapter 5 described the affect system which underlies both consciously experienced emotions and hidden ones as well. Below the level of consciousness are all those preferences that lead us to be attracted to or avoid people, other animate beings, inanimate objects, places, situations, thoughts and inner sensations. This chapter looks at how this system relates to various aspects of language within and outside the core. It will turn out later to be crucial for a proper understanding of language acquisition, in other words of how development in the individual proceeds or seems to come to a halt despite continued exposure to the language being acquired.

The Relevance of Affect to Language

The relevance of affect to language cannot be underestimated. This will have been made clear in the earlier chapter on affect where valence was shown to influence us sometimes in radical ways according to the different levels of intensity and combinations of positive and negative values that are associated with practically everything in our mental system. In actual fact, its role has been somewhat underestimated until recently both in cognitive science in general and in theoretical issues in linguistics and language acquisition. This has perhaps been because its influence was generally understood to be limited to *conscious* emotions or 'feelings' as Joseph LeDoux would classify them. It has also had to do with the compartmentalisation of research fields with emotion set aside from areas focusing on cognition, a general problem in academia that was discussed in the introduction to the book. Nevertheless, the all-pervasive influence of affect is now becoming more generally accepted, also in matters concerning language.

The emotional side to language and language learning, when this refers to *feelings*, as conscious, reportable experiences, has had a longer history. This is especially true in more applied areas and in sociologically oriented studies since it is directly related to the study of *attitudes* to language and, in learning, to *motivation*. These have long been important topics in studies related to education (e.g. Gardner & Lambert 1972). This includes a body of research on emotions and language in areas like bilingualism and second language acquisition (see e.g. Dörnyei & Ottó 1998; Dörnyei 2001; Pavlenko 2005; Dewaele 2010) and also some work, more relevant to present concerns, on neurolinguistic issues in language acquisition, notably by Schumann (1997).

Affect within the Core Language System

One interesting question raised by adopting the current framework is whether there are areas of the mind that are protected in some other way from influence coming from the affect system such that changing the valence of structures in those areas from positive to negative, say, is not possible, at least in any direct manner. What possible way could this be explained? In the simplest account, those structures would be *immune* to any valence, positive or negative because there would be no interface to permit this to happen. They would have no valence in the first place.

What would the possible reason for such protection be? Firstly, not all systems have to be directly linked by interfaces. For example it is hard to see, at least within the current framework, why the syntactic system would be connected directly to the motor system for example. Secondly, there is the question of evolutionary benefit. If something has turned out, in the course of evolution, to consistently represent a threat or a dire necessity, we may have developed a way of placing obstacles to any easy way of switching a positive valence to a negative one, or vice versa. In other words it may have turned out to be safer and more convenient to keep certain types of structure permanently valenced or simply neutral with regard to valence. Either way, it is an interesting question to explore empirically and it also demonstrates the open-ended character of the framework.

A possible counterargument to the evolutionary explanation would be that mental flexibility (the psychological counterpart version of neural 'plasticity') has turned out to be the most powerful insurer of survival. This would lead to giving affect access to every system in the mind. Anything positive could be changed to negative and anything threatening could be changed to 'unthreatening' (or even attractive) by removing its negative valence. These are empirical questions of course, in other words hypotheses and not claims, and as such they would need to be tested but the hypotheses spring naturally from the way this framework is organised.

As far as the core language system is concerned, one reason for *protecting* the two modules against changes of valence, particularly negative ones, would be that human beings as social animals would need to retain their positive valence under all adverse circumstances. In particular this would hold for the child acquiring the language or languages to which it is exposed from an early age. By way of contrast, one reason for *allowing* the direct influence of affect, apart from the general flexibility argument mentioned earlier, would be to permit the child exposed to more than one language or different versions of the same language to develop

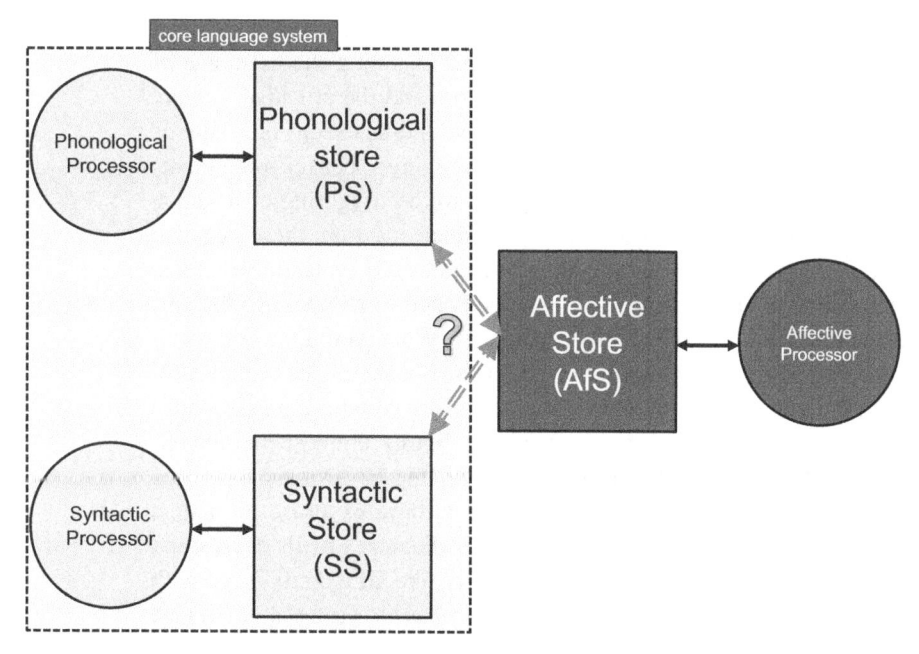

Figure 13.1 *Affect interface options for the core language system.*

preferences for certain linguistic structures (PS and SS) over others because those structures are the ones that give it the most communicative potential and the most power over its environment, in other words they are the ones that come to be associated with the particular language(s) of its caregivers or with members of its peer group. This language or set of languages would thus acquire privileged status for the child. It would provide an extra boost to any advantage accrued as a simple response to input frequency. However, the development of such preferences could still be handled outside the core system keeping the core immune and valueless since those positive values might easily could be attached just to the sounds (ASs) and not to the PSs or SSs triggered by preferred input. In other words it would be the auditory structures that acquired positive valence and the same ideas could be extended to cover handwriting and signs as expressed in VS.

As regards the access of affect to the core language system, Figure 13.1 expresses both options by rendering in thick, grey dotted lines the interfaces which are supposed to directly connect the affective system on the right with the two core language systems in the box on the left. In other words, this figure represents the two possible associations between the AfS store with, respectively the PS and SS stores as *open to question.*

It may be difficult to account for negative judgments, responding to a feeling of wrongness,[1] that native speakers of a given language make when presented

---

[1] Note that this is absolutely not about any conscious knowledge of grammatical rules that the native speaker may or may not have, just 'gut feelings'.

with examples of incorrect use of the grammar, in other words when exposed to a sentence that reflects a syntactic error, without assuming the existence of an interface between the syntactic system in the core and the affective system. Take for example sentences in English like *'I have the bus seen' or *'This is the woman that I don't know her name'.[2] Negative native speaker judgements of such examples would in this way, be attributed to the triggering of negative AfS during the processing of the sentences: in a chain reaction, these negative valence structures would have been triggered in response to syntactic structures (SS); the syntactic structures would have been activated in response to the earlier stage in the processing of the (faulty) sentences. What would the end result be? It would be a *feeling of wrongness* in the native speaker. This includes, of course, the same feelings in those many native speakers who have no clear idea at all of what grammatical rules are involved but simply know them subconsciously. For perhaps the majority of people, the feeling of wrongness will be just that with no further insights. Even those who do have expertise in matters of grammar will often have the feeling *before* their diagnosis of its causes and may even not be able to analyse the reasons directly like art experts faced with a very clever fake but unable to pin down exactly what is wrong about it (see Gladwell 2006, 3–8).

One argument for accounting for native speaker judgements in a different way and therefore for *removing* the connection between AfS and SS will be presented later. For the time being, the reader can treat this debate again as a demonstration of not so much the adaptability of the framework but, more importantly, its potential for raising interesting questions that can guide empirical research.

Affect beyond the Core Language System: Sounds and Meanings

Beyond the core system lie those systems which have other functions but that are also recruited for language-related purposes. There are various possible ways of presenting the different connections beyond the core with affect but let us just begin first with the *auditory* and *conceptual* interfaces with affect (and with each other) as, represented in Figure 13.2 as a two-way arrow, labelled CS/AS and then move on later to look at connections with visual and motor systems.

All three labelled interface arrows, CS/AS, AfS/AS and AfS/CS, now included in this second figure are not shown as grey dotted lines: the connections they represent are not controversial in the same way as are the links with the core language system in Figure 13.1. It would be difficult to argue that the conceptual and auditory systems are sealed off from any association with affective structures

---

[2] The convention, used in linguistics, of adding an asterisk (*) to incorrect, i.e. non-native linguistic forms will be followed here.

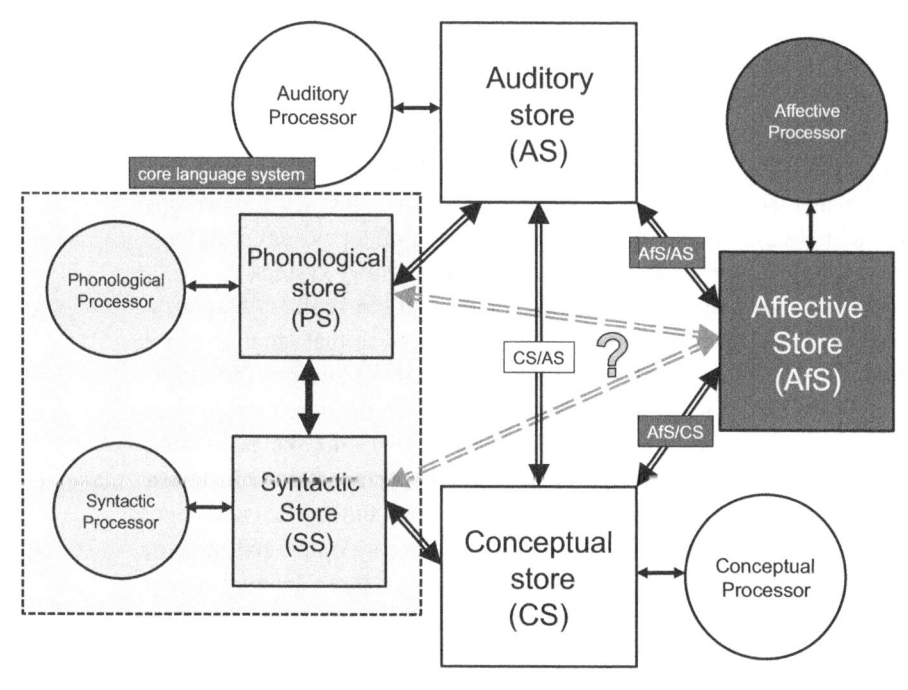

Figure 13.2 *The AfS store interfaced with the sound and meaning structures.*

precisely because they have uses other than ones to do with language. This holds for all other language-related systems lying outside the core language area. Affect is interfaced not only with both sound and meaning systems in Figure 13.2: these two systems, the AS and CS stores are also interfaced with each other. In this way, any sound may be paired with any meaning whether language meanings are involved or not.

Affect and the Auditory System (AfS and AS)

To take audition first, sounds of all kinds represented in the auditory store will have valences in the form of AfS associated with them; this includes those sound structures (AS) which are associated with language and therefore also interfaced with the core language systems and it includes those that are not. In other words, the sound of a lion's roar will have a negative valence associated with it but the sound of a particular word or any word associated with a particular accent may also have acquired a negative, or indeed positive valence. Let us assume now that there are no direct connections between the affective and core language systems (see the earlier related discussion) so this would mean that, if, for instance, French speech sounds attractive to the ear, it is not French phonological structure that has been assigned a positive value: rather, it is the *auditory structure* of French sounds. The interface between AfS and AS outside the core is sufficient to explain this preference. It explains sentiments such as 'I love the sound of French although I have absolutely no knowledge of the language' and 'I think Italian sounds nicer than French although I have no knowledge of either'. This holds even if our phonological systems kick in every time we hear French or Italian because the core language systems respond automatically to any language and have been doing so since infancy and perhaps before. They will always attempt to assign a PS but the affect system need have nothing directly to do with this. It only deals with the auditory system.

Whatever positive or negative valence is attached to the sounds (ASs) of a language will of course influence other structures related to that language: any activated chains and networks of structure that include those auditory structures will accordingly become boosted or depressed and hence become more or less effective in any competition. If the valence is a negative one, the expression 'a chain is only as strong as its weakest link' will apply and this will pose a general obstacle to be overcome for those required to learn and use that language. Guttural sounds as are evidenced in languages like Dutch, Arabic and modern Hebrew can have this negative effect on nonspeakers of those languages and Danish, which people, including Danes themselves, jokingly refer to as a mouth disease, is another case in point. Learn any of the languages well and you can sit happily listening to beautiful songs and poems without a slightest feeling of disgust at just those sounds that may have once made you recoil in horror. Luckily, affect can work in different ways given that it is interfaced with most of the mind's systems. The more you persist with a language with sounds you do not find attractive, the more the meanings conveyed in that language seem to dominate over the original negative response so that sensitivity to its sound seems to fade away. Clearly the sound was most objectionable when it was meaningless. Positive affect has been accrued to CSs, that is, the way you conceptualise the language and its usefulness. The positively valenced structures activated during use of that language militate against the effect of the original negative appraisal of its auditory structures and the ultimate result is networks of language-related chains with an overall valence that is positive. That still means that the individual sounds pronounced in isolation and therefore meaninglessly may still retain their original negative affect and sound unpleasant.

Affect and the Conceptual System (AfS and CS)

As far as affect and language-related meaning, i.e. conceptual structure is concerned, the same kind of argument used to explain affect and sound structure can also be applied. As discussed in Chapters 4 and 5, meanings of all kinds, expressed in terms of conceptual structure, i.e. encoded as CS, will have valences associated with them and these valences will be encoded as AfS. Many of these meanings may well have some form of linguistic expression but many will not. This may be because a given individual may not have acquired any word or expression for a concept[3] or perhaps the language he or she speaks may just not happen to make available neat, concise ways of expressing that particular concept. Sometimes the putting into words of some meaning may frustrate the attempts of even the finest poets in that language. T. S. Eliot, in his poem "Burnt Norton," expressed this frustration well when he wrote:

> Words strain,
> Crack and sometimes break, under the burden,
> Under the tension, slip, slide, perish,
> Decay with imprecision, will not stay in place,
> Will not stay still.

Some of the myriad interactions between affect and the conceptual system are briefly discussed in the following sections as well although the topic itself could easily take up a whole book in its own right.

Grammaticality Judgements and AfS

To return to the question of direct interfaces, the question was whether syntax and phonology[4] may only be influenced *indirectly* by affect, in other words whether the dotted lines in Figures 13.1 and 13.2 should simply be removed. If they are removed, what then might explain the feeling of wrongness triggered by exposure to linguistically anomalous utterances? Why does the native speaker of English or anyone with similar levels of ability in that language respond immediately to sentences like the one mentioned earlier, namely: *'This is the woman that I don't know her name'? We cannot attribute this instant response to the conscious knowledge of grammatical rules – metagrammatical knowledge – since the majority of native speakers, not being academic linguists, have little or no idea of what exactly is wrong in such examples. They just 'feel' wrong. Also, any conscious judgement of the sentence structure would normally not be instantaneous – a moment's reflection is required – so conscious assessment cannot explain the instant feeling of wrongness. Any conscious inspection of the sentence offered for assessment will follow on from the spontaneous feeling. This feeling has at least to be a sign that something has triggered a negative

---

[3] The internet is full of sites that list words that don't exist in a language or that exist in one language but not in another. A frequently recurring one is Japanese 'age-otori', which is supposed to mean 'to look good after a haircut'.

[4] Note that 'syntax and phonology' is just one definition of the term 'grammar'. Grammar, while not as vague a concept as language, is still open to a wide range of definitions. For instance, most will agree that *I told to him that I was ready* is incorrect. Is *tell to someone*, on analogy with *say to someone*, a grammatical error because it has to do with the way words combine in sentences? Or, is it a lexical error because the grammatical construction – verb + to + (pro)noun – does exist in English but is just associated here with the wrong word? One could say the same thing with articles. If you already know the set of articles in English to choose from – 'the', 'a' and 'a(n)' – and also know where to place them, how would you classify the error in *I climbed the Mount Everest*? In both cases, there is no right answer. It just depends on how you define grammar.

valence structure, in other words a particular structure in the affective store. The question then is what is that (negative) AfS coindexed with? If it is a conceptual structure, it *may* be some CS other than conceptually encoded knowledge of how grammar works in the language concerned, that is, metalinguistic knowledge. If the individual has no appropriate knowledge of the relevant grammar principle involved, then it *must* be something other than a metalinguistic CS.

A feeling of wrongness might seem vague and insubstantial but, in a way, it is supported by neurolinguistic evidence which appears to show different neural responses that appear to distinguish the processing of, respectively *syntactic* and *lexical* anomalies (Foucart & Frenck-Mestre 2013). In terms of the framework, 'lexical' would mean something in the conceptual system, a semantic or pragmatic anomaly in a stretch of language that is from a purely syntactic point of view, well-formed. The classic Chomskyan example, 'colourless green ideas sleep furiously' might spring to mind here. Research in the nineties already associated syntactic error with a so-called *P600* response. Briefly the P600 is a positive spike in electrical brain activity reaching its peak at 600 milliseconds after the onset of processing: this is regarded as a late response in processing terms (Osterhout & Holcom 1992). In this type of research, semantic anomaly where the listener is reacting to meaning, i.e. conceptual errors rather than syntactic ones, had come to be associated with an earlier peak in the opposite (negative) direction, called the *N400* response (Kutas & Hillyard 1980; Osterhout & Nicol 1999). Ultimately, it is a question of how to interpret these different responses and this is where a theoretical framework of one kind or other should come in useful and be developed alongside and in association with the empirical investigation. Ultimately, it is not yet clear what exactly the brain is responding to, especially in the case of the P600. It has been suggested, for example, that it is a general response to oddness of any kind rather than a response specifically to the syntactic structure itself analysis itself, an effect already associated with the P300 spike which, in one variant (P3a) has been tied to responses to novelty and in the other (P3b) to improbability (Chapman & Bragdon 1964; Polich 2003).

In sum, the intriguing neurolinguistic evidence that reveals particular subconscious responses to linguistic anomalies of various kinds could also be associated with the conscious feeling of wrongness but does not fully explain either. However, note that in the case of syntactic anomaly, whereas the occurrence of a P600 neural response seems to be more reliably present, the *conscious* feeling of wrongness may not always co-occur with it since we normally focus on the *meaning* of utterances and syntactic anomalies may pass us by as long as the utterance is perfectly comprehensible. Even language teachers with all their expertise find it hard to consciously monitor the spontaneous performance of their students for errors while at the same time interpreting the meaning of what they are saying. By way of contrast, meaning-related errors are much more disruptive and their presence therefore more often raised to awareness, whether the cause is a syntactic error or what would, in the framework, be classified as *conceptual* anomaly, that is, semantic or pragmatic errors of some kind based as they would be on an anomaly at some level of conceptual structure. As has already been discussed, conceptual as opposed to syntactic or phonological structure, can in principle be projected into consciousness. This should make conceptual anomalies more immediately recognisable, supplementing any feeling of wrongness with the ability to consciously identify the (conceptual) source of the wrongness.

Syntactic errors can cause comprehension problems ranging from momentary to complete breakdown and in either case sounding 'alarm bells' during conceptual processing but other syntactically anomalous utterances may, of course, be perfectly comprehensible as in *'Me go tomorrow' when intending to speak Standard English. Apart from any degree of disruption in *comprehensibility* caused by an anomaly, and the lack or otherwise presence of conscious awareness in the hearer of the actual source of the anomaly, there will presumably always be some delay in the processing of a faulty syntactic construction: the syntactic processor will not have a ready-made response to it (see Friederici & Weissenborn 2007). Hence, in the to-and-fro activity as the mind tries rapidly to assemble a best fit between all the structures involved in utterance interpretation, it is the *delay* in getting the syntactic part of the chain resolved rather than the syntactic nature of the anomaly itself that triggers the activation of negative valence (an AfS).

With reference to the event-potentials mentioned earlier, if delays in processing can be regarded as provoking a response to oddness, this effect might be part of the explanation of the P600 response or indeed, if delay counts as novelty or the unexpected, then it might have to do with the P300 responses. In any case, to register the fact that a train is delayed, you need not analyse why or where the train is held up. By the same token, it seems to be an open question as to whether direct access of the affective system to the syntactic system is really necessary to explain responses to syntactic anomaly. They might rather be attributed to interactions between affective structures and other structures from systems beyond the core, that is in the case of responses to anomalies in *spoken* language, between structures in respectively the affective and *auditory* systems.

Expanding the Connections: Affective, Visual and Motor Structures

Let us now continue exploring affect outside the core by looking at the interaction between affect and vision on one hand and affect and the motor system on the other. The systems actually displayed in the third figure in this chapter, Figure 13.3, include, in the top left corner, the *core language* system

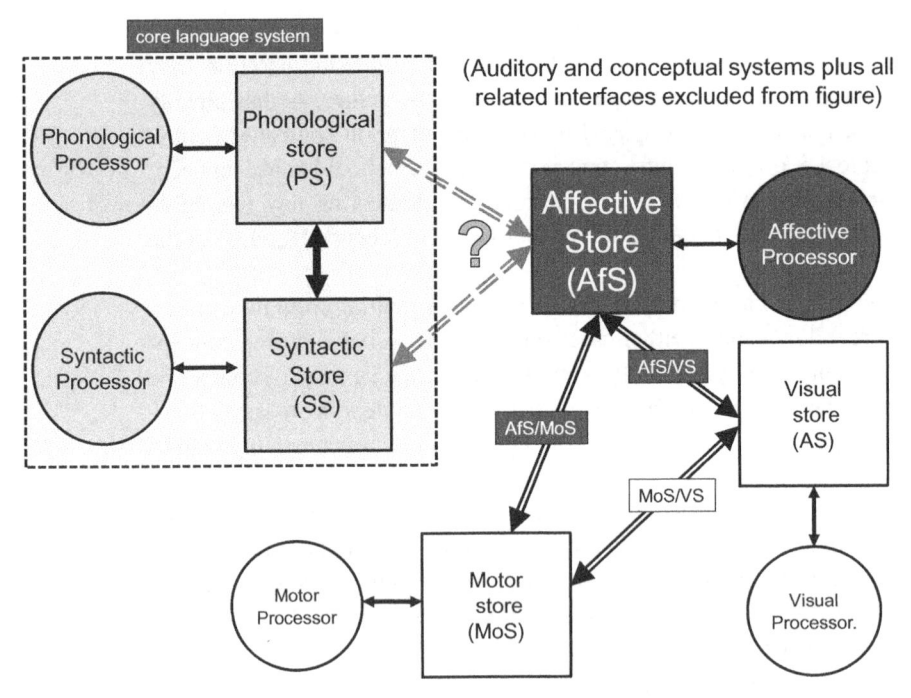

Figure 13.3 *Affect interfaced with motor and visual systems (MoS and VS).*

plus, beyond the core, the *affective* system and the *motor* and *visual* systems. Just to simplify the picture a little, the *conceptual* and *auditory* systems, shown in the previous figure, have now been excluded from view.

Affect and the Visual System (AfS and VS)

The audible sounds of language and their affective associations have been dealt with. Looking at affect, language and the visual system means looking at the mind's evaluations of the *visible* signs of language and associated meanings. This includes the various writing systems, but it also includes the visible patterns, gestures and facial expressions, used in sign language. The visual structures (VS) associated with sign language will certainly acquire associations with valence from an early age in children with deaf caregivers and those associated with positive meanings will be associated with positive AfS. In the case of reading and writing, that is to say at the onset of *literacy*, this process of association will begin once the child is exposed meaningfully to stretches of text. This literacy stage will happen long after the child has used its core language system and *auditory* input to develop a knowledge of how that language works. In other words, the child approaches learning to read and write as a little native speaker. However, the child of deaf parents may only effectively become a native speaker by acquiring the sign language system via visual structures associated with native-speaker sign language production: both types of language acquirer will normally become native speakers within the same time frame.

Affect and the Motor System

If we wished, in the functional map of the mind, to base the links between affect and the motor system on neuroscientific evidence, there would be plenty of reason to do so. There are parallel pathways in the brain reflecting on one hand *voluntary* control of the motor system and, on the other hand, emotional expression via the motor system on the other. Predictably, the second set of pathways, which control *involuntary*, emotionally driven movements are projected from areas in the 'limbic' system to motor neurons. The first set of pathways also engage the same neurons but are projected from the motor cortex. Affect will be involved in both cases. In the case of the first, voluntary system, affect will influence the planning of such movements, i.e. indirectly. In the case of the second set of pathways it will be a more direct route since it will involve rapid fight or flight related responses. These two possibilities are easily represented in the framework as was shown in Figure 13.3. The direct route is represented by the interface linking affect structures and the motor structures. Less direct routes from affect involve the other systems with which is it interfaced. One, some or all of these may of course undergo simultaneous activation but the direct route is most likely to show the fastest response. In this way we can be responding to danger physically before we have any understanding of the presence and nature of what poses the threat.

Affect as an Inhibitor of Language

The idea that affect might be associated with inhibition has long been recognised in connection with taboo words. Negative emotions need to be intense to trigger a spontaneous taboo word, such as a curse or obscenity, assuming it really is a taboo for the person concerned. Different individuals will have different valences of such words. For it to be a taboo specifically for *them*, as opposed to the language community at large, it needs to have strong negative valence. The stronger this is, the more relief a curse can bring. At the same time, in certain social contexts there may be inhibiting factors, such as finding oneself in a very formal situation, that cause the individual to suppress that taboo word. The relevant structure here would be conceptual structures representing the meaning associated with formality. At the neural level of description, inhibition is caused by mechanisms that are quite well researched, in particular with regard to the neurotransmitters that control (excite or inhibit) communication between brain cells, the most notable one in this context being GABA (gamma-aminobutyric acid) which is a predominantly inhibitory neurotransmitter. Normally, in the

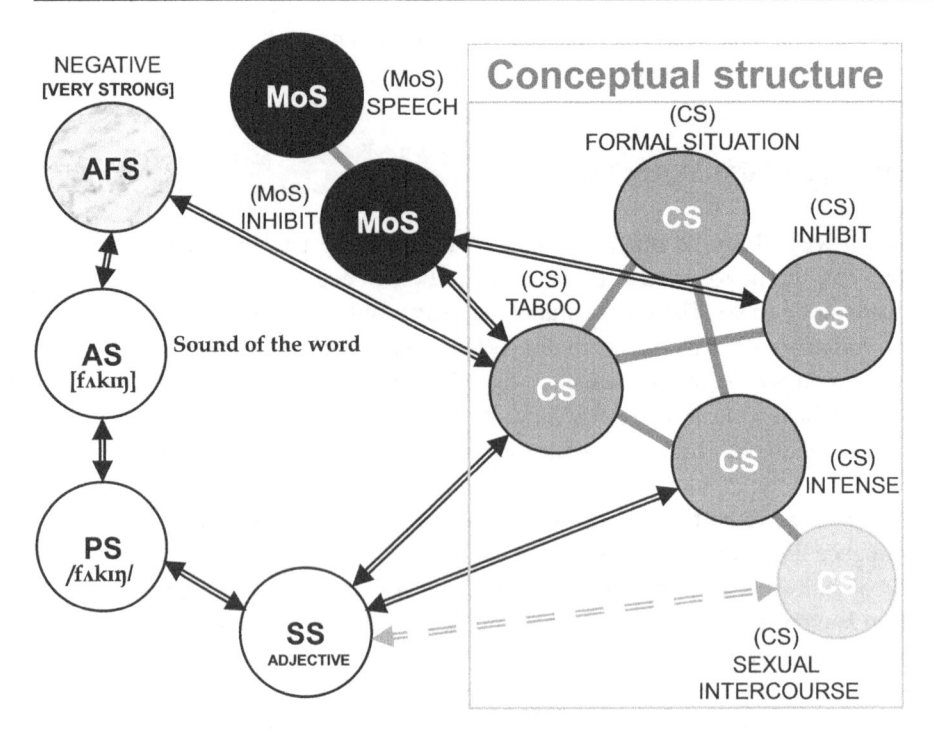

Figure 13.4 *Example of a 'taboo word' network.*

current framework, any kind of valence, negative or positive, boosts the activation levels to the structures involved. A taboo word will have a strong negative affect and therefore be very accessible and easily triggered, that is, it will have a high resting level of activation. How then, now in terms of the framework and therefore talking at the mind level of description, can the inhibition of such easily accessible structures as taboo words be explained? A concrete example is in order (with advance apologies to those with delicate sensibilities in English).

Figure 13.4 shows in a highly simplified manner the way in which a taboo word in English ('fucking') might work when the context is a formal situation where the use of that term would be inappropriate. Again, this example assumes that, for this individual, this word has not lost its full taboo status and its meaning is not become so 'bleached' that it is now, if at all offensive only mildly so. If, then, the individual, experiencing intense negative emotion is driven by the situation to utter the taboo word which would be activated under those affective conditions but is nevertheless sensitive to the social context inhibiting the use of such words, then the motor structures that would be responsible for fully articulating the word need to be suppressed, hence the complex of two (black) motor structures at the top of the figure, including one responsible for inhibition. In reality, the complexes of motor structure (and conceptual structure) would probably be much more elaborate, that is, if everything were fully specified in the display.

As always the *two-way arrows* represent the interfaces between different systems. The *thick grey lines without arrows* are reserved for combinations of structures within a store. The right half of the picture shows the complex conceptual structure that is activated. This relative degree of activation will be determined by whatever other structures are participating in the current chain or network. In this figure, then, the meaning 'sexual intercourse' is activated but much less strongly than the one representing the currently relevant meaning 'intense', both associated with syntactic structure 'adjective'. Any meaning that is associated with the meaning TABOO will trigger the meaning INHIBIT as part of its combined meaning. Any meaning that involves the CS TABOO combined with CS FORMAL SITUATION (a simplified representation for graphical convenience) will trigger an appropriate (inhibitory) structure in the *motor system*. In this case, the word will spring to mind, not necessarily to the extent that it enters awareness, but it will be suppressed, i.e. not uttered. In some cases, the activation of the 'inhibit' motor structure might kick in a bit late with the result that the articulation of the initial consonant ([f])[5] takes place before the relevant motor program is closed down properly. The individual begins to utter the taboo word but stops after the initial consonant. A similar set of structures to the ones displayed in Figure 13.4 will be activated if the same (sensitive) individual *hears* the word uttered by someone else in a formal context although the levels of activation involved might not be comparable.

Motivation and Attitude

This may not be the whole story as far as inhibition is concerned and we will return to the subject in the chapter on multilingualism where an interesting inhibitory effect noted in Wu and Thierry (2012) will need to be discussed in terms of the framework. From this example, however, it should be clear that the great richness of the conceptual system and the way CSs are combined with many others yields insights into areas much more wide-ranging than just taboo words. Attitudes to language and the motivational issues that spring from that clearly also originate in the interface connections that mediate between the conceptual system and the affective system. The way an individual conceptualises a particular language, language teacher, fellow students in a group or indeed acquaintances speaking that language, for example, will always involve associations with one or other kind of valence. A very strong positive valence or the opposite, a very strong negative valence will play its part in activated networks in the same kind of way as illustrated in Figure 13.4 causing an attract or avoid response to a given language using or language learning situation.

---

[5] At this point speakers may only have just become aware of the word about to be offered if they haven't already been aware of it before.

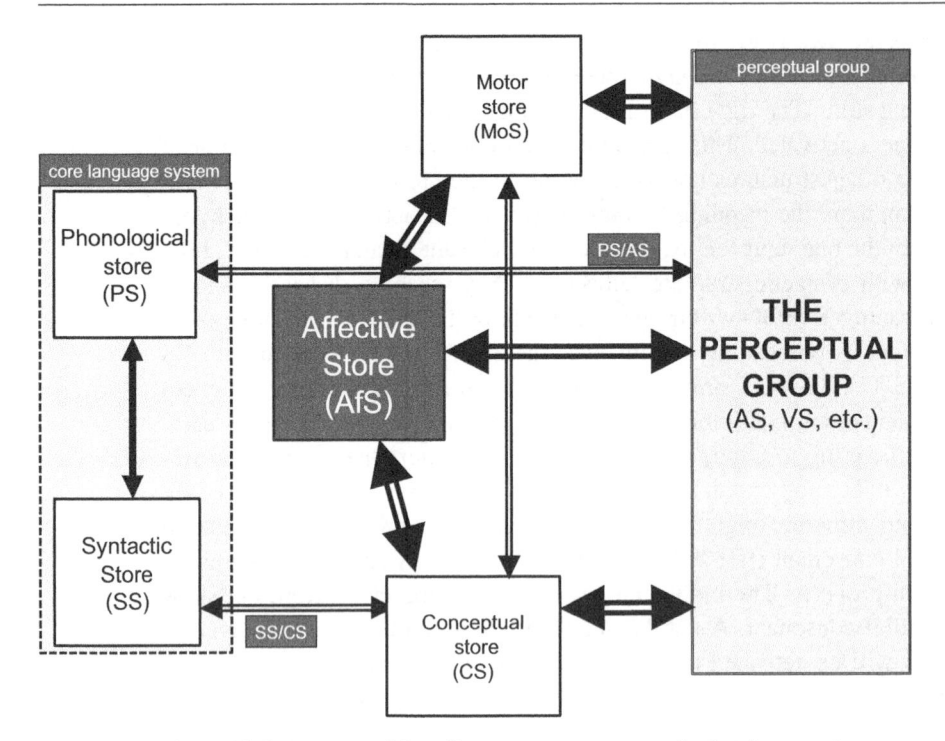

Figure 13.5 *Overview of the affective memory store and related connections.*

Summary

By way of summing up, Figure 13.5 displays just those memory stores showing the place of affect in the mind as a whole. There are two more simplifications in this particular figure. The connections with the core language system, previously represented as interrupted lines have been removed. Secondly, to save space, the separate perceptual processors and stores have not been differentiated but lumped together: although they are highly interconnected, tend to co-activate all the time and so often work together as a group, they are still separate systems. Affect is involved in practically everything we do and think. It is, therefore, not surprising that it plays a large part in aspects of the mind related to language.

Although there is a prima facie case for connecting the core language system directly with affect, everything can actually be explained with indirect connections. This explains positive and negative responses to accent, to particular spoken or written words and expressions, to a whole language, to people using language, to language teachers and so on and so forth. In many cases complexes of conceptual structure and their particular associations with affect play a major role.

This chapter continued the discussion of the system which underlies our consciously experienced emotions as well as all the subconscious biases that steer our perceptions and decision making one way or the other. In the case of language, there has been much research in areas involving emotions, especially applied and sociologically oriented studies where attitudes to language can be directly and indirectly elicited using methods such as questionnaires. More research is needed, however, on learning especially how affect operates at the subconscious level to produce 'attract' or 'avoid' behaviour where language is concerned. The framework provides one particular way of conceptualising the processes at work and guiding future theory and experimentation.

14 Language Development in the Monolingual

In This Chapter

We return now to the development of new knowledge and ability. This time we zero in on *linguistic* growth and how it can be studied using the proposed framework. Keeping in mind the fact that 'language' is a complex of different things, it is good to remember that linguistic development is more than growing grammars and a repertoire of words. It is the establishment of a whole set of structures and a 'mind-web' of structural connections across numerous mental systems, many not specifically custom-designed for language. This is why linguists[1] of all kinds need to be reasonably familiar with much more than the most obvious aspects of grammatical and lexical structure to have a wider understanding of language and also why people working in other aspects of the mind-brain need to establish how language fits into their scheme of things since language is so all-pervasive. To reiterate the fundamental principles of the framework, this time with regard to language, the growth, over shorter or longer periods, of this mind-web relies on three things. These are, apart from the various expert systems themselves, the *building blocks*, *the building principles* and the *raw materials*, or, to put it another way,

1. the *primitive elements* in each memory store and any combinations that happen already to be present;
2. the *unique set of principles* that handle/build structures out of the elements in each particular memory store that is involved in language development;
3. not words and sentences as such but *raw sensory data* that come in via our senses and are registered and stored (briefly or for longer periods) in our perceptual system, that is to say, in the case of language, mainly in our auditory and our visual stores (Figure 14.1) and in the two stores that handle only language structures.

---

[1] A quick reminder to non-linguist readers that 'linguist' here is not the practical, everyday sense of the word (someone who speaks more than one language) but the *academic* sense of the word, meaning someone involved one way or another in *linguistics*, the study of language.

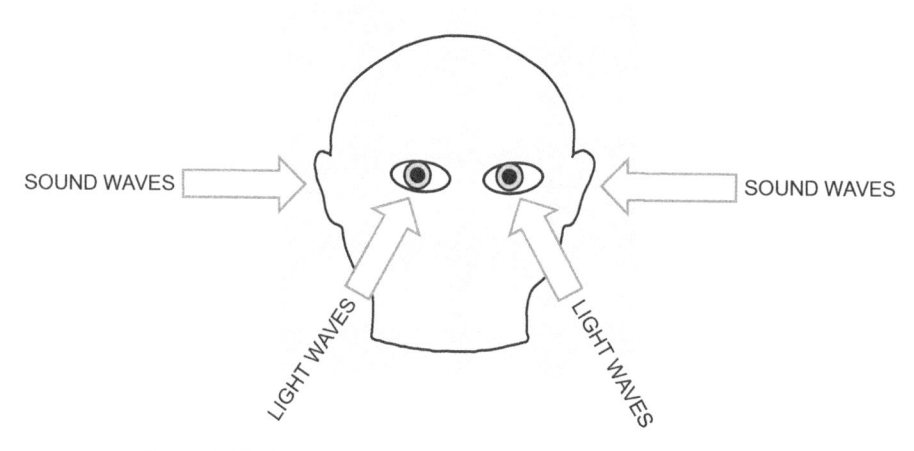

Figure 14.1 *Raw input, not 'words and sentences'.*

With these three components plus the set of systems that make up the framework, language construction of whatever kind can get going following the overarching 'acquisition by processing' principle (APT) discussed in Chapter 8.

Completely new structural combinations can be created *within* each system where required. Also, their resting levels may be raised or lowered reflecting their activation history. Finally, new connections can be established *across* systems via the interfaces with adjoining modules using indexing as described in Chapter 8.

Note that this linguistic growth works in essentially the same way whether we are talking about *first* language acquisition, that is acquiring one or more languages from the very beginning, as very young children, or acquiring *new* languages later on, when we are older. If we are in a monolingual environment acquiring just one language with no prior linguistic experience, our minds will have to make do with just the initial set of structures. These are the 'primitives' in the core language system, like the *syllable* and *noun categories* that all languages would seem to possess and which many but not all linguists assume are available from the word go.[2] They are, of course perfectly adequate for developing a native language from scratch in collaboration with all the modules that exist outside the core language system and which are involved in language, namely perception, articulation, affect and the conceptual system.

---

[2] Some claim that noun and syllable are categories that can, with sufficient exposure to language, be assembled from scratch in what in the framework would be the conceptual system, in other words using general cognitive ability without any need for a core language system. The fact that only humans do this would be attributed to the greater power of human cognitive ability but not to any special 'language faculty' (see e.g. O'Grady 2005). This much debated issue remains one where opinions are highly polarised.

INCORRECT!   **CORRECT!**

LANGUAGE SYSTEM 1   LANGUAGE SYSTEM 2   LANGUAGE SYSTEMS 1, 2 & 3

LANGUAGE SYSTEM 3

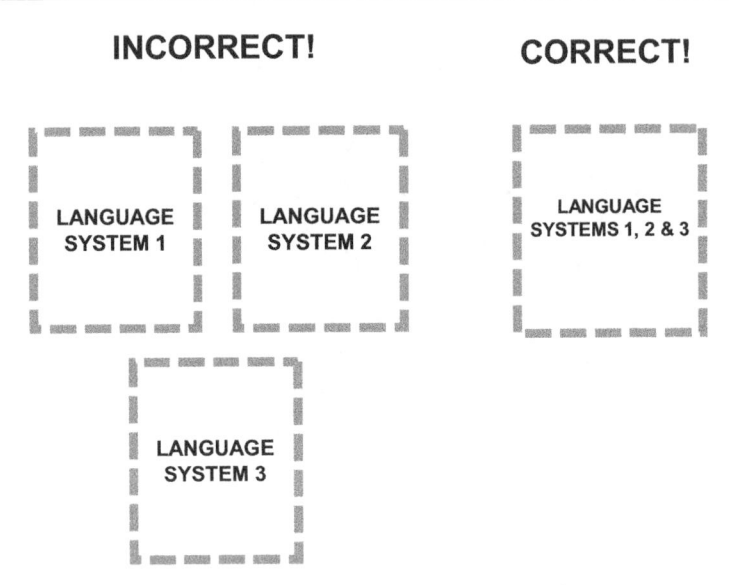

Figure 14.2 *All language systems stored and processed the same way.*

One Size Fits All

As far as growth is concerned, in some important respects the process of constructing a new linguistic system is the same. There is certainly no need for a special location in the mind (or brain) for storing and processing an extra language or an extra dialect. The same goes for accents, since a dialect, especially one that is considered to be the standard dialect, may be spoken with different accents. In other words, there is also no special location for even an extra accent used with the same dialect as when Standard American is spoken with a Californian, Texan or New York accent or Standard British English spoken with a Scottish, Welsh or Yorkshire accent. Everything gets processed, develops or declines in the same way using the same repertoire of systems. In other words it is not correct to imagine dialects, varieties, registers or even whole languages as though they resided in different mental boxes (see the left side of Figure 14.2). In the act of processing any one of the linguistic systems we happened to have acquired, there will be simply more phonological and syntactic competitors around. They will all be fighting for a place in the chain of structures being built in any act of language comprehension or language production.

The Tower of Babel

It might seem that handling everything in the same set of systems is a recipe for total confusion and representation of what might happen in a Tower of

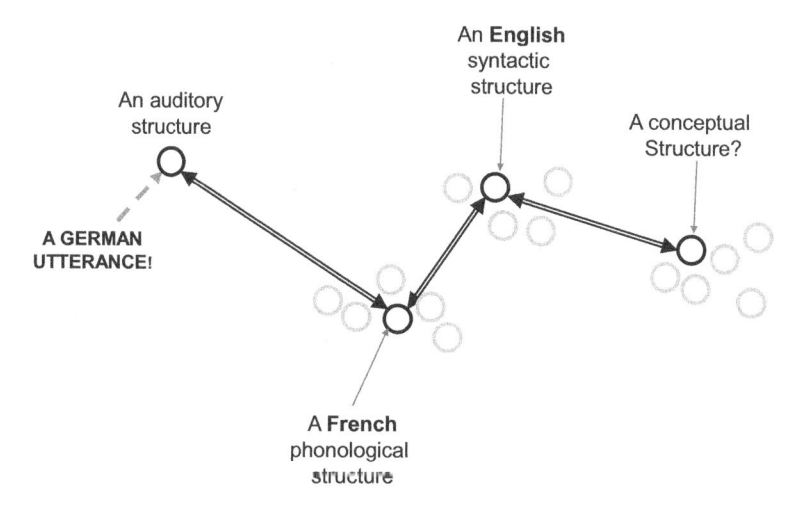

Figure 14.3 *A recipe for confusion?*

Babel[3] (Figure 14.3). Surely, won't everything then get mixed up all the time like this? There have to be pathways linking certain structures and not others together in all the relevant working memories, all forming appropriate chains or networks that serve in a consistent manner the interpretation or production of utterances in one language system. How then, in this single, undifferentiated set of systems, does a bit of *German* phonology end up tied to an appropriate bit of German *syntax* and linked to the right sound at one end and the right meaning at the other, so to speak? We will leave that question hanging in the air for the next chapter. In the present chapter, we will concentrate on development in monolingual, first language acquisition.

Language 'Input': A Misleading Term

It is perhaps useful to remember that mental processing in response to stimuli from the environment includes many stages. In some research traditions involved in the study of language acquisition, the term 'language input' is used, especially where adult second language acquisition is concerned. In these contexts it means any language to which the learner (acquirer) has been exposed.

Generative linguists tend to use the term 'primary linguistic data' for input. This has the advantage of not assuming in advance that mere exposure implies any processing at all. Any form of environmental input, as will already have been

---

[3] Strictly speaking, the Tower of Babel as described in the Christian and Hebrew Bibles was a tower from which everyone, all speaking the same language, was scattered after having the numbers and the temerity to build a construction so high that it would reach heaven and reveal all the world's secrets. God is supposed to have taken great exception to this idea and made absolutely sure it would never happen by rendering everyone's speech incomprehensible to everyone else.

emphasised in earlier chapters, is in effect sensory in nature. Language 'input' is no different. It is registered first as signals that impact upon and stimulate the sense organs along with other signals that may or may not have anything relevant for further processing as language. It is only *language* input because we as outside observers know it is. To the basilar membranes on our ears and the retinas in our eyes and indeed to the initial, internal processing of this input, the linguistic content of the input is not recognised at all. There is no label, as it was, saying 'this input is language'. Our ears and our eyes are, as it were, 'stupid'. They naturally have no way of knowing the significance of what they are dealing with. The initial processing of *acoustic* input, for example, is followed by *auditory* processing and only then, if the conditions are right, it engages the core language system where language alone can be processed. At the same time, some of the other sensory signals that are registered at the same time as those that constitute language input will get processed by the relevant perceptual system and then end up in the conceptual system where they will also take part in the interpretation of the utterance by providing a meaning context. This means, strictly speaking, that we should talk about inputs in the plural, as each successive stage is completed in the processing of an utterance. Susanne Carroll has, for this reason, suggested that the term 'input' for the sensory signals that trigger responses from our perceptual systems should be dropped and accordingly proposed that we replace it with the term for that type of input by 'stimulus' (Carroll 1999).

Early Speech

Now, to begin at the beginning, we know that infants are attracted to speech sounds as opposed to nonspeech input from a very early age (Eimas 1975). This suggests that auditory structures of a certain type, i.e. bearing the general characteristics of human speech, have a preassigned positive value as has been discussed in Chapter 13 (the section on affect and the auditory system). Research, stretching back to the 1970s investigates infants' responses to samples of sound. This is done by means of a sucking device that does not supply any nutrition but simply registers sucking activity, which slackens off when babies lose interest. In this way the machine can record the degree to which they find a particular type of sound interesting. Another way is to register the ways in which infants fixate on or do not pay attention to different types of sound played to them from a single source. It shows that between the ages of 9 and 11 months babies acquire the ability to recognise the vowels and consonants specifically of the language(s) spoken in their presence.

By the end of their first year, there is a new development: babies lose interest in any kind of speech sound which doesn't figure regularly in their immediate environment. In other words, they will first show equal interest when exposed to the sound of, say, Dutch, Hindi and Vietnamese speech to begin with but later they will tune out those languages which they do not hear frequently around them.

In this way they become desensitised to any speech sounds that are not relevant to them by virtue of their infrequency or their complete absence. In other words they concentrate only on the frequent language around them and treat the rest as extraneous sound. In terms of our framework we can say that one particular group of frequently occurring auditory structures that happen to be relevant for speech interpretation have acquired higher resting levels of activation due to their frequency. Other ones, those that have become infrequent, have according acquired lower resting levels and their positive valence has declined. The child is henceforth guided towards just what it needs to process linguistically not only by virtue of its frequency alone but by the increased value placed on it by the affective system.

There may well be other frequent nonlinguistic sounds in the environment which originally attracted its attention but to which it has now become accustomed and for that reason no longer attracts its attention. This process of habituation is the normal course of events. In the case of language input we see that the child continues to pay close attention to it and his or her core language system will more often than not persist in trying to make sense of it. The type of sound that the human voice makes has this predetermined positive value to 'guide' every child towards a source which will ultimately give it language ability as well as food, comfort and protection. The question of whether the core system is actively engaged in the processing of speech sounds from the start or whether it kicks in later is an interesting question and one which will be returned to later on in this chapter. It is possible that some initial processing by the phonological system very early on could account in part at least for the special attraction the infants have for speech sound. This is both a theoretical and an empirical question that the framework encourages us to ask.

Babies, Birds and Monkeys

How do infants, in the processing of the acoustic input around them, compare with other comparable species? From what was said in the last section, already at the age of three months babies will be more attracted to the sound of human speech than to the sounds of macaque monkeys (Vouloumanos et al. 2010). We can reasonably conclude that research on early infant speech seems to show a natural (innate) bias towards speech sounds. However, at least one species of monkey, the cotton-top tamarin, has demonstrated a similar ability to recognise sequential patterns of human speech sound even though it would appear to us that they have no need to do so, i.e. the evolutionary advantage of this particular ability is not clear (Hauser et al. 2001). They can distinguish between different syllables and can keep track of the order in which these syllables occur. Does this really mean that they must have, in the relevant system, a primitive element that is equivalent to *syllable*? They surely cannot develop this ability further by proceeding to acquire human language (although intensive exposure to human language would of course be needed to prove that conclusively). This would suggest, then, that the sound distinctions that cotton-top tamarins are able to recognise are not really based on a phonological category (syllable) as such but rather something that has a different function in their vocalisation system that we have not yet been able to determine.

In humans, the syllable category comes into play once auditory sounds are matched with phonological structures and are by virtue of that fact then processed as speech. Young humans alone can capitalise on the auditory representations that are created in the early months from speech input by creating phonological representations using the phonological primitives available in their phonological store.

Research with apes indicates that other species can demonstrate human-like communicative behaviour both in what they can *recognise* and what they can *produce*, i.e. a signing system. However, they never develop anything but the most basic grammar. Nevertheless they do all proceed to develop their own innate abilities as communicators in their own different ways. Exposure to human speech can never take other species very far. The ability of some birds, like parrots and mynah birds, to accurately mimic, that is 'fake' fragments of speech only results in an illusion of language ability. Danish researchers carried out research that showed that orange-fronted conures, a type of parrot, use their mimicking ability to address specific individuals in their own flock (Balsby et al. 2012). Various interesting similarities between humans and other species with respect to their communicative systems – the processing of both birdsong and human speech is located in the left hemisphere of the brain, for example – only serve to emphasise the essential, striking difference.

Babies and Dogs

To sum up so far, the innate bias in speech perception as demonstrated by infants may reflect an early collaboration between two different systems, one outside the core language system and the second one within it:

a. the general auditory system that processes and represents any kind of sound;
b. the phonological system that matches auditory input with speech categories.

It is not clear how early the phonological system starts to attempt to build representations from sound input, i.e. auditory structures. In any case, in the earliest stages, infants and certain other species process and create representations from acoustic input in similar ways. One view is that they employ statistical strategies to tune into frequent patterns detectable in what they are hearing and they construct many perceptual (auditory) categories based on that acoustic input.

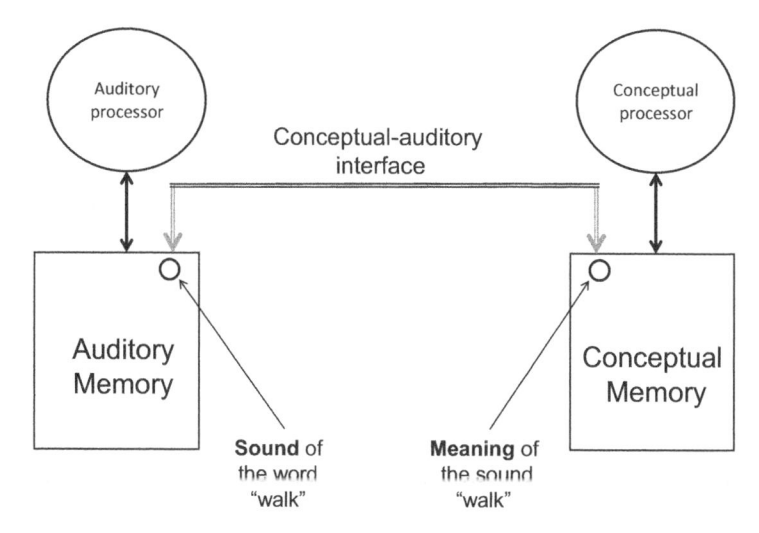

Figure 14.4 *Nonlinguistic comprehension.*

It is worthy of note that animals can also, in this 'prelinguistic' (or 'nonlinguistic') stage, make such auditory representations meaningful: they can already link these auditory categories to conceptual categories. Long and intensive exposure to human speech, however, will never produce the same results in other species, which have different innate biases and acquire their own specific systems of communication in the form of various types of vocalisation.

This strongly suggests that any links between sounds and meanings that are made by other species do not involve any phonology or syntax but represent direct connections between the relevant perceptual systems and the meaning system. In the case of nonhuman species, we must assume that the conceptual system, if we can speak of some nonhuman equivalent, must be comparatively limited in scope and complexity but it will be sufficient to, say, identify a particular parrot in a flock or convey a warning to a rival. Figure 14.4 illustrates this auditory-conceptual collaboration in simple terms. Both a dog and the humans who look after the dog are perfectly able to attach a meaning to the sound of the word "walk" without resorting to a core language system; the content and degree of complexity of the two resulting conceptual structures will naturally differ.

Acquisition: The Early Stages

Language involves many different parts of the mind. According to most accounts, its development in the individual mind gets seriously under way about the age of 18 months. However, there is what you might call a 'preparatory phase'. This shades off into the first stage of language acquisition where we can more clearly see recognisable signs of a new language system forming in the child's mind.

In the preparatory phase, there is *cooing*, when babies already show a clear interest in the human speech around them, and then there is *babbling*, which begins at around 6 months when the baby produces syllable-like sounds, often repeated. Cooing and babbling would appear to be the baby practising the articulatory bases of speech, finding the right physical movements and experimenting with different sounds including what would be the precursors of stress and intonation patterns. The auditory and motor systems are involved in this together but this phase could be called prelinguistic. That is to say, the auditory structures involved in babbling may well be, but are not *obviously* linked up with the phonological system and, if they are, it is because the baby utters syllable-like sounds. More detectable linguistic progress is made only a couple of months later. This is when the first single-word utterances begin to emerge in production.

As implied in the discussion thus far, production is the way in which the early stages of language acquisition are usually charted. Produced language is easy to detect, record, measure and analyse. To start with, there is a one-word utterance stage (usually assumed to begin at about 10 months), a two-word stage (beginning at 14–18 months). When the child gets around to producing three-word utterances, there is an explosive development too rapid to really talk about a proper three-word stage. However, we know that acquisition starts earlier than speech production might suggest. Something is going on before the child has uttered its first word. Producing it does not mark the beginning of language acquisition.

The Silent Period and Baby Signing

The stage at which children begin to produce their very first words is, then, not the point at which language growth actually begins. Word comprehension generally precedes word production. This puts the actual beginning of the first, one-word stage of language acquisition somewhat earlier, that is to say, at the start of the so-called silent period of language acquisition. How can we tell this is part of the first stage of language acquisition? First and foremost, simply by registering the fact that babies begin to respond meaningfully to certain words that are spoken to them. In general, comprehension precedes production at all stages of language development. The silent period is only the first indication of this.

Hidden progress before speech is produced, i.e. during this silent period, can sometimes be revealed in another interesting way. This is when children are exposed to 'baby signing'. *Baby signing* is a simple signing system, not a sign language in the normal sense, but more like a simple pidginised variety of sign language (Acredolo et al. 1999). *Pidgins* are simple language systems each developed as a lingua franca by adolescents and adults with no shared language. They have a limited vocabulary, fixed word order and little grammatical morphology such as forms attached to words indicating plural, gender or number for example. In the case of baby signing, each baby sign system can differ from

LUKE BABY SIGNING

ALL GONE!   APPLE   BATH   CEREAL (Loops)

ELEPHANT   PIG   RAIN   (INCY WINCY) SPIDER   TORTOISE

Figure 14.5 *Luke's signs.*

any other in some respects since both child and caretaker can invent their own signs in addition to those suggested by others or taken from a book (see examples in Figure 14.5 depicting Luke's signs partly made up at home and partly borrowed from American Sign Language). In this situation, babies and parents typically start communicating even before the onset of early speech, at around eight months. This is mainly done with the baby producing single signs but occasionally, later, they can sometimes put signs together to form more complex structures.

Apart from revealing something about the silent period, baby signing appears to give much pleasure to both parties involved and also seems to have no negative effect on normal language development and indeed some positive effects (Doherty-Sneddon 2008). The child can communicate ideas and emotions more effectively and seems to learn more about socialising with others at an earlier age. However, we cannot draw any dramatic conclusions about its significance at this point. We need to keep in mind the fact that, as mentioned earlier, some great apes are also able to do this, at least as adults, the bonobo Kanzi being a classic example with his 500-sign vocabulary and the ability to work to a limited extent with signs strung together (Savage-Rumbaugh & Lewin 1996). At the same time overhasty conclusions could be drawn on the basis of similar levels of development in communicative ability observed in some great apes and young children. In the case of the apes, development comes to a definite halt in what can arguably still be called a prelinguistic stage.

With children, we know that this stage is one step in a series of steps of rapidly increasing complexity undertaken without explicit instruction and no effective grammatical correction, if any correction at all: most parents recognise there is no need for this. Apart from that, adults often find the child's creative grammatical constructions entertaining, arguably rewarding the 'errors' with increased attention and thereby discouraging self-correction, a reward system that, however, clearly fails to work. Given the significance of what we have tentatively labelled the child's *pre*linguistic development, as opposed to that of the apes, we may well ask whether the core language system is in fact, already at this early stage, attempting automatically to assign some linguistic structure to the input originating in the visual and acoustic environment. Despite the similarity between the child's early communicative abilities and those of chimpanzees, once we can show that the core language system has been engaged, even minimally, we must, following the framework, talk about an initial and uniquely human 'linguistic' stage. The child is making some use of a system that even the apes do not possess, at least at the present stage of their evolution.

Language Acquisition by Processing

How can we make sense of the language acquisition process using the mechanisms of the framework map outlined thus far? Following the principles of *Acquisition by Processing Theory* outlined in Chapter 9, a set of auditory representations is created in the mind to match patterns encountered in the acoustic input from the environment. This is stored in our 'sound library', i.e. the auditory store. For those acquirers with hearing problems, the relevant perceptual system will be the visual one and the source for building linguistic representations will be the visual library.

Gradually the resting levels of activation of these two perpetual stores are built up so that the sounds (or visual patterns) we encounter later become instantly recognisable. For the majority of children, i.e. those with no hearing impairment, the main environmental input for language will be auditory. For the literate, older learner, the visual store also becomes important: additional or alternative *visual* input will then be supplied, in the form of written text, that also needs to be given generic visual representations. So, of all the many and various perceptual representations created in the learner's mind when exposed to language in the environment, a number of representations will be processed further in automatic attempts to find linguistic – phonological and syntactic – representations to match them.

As far as most young children are concerned, visual representations only come into play when learning to read, which is *after* the serious bit of language acquisition has taken place, i.e. cracking the grammatical system. In other words, when the child is ready to read, *s/he is already a little native speaker of the language concerned*. What then remains, as far as linguistic growth during the period of formal education is concerned, is mostly refining, enriching and polishing the basic language system that is *already in place*.

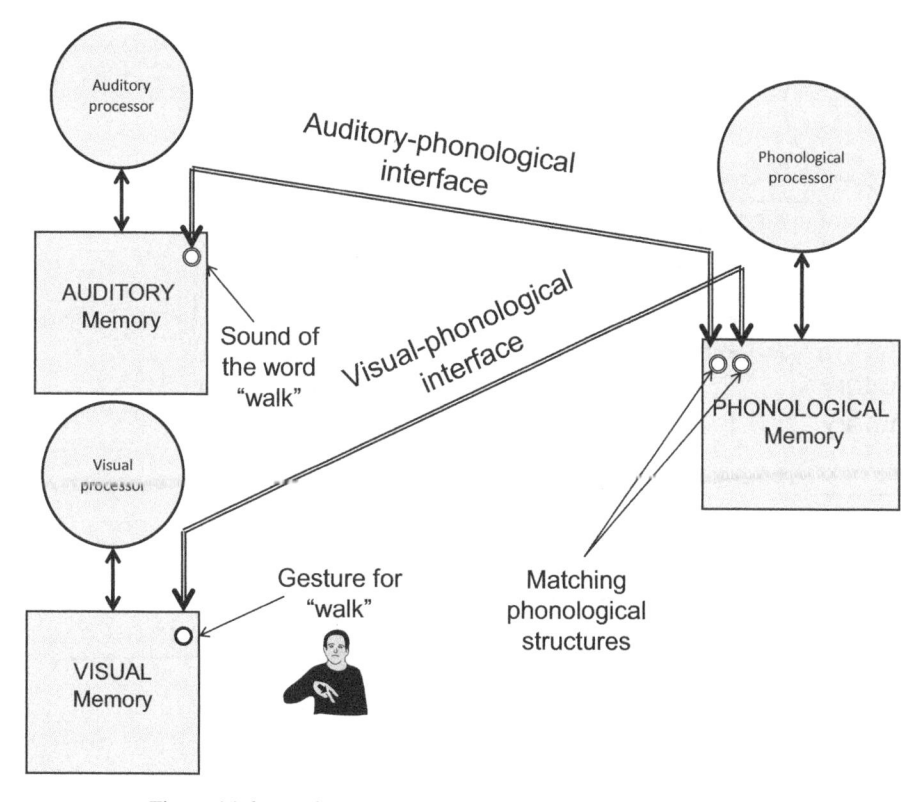

Figure 14.6 *Matching perceptual and phonological representations.*

Whether the perceptual representations of language input from outside are auditory or visual, those that feed into the core language system will always feed into the *phonology* module (see Figure 14.6). At the moment we have no neutral name[4] for this stage of language processing that covers the linguistic processing of both visual and auditory input but ever since the 1960s it has been recognised that gestures in sign language, for example different hand shape configurations, can be broken up into different structural components just like speech (Stokoe 1960). Accordingly, as was mentioned earlier, in accounts in the sign language literature, the process of converting visual structures into language is seen as a being a phonological one (Sandler 1989).

We will now concentrate, for the sake of convenience, on the processing of speech. As the auditory system responds to repeated patterns of acoustic input transmitted to via the ears, the resulting auditory structures that are created will move from a relatively low resting level of activation to a higher level more accessible to working memory and therefore with an increased chance of participating in coactivation with a structure in the phonological system (Figure 14.7).

---

[4] The term 'chirology' has been used, but it is also used for fortune-telling via hand-reading and so might be best avoided.

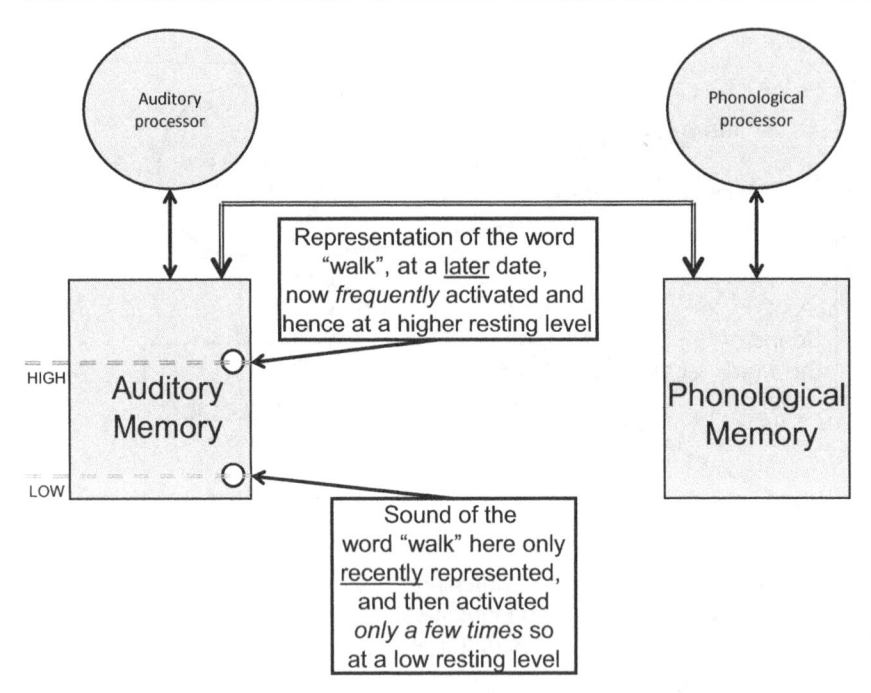

Figure 14.7 *Matching activated auditory representations with phonological ones: comparisons of resting level status at two different times.*

We quickly become able to recognise frequent sounds like the sound of a door bell, the opening of a door, the bark of a dog. Some of these frequent environmental sounds will be linguistic in origin, i.e. speech. Easily activated *auditory* representations created in response to frequent speech sounds should, by virtue of the frequency and the corresponding gain in value acquire increases in their resting levels of activation: this should make them good candidates for further processing at the *phonological* stage, i.e. as language. They, that is the auditory structures, should quickly rise into working memory competing strongly with other candidates and become ready and available for matching across to some phonological structure although such a matching across the auditory/phonology interface is never guaranteed: it all depends on what phonology can make of it.

Apart from frequency, several other factors will influence this whole process that goes from acoustic input from the environment, to the establishing of corresponding auditory (memory) structures and the eventual use of those auditory representations in phonological processing.

Firstly, the *quality* of the auditory (or visual) input itself. The sensory abilities of normal hearing younger children will ensure the optimal processing of sounds although gradually diminishing hearing ability in older learners should pose problems: low quality input will be correspondingly harder to process. Many older learners will experience age-related hearing loss both in terms of changes in their ears as also in terms of changes in their central auditory processing although there is nothing in principle to stop learners at an advanced age learning another language and indeed profiting from it in terms of their cognitive abilities (Long et al. 2015).[5]

Secondly, as mentioned earlier, affect will play an important role. Any auditory input from speech already has preassigned positive value. This reflects the innate bias to attend to speech sounds described earlier. In addition, auditory input from speech addressed to infants by caretakers may acquire even higher positive values. This, as was explained in Chapter 5, will boost its activation levels rendering caretaker speech best of all for getting phonology, as it were, to sit up and take notice where young children are concerned.

In later life, affect will continue to play an extremely important role in facilitating language acquisition by boosting activation levels during various stages in language processing. Because we are built to acquire language(s), our core language system will not be dormant while we are awake: it will be constantly on the watch for relevant auditory input whatever age we happen to be and whatever physical obstacles are placed in the way.

Early Grammars

Producing single words only may or may not reveal the early operation of the phonological system but it will certainly say little or nothing about syntactic structure during this first stage of language acquisition.[6] The moment the child begins producing two-word utterances, however, the question of word order comes up for consideration. Is it to be 'doggy ball' or 'ball doggy' (McNeill 1970)? If the word order is not random at this stage, and it has long been observed that it is not random, the question then arises as to whether the order is determined *syntactically*, according to categories, always putting, say, a subject noun in first position. In this case, we can definitely talk of the child leaving the prelinguistic phase and finally beginning to make real use of both modules within the core language system, i.e. phonology and syntax. However, a number of people have argued that the word order observed in early child speech[7] is initially determined by meaning, on *conceptual* grounds, which in standard linguistic terminology would be usually termed 'semantic' or 'pragmatic' grounds. This way of determining the position of different words would manifest itself by not

---

[5] The Long et al. study reports improvement in participants following a course in (Scots) Gaelic immediately and much later after the course. This study will be discussed again in the next chapter on multilingualism.
[6] Here, the only possible information to had from a single word would be the appearance of a bound morpheme, say, signalling plural as in 'toys', and even there the child may have chosen 'toys' as the word for toy, whether plural or singular, in which case the 's' in the child's version of the word will not signal anything.
[7] Similar claims have been made for adults learning a second language 'naturally', i.e. in the workplace, and generally in the language community, that is, not in a formal learning environment (Klein & Purdue 1997).

making syntactic categories like *subject, object* and *verb* dictate the word order, but using conceptual categories, for example by putting the *agent* in first position in the sentence (the 'doer' of an action) or the *topic* of the utterances first (who or what it's mainly 'about') followed by the *action* and then the *patient* (the person or thing acted upon).

At this point the question is whether the prelinguistic phase has been properly left behind yet. If categories like *agent, topic*, action and *patient* are conceptual representations, then it looks as though the child is still linking auditory structures *directly* with conceptual structures as shown in Figure 14.4. Utterance production is therefore, *bypassing* any core language system, and operating uniquely with systems that are not specific to humans. At this stage in development, then, the child would be using a system that did not differ dramatically from that used by Kanzi, the bonobo ape. Or has the child at this stage associated the auditory structure of what it has heard with a *phonological* structure but has not yet managed to match this with a *syntactic* structural element in the syntactic module like *noun* or *adjective*? In such a case, utterance interpretation will, still have to rely on the auditory-conceptual match as in the previous example: the child has only begun to use part of the core language system but is relying on the conceptual system for ordering 'doggy' and 'ball' as, for example, *agent* + *patient* to mean (roughly) 'the dog has picked up the ball'.

Applying the Framework

The framework helps us to formulate questions like 'when does the child start to produce language?' in a way that simultaneously involves the real-time processing dimension, the properties of the representations themselves and also the transition over time from one stage of development to the next. Empirical research may provide reams of potentially useful data but a combination of language processing theory, linguistic theory and theories of development are needed to understand the patterns observed in the data. This applies to both first and second language acquisition, so it is not just about small, immature learners.

It is true that older learners do not show a regular pattern of early development in quite the same way as monolingual first language learners going from a one-word stage to a two-word stage and then a rapid spurt. They have, in their first language, a fully fledged linguistic system at their disposal which will undergo activation whenever they are engaged in language activity. This will inevitably affect their interpretation and production of a second language allowing them to produce longer (nonnative) utterances at a much earlier stage. Nevertheless, research has indicated that second language learners, particularly those who are picking up the language in the community, are not relying on formal instruction and are free to use their second language for communicative purposes, will also go through a preliminary stage of development where their spontaneous utterances are structured largely according to pragmatic principles. There will be more to say about second language learners in the next chapter.

Conceptual Bootstrapping

At a certain point – perhaps during the two-word stage or later in the three-word stage in the case of child learners – syntax kicks in and the core language system becomes fully engaged in processing the language. Pinker believes that, this is at the point when the child (1) has sufficiently developed appropriate conceptualisations of objects, states and events and (2) has become able to associate them with bits of the utterances it hears. This is the stage when it, the child, becomes able to match these concepts to specific syntactic elements that it has in its repertoire, i.e. as syntactic primitives, but which have hitherto been unused. At this point the syntactic processor can get to work on any activated elements from its syntactic store and order them according to syntactic principles.

For this process of matching conceptual structures with syntactic ones, Pinker introduced the term *semantic bootstrapping* (Pinker 1987, 1994).[8] In the framework, how long and when the transition to full (core) linguistic processing of auditory and conceptual input takes place can be roughly determined empirically by the structural patterns in production data, 'roughly' because in the case of child language acquisition, it is not an easy matter to collect data that would reveal how language is currently being processed and interpreted. Such data would provide the best indications of the earliest deployment of the core language system. It is to some extent possible to detect the working of the core language system by giving children's utterances exhibiting some significant linguistic principle that cannot be acquired any other way and seeing if they interpret them appropriately. This can give an early indication of the operation of phonological and syntactic processing but the largest body of child language data to date comes from production not utterance interpretation. Whatever particular theory is used to explain how acquirers of language shift from the prelinguistic phase to the first properly linguistic stage, it can be incorporated into the framework using APT.

Acquiring Language by Interpreting Utterances

It is important to understand how, respectively, the interpretation and production of utterances is related to growth in the core language system. We often think of language learning as learning to *speak* a language. Speaking certainly provides *tangible* evidence of new knowledge and also of an ability that can be used to fully exploit the communicative possibilities that language offers. As was mentioned previously, language acquisition research has, for practical reasons, focussed on production data. In fact the most important part of linguistic growth – making new connections, within and across stores – takes place during the *interpretation* of utterances. In other words, it takes place during attempts to make sense of what we hear (or read), and not during attempts to produce

---

[8] This would be 'conceptual' bootstrapping, using the terminology employed in the framework.

language. It is the act of trying to understand that leads to new structures being assembled within a given memory store and new matches being made, via interfaces, between structures in other stores such that matched structures get assigned the same index and can therefore be coactivated later. In terms of the framework, if no interpretation at all is achieved the current processing enterprise falls flat: any new combinations temporarily created in working memory have no effect so there is no growth and no changes made to any resting level. Still, that said, even partial comprehension can trigger growth.

Utterance production will certainly play a role in the acquisition of language. Production may not necessarily push development by generating *new* combinations of structure or chains of representation. Nevertheless, it may help by boosting the resting levels of *existing* structural combinations, ones that have been created earlier via successful utterance interpretation. At first, these recent creations will usually not function well in fast spontaneous production because they will often be out-competed by more well-established candidates. These rivals will have higher resting levels of activation and easy access into working memory. Although the raising of resting levels will develop with continuing experience in interpreting utterances, every time a speaker manages to use the new structures in production, this will also contribute to the raising of resting levels in the relevant stores and the increased likelihood of the new combinations making it into participating in an actual utterance and hence beating older rivals. In sum, both comprehension and production play their part in the growth of knowledge in language, as they do elsewhere. The old adage as used in educational circles, apparently dating back to Aristotle, which says that 'you learn by doing' should be interpreted in this light.

There are still situations in which you might say that production is the main driver of growth. This is when we consider changes in the system having to do with the physical act of producing languages, i.e. the motor structures responsible for the articulation of speech and writing? Consider speech, for instance. Although mechanisms associated with speech production are not used in any obvious way when listening and interpreting, there is reason to assume that they are still activated. We know that, when reading for example, we 'subvocalise', that is, we imagine speaking what we are reading and this, in turn, triggers movements of the muscles associated with speaking without any actual speech taking place. Since this is supposed to have a delaying effect on reading speed, we can be made conscious of this and try to eliminate it in order to be able to read more swiftly. The movements of the larynx[9] can be detected even when they are not felt by the speaker. This suggests the brain and corresponding mental mechanisms responsible for speech are regularly active during utterance comprehension. This would also suggest that the motor structures associated with producing a newly acquired linguistic construction may also be first activated during the earliest

---

[9] The larynx is the organ in the neck that contains the vocal cords. Apart from their role in shaping speech sounds, the vocal cords have a nonlinguistic function, stopping food, for example, going down into the trachea, which connects up with the lungs.

successful acts of comprehension and not when the new construction is actually spoken aloud for the first time. Still, it would seem that actual utterance production, with the required coordination and muscular activity involved, is the obvious main driver of progress in articulating newly acquired structures, in other words in developing the right production skills. The role of production in growth will be returned to later when we get to the effect of learners trying to control their language use *consciously*.

Building Core Linguistic Structure from Speech Input

Returning now to growth triggered by comprehension, let us consider how the core language system responds to an unfamiliar chunk of speech. Recall that the processes involved necessarily occur below the level of consciousness. Take for example a word like 'doki', the Hausa word for horse, and the various ways in which it is used in the language. In processing terms, arriving at the appropriate meaning of the sound of even this single word (more properly, the auditory structure triggered in response to it) is not a simple matter.

One crucial problem in making sense of an unfamiliar chunk of speech is that of the *segmentation* of sounds into different units. A lot depends on how the utterance 'doki' is encountered, that is, whether or not the 'doki' part of the sound can be identified as somehow separate from the surrounding auditory context. For example the sound 'gidanmaidoki' is an uninterrupted stream of sound which might, as far as the learner is concerned, be any number of units beginning with a single one. If a learner of Hausa hears this chunk of speech for the first time they will have no way of knowing that AS [gidanmaidoki] is not one word with one simple meaning, to be derived by guesswork from the situational context.[10] A Hausa speaker, on the other hand, will immediately recognise it as the three-word phrase meaning 'the house of the man in charge of horses' – gida-n (house-of) + mai (master) + doki (horse). Analysing what this instant recognition entails helps to spell out the problem for the learner of Hausa. The sound 'gidanmaidoki' has to be to be segmented by the listener, using the core language system, into at least three distinct units before 'doki', as part of the stream of sound, can be processed as a separate unit and related to the other units to yield a complex meaning. In actual fact, the word 'gida', has an additional fourth unit, that is the 'n' attached at the end of it ('gida*n*') indicating possession ('house *of*').

For the learner of Hausa, increasing exposure to both Hausa utterances and situations which make clear the meaning will eventually make it possible to assemble a complete chain of representations including a phonological

---

[10] *Written* input, available to older learners and hence characteristic of *second* language acquisition, at least gives some advance help with segmentation because words are usually separated out using spaces. Note that this would not help with analysing 'gidan' into two units. Moreover written input can either be no help for learners or mislead them in another ways, namely with regard to pronunciation depending upon the writing system and, if the system does relates at all to the sounds of speech, the relative reliability of the spelling for guessing how words should be pronounced.

representation (PS) and a syntactic representation (SS). Then the stream of sound – 'gidanmaidoki' and its auditory structure (AS) can finally get a full linguistic interpretation (syllables, vowel and consonant structures, etc., plus nouns, verb, tense, gender, number and person, etc.) and can be paired with an appropriate meaning structure (CS) to yield the full intended message. 'Doki' by itself can then take part in the interpretation and production of different complex linguistic structures such as 'doki goma' ('ten horses') and, eventually also develop further meanings (CS) alone or in combination with other CS as in 'dokin wuya', meaning 'back of the neck' but also a form of children's game, another example being 'dokin Allah', meaning 'horse of God' but also a children's name for a praying mantis.

It should now be clear that what is involved in the learner's subconscious analysis, over time, of 'mere' words and phrases such as the preceding examples is already a far from simple matter even leaving out the more complex business of working out all the structure of more extensive chunks in the process of acquiring a complete grammatical system (for a more detailed discussion of syntactic growth see e.g. Sharwood Smith & Truscott 2014, 44–61, 107–129).

Not only do we have no sensation as structural elements are combined and recombined, activated and bring about changes in the resting levels of various structures. We also get no splitting headaches as a result of the frantic competition between rivals attempting to gain access into our working memories and play a role in forming a representational chain. All we are really aware of is trying to understand something we have heard (or read, in the case of older learners) and the *result* of all this activity: a feeling of understanding something, or a feeling of *not* understanding it. And it is just as well that we are spared all this because, as suggested already, we would very quickly be driven out of our minds in the resulting pain and confusion.

Research has showed that no matter what the language, the acquisition of phonology and syntax in the early years proceeds without any need at all for conscious intervention and manipulation; in fact, in the immature learner, that is not even a possibility since becoming a native speaker happens well before the requisite knowledge is in place to be able to even think about grammatical concepts. Anyone conversing with a four- or five-year-old will be aware of that. This is something that needs to be taken on board by those who would wish to attribute success in early childhood purely to enhanced perceptual sensitivity, higher motivation and in some way more effective memory ability.[11]

This subconscious acquisition of grammar also proceeds not in just any logically possible way but rather in specific directions that research is uncovering and becoming able to predict. Secondly, it does so without the need or indeed the availability of correction by parents or others. This is in marked contrast to what happens later in life in formal classroom environments. Parents do not correct

---

[11] The claim concerning memory would have to be qualified in view of all the tests that show working memory is more limited in very young learners (Gathercole & Alloway 2007, 7; Cowan 2010, 52).

their children's grammar because they know perfectly well it will sort itself out independently of any teacher-like intervention. Many of the alternative views propose processes to account for grammatical acquisition within the core that actually seem more fitted to explaining linguistic growth *outside* the core system, which is the topic of the next, final section in this chapter.

Language Acquisition outside the Core System

One notable thing about language is that it involves so many different parts of the brain within and especially beyond the core system. That is why, for example, that some have recommended learning a foreign language as an excellent means of increasing your cognitive reserve, especially in later life when the increased mental flexibility can delay the symptoms of dementia for between four and six years (Alladı et al. 2013; Antoniou et al. 2013; Bialystok et al. 2010). The topic of language acquisition in the later years will be discussed in the next chapter.

One notable feature of language outside the core is that we can become aware of some of its contents, within limits. This is particularly important with regard to conceptual structure. As was explained earlier, the experience of conscious awareness is something that, in the framework, is enabled elsewhere, via the perceptual system, so that means anything that happens *within* the conceptual system, the prime source of our thinking activity, still remains inaccessible. Some small part of the conceptual activity involved in mental operations may be projected outside and become a conscious, perceptual experience. This means that aspects of language that fall into this category may be open to conscious interventions of various kinds, the most obvious one being the acquisition of vocabulary, that is to say, of the meanings of words but also how they are used in particular contexts. This is precisely because of the opportunities for conscious reflection that the conceptual system permits.

Setting issues of consciousness aside, linguistic growth outside the core module proceeds in the way all mental development occurs, with the step-by-step processing of environmental input. This was briefly discussed earlier using the Hausa example 'gida'. Gradually the smaller-scale linear chains centred on the core language system that co-index respectively auditory, phonological, syntactic and conceptual structures by means of common indices widen out to become whole networks of representations. Looking at the example in Figure 14.8, imagine the network of structures that are activated together. When you have the concept of a banana in mind, for example when you see one, taste one, imagine, dream about or remember one, the structures are all coindexed with one another and therefore can all, with various degrees of intensity and depending upon personal experience, be coactivated. This figure displays only a small fragment of the actual network of coindexed structures that might be triggered including representations of the smell, sight and sound of the word banana. The letters A-I show some of the internal interfaces that match up coindexed structures in the various stores in this 'banana' network. The associations to be triggered are listed:

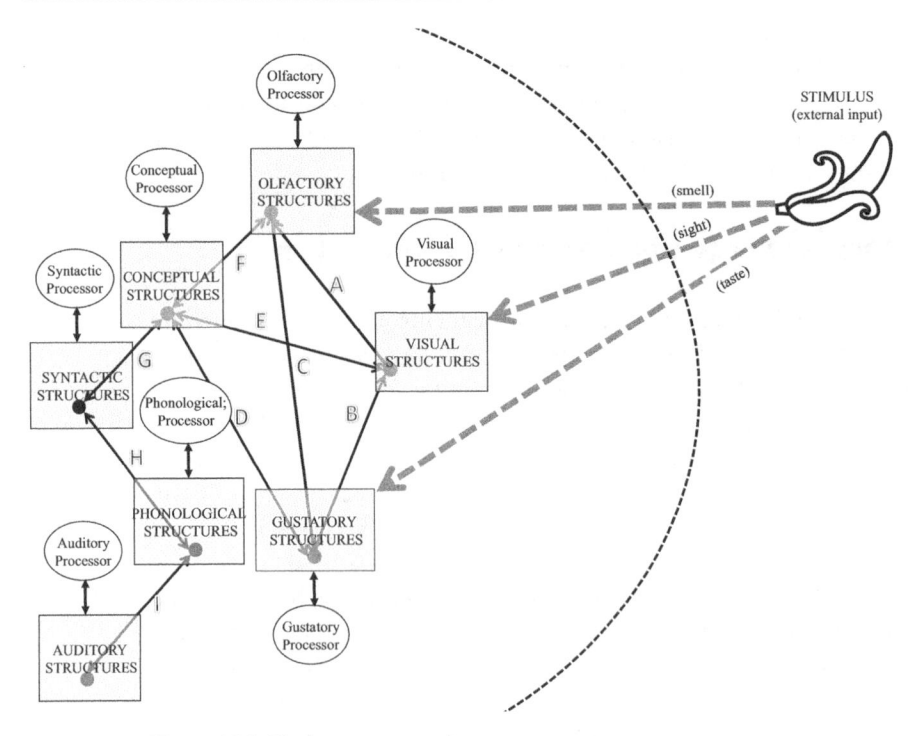

Figure 14.8 *The banana network.*

INTERFACE A: smell – vision association
INTERFACE B: sight – taste association
INTERFACE C: taste – smell association
INTERFACE D: taste – meaning association
INTERFACE: E sight – meaning association
INTERFACE F: smell – meaning association
INTERFACE G: syntax – meaning association
INTERFACE H: phonology – syntax association
INTERFACE I: phonology – sound association

G, **H** and **I** (listed in boldface) are the specifically linguistic part of the network. This means that the interface operations in this part of the total network associated with the words 'banana' are governed by domain-specific, linguistic principles giving the auditory structure [bənana] a phonological and syntactic identity.

Note that all the meanings associated with banana would certainly involve an extremely complex set of conceptual structures inside the conceptual store alone. They would include not only the basic semantic meaning of banana and its meaning in the immediate context but a whole web of elements representing all the many conceptual associations that have been formed over the lifetime, for example with particular houses, countries, places, pictures, people and also with various idioms in the language involving bananas. This web of structural associations form what is often called *episodic memory* although in the framework, that is to say as it is currently conceptualised, episodic memory has no independent status: it is manifested as a web of associations within and across different modules.

One notable absence in this figure is any association with the affect system and the particular positive or negative values the different banana associations have for the individual concerned all of which will influence the degree of activation in a given situation and any immediate or subsequent behaviour. Then again, another module that will be engaged one way or the other is the motor system and its connections with somatosensory system. This is because a banana is a physical object that can be felt and manipulated.

In the light of how language involves so much more than the core system, it is perhaps not surprising that there continue to be persistent attempts to explain language in its totality without resorting to the idea of a domain-specific human language core. Time will tell whether these attempts will find ways of eliminating the need for including a language module(s) in the map of the mind, carrying convincing enough arguments for the so-called nativists to relinquish their claims for good. The arguments for the domain-specificity of this core system, however it is conceived, remain well established in the research literature. This framework as implemented in this book happens to promote a processing view of the matter with a design that, as already mentioned, owes much to Ray Jackendoff but also builds on the work of other leading figures in the scientific study of the mind (see discussion in Jackendoff 2011).

Simple Linguistic Systems

In the normal course of events, the young child exposed to a sufficient amount of input from the languages to which it is exposed, will develop language systems that the outside world recognises immediately as 'native'. As mentioned earlier, deciding what counts as 'native' or 'fully acquired' depends on what the relevant community of speakers generally agrees on or recognises as such. Depending on the individual acquirer, at any given moment he or she will have in place a given linguistic system that meets the external norm or otherwise can be classified as deviating from the norm. In some cases, where the exposure to language input has not followed the normal course of events, the current system can be described as 'simple' or 'incomplete'.

Linguistics, of course, includes the study of such simpler systems, not only because they are interesting from a sociological or anthropological point of view but also because they have identifiable linguistic properties. For example, when people speaking different languages are forced into a group and a place, like a plantation, where they cannot communicate with one another but desperately need to do so, they develop, alongside some ability in the language of their oppressors, simple system called *pidgins*. These were referred to earlier in connection with baby signing.

As a result of the way and the circumstances in which they were originally acquired, pidgins have certain structural characteristics wherever they are developed (this being typically wherever the slave trade has operated). These include a fixed word order, a limited vocabulary and little or no inflectional morphology: in other words concepts such as number and time reference are not marked by adding forms to words or changing the forms within a word but by adding an extra word. For example, time adverbs like 'nownow', 'bin' and 'goin' can indicate present, past and future time while the verb form itself remains fixed.

Pidgins may vary in complexity but something fundamental happens when children are born into a pidgin-speaking community and the ultimate result is a *creole* language in which all the typical characteristics of a standard native language are manifested as the child, having, as yet no mother tongue and little exposure to the language of the slave-owners, develops from the only input it has a much more elaborate version of the adults' pidgin with all the extra expressive power that brings. Whereas the pidgin served as a means of basic communication between adults who already have their own native language which they are unable to use, creoles function in all the usual ways associated with any native language. The child, having no other language to function in this way and faced with a situation where it is exposed only to input that does not fulfil all its communicative requirements, creates a more complex system out of a simple one.

This is a very basic account of pidgins and the process of creating a fully fledged language from simple input. Nevertheless, in terms of the framework, it is the phonological system and most especially the syntactic system that are the engines that drive this development boosted, naturally, by the drive to develop a way of communicating all kinds of thoughts and feelings with the outside world, especially with parents and other family members. The core language system works blindly with anything, that is any auditory structure that it can process. In the case of the very young child, it has not implemented any other system beforehand. This means that there are no PS-SS chains to compete with whatever new phonological and syntactic structures are being put together in response to the auditory input. Those not espousing the view that humans are equipped with a language faculty (however it may be defined) will of course claim that this is just another case of general cognitive learning, that is, with no core language system controlling the construction of the new system. Either way it is generally understood to be the child that creates complex inflectional morphological systems to replace the simple versions typical of pidgins. For a fascinating account of this process, it is worth reading how Nicaraguan sign language developed in the 1970s and 1980s with children creating a complex system from the pidgin-like variety used by adolescents and adults (see Kegl 2004). The motivation for including pidgins in this chapter was in connection with the way creoles were developed. However, there are other types of language acquisition which are related to this discussion but which will be kept over to the next chapter on multilingual development. They include *The Basic Variety*, a special term coined by Klein and Perdue, and *heritage languages* (Klein & Purdue 1997).

Language Acquisition and Age

Something has already been said about the development of language in early childhood. The whole question of the varying ability in language acquisition over the life span has a rich literature, sparked off, most would agree, by Lenneberg's Critical Period Hypothesis (CPH) in which he argued for a cut-off point round about adolescence for the special ability children have to respond to exposure to linguistic input and become native in the language(s) to which they are regularly exposed (Lenneberg 1967). If sufficient exposure to a language has taken place within that critical period, then native ability is assured. Lenneberg attributed this to brain maturation suggesting in an aside that the difficulty in learning a foreign language experienced by older learners may also be implicated in this. That said, his CPH was not about second language ability as such and this aspect of the claim has also been the subject of much research and controversy (Bialystok 1997; Johnson & Newport 1989; Singleton 1989; Hyltenstam & Obler 1989; Hyltenstam & Abrahamsson 2000; Herschensohn 2007). The general opinion seems to favour a more gradual decline in *sensitivity* to language input with no sharp cut-off point. This does not preclude, in other words, any older learner (adolescent or adult) becoming native in a new language or becoming at least good enough to convince many who have learned the language from early childhood that the older learner is in fact the same as they are.

Viewed now from the framework perspective, it should not be surprising that resolving this question of age effects has proved difficult. The large mind-web involved in language acquisition and use engages many different systems and each of these can experience different age effects. To pick out just one factor, already referred to earlier, the ability to discriminate sounds will vary depending on auditory acuity. This acuity declines with age starting quite early and ending up with situations in later years where people will withdraw from social situations and thereby reduce the frequency of their exposure to language: this reduction in language input from outside adds to any reduction in language processing as a result only of declining acuity. A similar story can be told with regard to visual acuity and the written language.

With regard to reduced perceptual acuity, then, there might *in principle* be no decline in the ability to acquire languages per se, say within the core language system, and changes *in practice* then would be attributable only to a lack of sufficient or sufficiently clear input for all the different stages of processing to be completed efficiently. Again, age-related change in the effectiveness with which their working memories deal with all the activated items currently competing for participation in a representational network can also, by itself, bring about decline in performance without implying decline elsewhere. A chain is as strong as its weakest link so any reduction in efficiency of one link will have a negative effect on the ultimate result.

Summary

In this chapter, the following points were made. Firstly, development in all areas whether they have to do with language or not, works in the same way as was explained in Chapter 8: the general principle of acquisition by processing (APT) holds everywhere. Secondly, the first steps in acquiring language as a young child begin very early and initially bear some resemblance to what happens in other species developing their own system of communication. Baby signing gives us the most obvious source of comparison between humans and apes like Kanzi, that is, especially during the silent period before children utter their first words. It is hard to identify exactly when the kind of growth that is unique to humans is triggered but at some point there is a dramatic difference in development between the two. This issue revolves around the involvement of the core language system which is responsible for this difference. Even once the phonological system starts to process perceptual input, the syntactic stage may not function properly: for a time, early grammars may be simpler systems organised according to conceptual principles. Thirdly, the notion of language input has to be understood as a series of inputs, that is, of separate processing stages beginning with sound and light waves impacting on the senses. This is because processing and storage is modular. At any point, processing can fail to pass on to the next stage. The quality, frequency and affective value characterising structures at one stage will optimise the chances of them being accepted for processing at the next stage, but without any guarantees. Then, a further point had to do with how much, respectively, language interpretation and language production drive growth forward. The major role was attributed to successive attempts by the individual to interpret utterances. Then the role of conscious awareness in language acquisition was briefly touched upon, to be taken up again in the next chapter. The main point here is that we are aware of only a fraction of what happens in the mind: what happens in the core language system is totally impenetrable while a little of the contents of the conceptual system, may on occasions be projected into consciousness via the perceptual system. However, the formation and consolidation of whole networks of associated representations across the various working memories takes place painlessly: we have no sensation or conscious insight into the operation and are limited to discovering the basic results and reflecting on whether we have learnt something, or not. These abilities last into old age although their effectiveness is challenged by other factors such as hearing acuity, working memory efficiency and competition from previously acquired languages.

15 Becoming Multilingual

> **In This Chapter**

'Multilingualism', including ability in just two languages, is a concept that needs some clarification. In this book, being multilingual is understood in a sense more generous than the one often used in day-to-day conversation. This means that anyone with some degree of ability in just two languages is already a (developing) multilingual. The precise point at which you start being multilingual is not so important; it can be defined in various ways according to preference. Either way, on being exposed frequently to more than one language enough to begin understanding some small part of what is being said, you become multilingual in this sense very quickly: it is just a matter of how useful and effective your linguistic ability is, that is, given the knowledge, fragmentary or otherwise, that you currently possess. This means that having established a case of multilingualism, it is then possible to go and define it in various ways from 'rudimentary' right up to the point at which someone can be described as highly functional in more than one language and in all kinds of different situations. This means there are all kinds of multilingualism and the categories differ according to where you look for them (Sharwood Smith & Truscott 2014, 182ff.).

As was suggested in the last chapter, certain kinds of multilingualism, defined in a way that extends even beyond the one just described, is a normal state for people to be in. Even monolinguals control different language systems within their one language as they adjust their grammar and vocabulary, their speech and writing style, even their accent, to fit different circumstances of use. In many parts of the world it is taken for granted that people should be multilingual and they find it strange to have only one language. People brought up in a monolingual community can develop a strange conviction about language, believing that communicating in another language is somehow only for the talented and, where children are concerned, it will always be confusing, educationally disruptive and may easily deprive them permanently of the treasure that is a 'mother' tongue. The chapter on affect will have shed light on how we come to value positively or negatively all kinds of things to do with language, sometimes in ways which do not really make sense if examined carefully in the clear light of day.

This chapter will discuss the growth and use of language when more than one language system is involved, whether this growth takes place in sequence, or simultaneously within the mental systems described in Part I. Beginning with how we distinguish between different languages in our heads, we will go on to look at often entirely subconscious processes of language acquisition characteristic of early childhood before tackling the subject of explicit grammars and their influence on the rate and manner of growth in adults who start learning a second language long after the first language(s) are in place. Finally a word will be said about how languages are acquired at much later stages when signs of ageing are becoming more apparent.

Accommodating Different Language Systems

Becoming bilingual and multilingual is essentially the same as mastering different linguistic systems that are generally regarded as belonging to the *same* language. For example, any language has different **registers** depending upon the circumstances of use, for example, a *casual* register and a *formal* register. Each involves particular selection of vocabulary, accent,[1] and grammatical constructions. Language varieties may also be associated with particular social groups or geographical regions. That is, the same language may also have different **dialects**. This includes the one generally regarded as the standard and typically not referred to as a dialect although, technically speaking, it is 'just another dialect'. Examples of such standard dialects are Standard Spanish (based on Castilian Spanish), Standard American English (not be confused with General American which is a standard *accent*) and Standard British English (not to be confused with Received Pronunciation which is a standard British accent spoken across the UK) and standard Chinese (also known as Mandarin, based on the Beijing dialect and which is the sole official language on the mainland and in Taiwan). In actual fact, there is no clear-cut, purely linguistic way of distinguishing dialects from languages: the choice as to which is which depends on external, social evaluation, Cantonese and Mandarin being classic examples of this. They are either separate languages sharing the same writing system or they are versions of Chinese. It is often difficult to draw the line between the two. There is an old joke which makes the essential point which goes 'a language is a dialect with an army and navy'.[2] In other words the version of the language that is *not* called a dialect but is treated as the standard is the one that happens to be spoken by the most powerful social group. Scots, a Germanic language with its own literature, closely related to English and the official language of the Scottish

---

[1] Accent should not be confused with dialect. Accent is only to do with pronunciation. To emphasise the distinction, even though particular dialects are normally associated with particular accents, it is still in principle possible to speak a dialect with an accent not normally associated with it. This can be done with comic effect.
[2] The joke was passed on by the sociolinguist Uriel Weinreich during a lecture.

court, lost its status as a standard language when the King of Scotland moved his court down to England after the union between the two kingdoms: it was not long before Scots was generally treated as a dialect and eventually only remained in regular use in a fragmentary sense, in separate dialects and with different degrees of closeness to the modern standard.[3] In any case, the main point here is that a language is not something that has a single, uniform set of categorical rules. It varies systematically depending on the context. This therefore makes almost all of us 'multilingual' in some sense, something that language acquisition researchers are beginning to acknowledge (see e.g. Cook 1992; Amaral & Roeper 2014, and related discussion in the same journal issue). Also, in some geographical regions, different dialects of one language are in common use and people switch easily between the two depending on who they are talking to. They are therefore bi- or multidialectal. In sum, it is the norm everywhere to control different linguistic systems even where they are officially all classed as belonging to one language and the speaker is classed as a monolingual. Acquiring more than one system is therefore an extremely normal thing to do, something that, in one way or another, everyone does.

Escaping the Tower

There is an important question that arises even where monolinguals are concerned, which is about how language systems are actually differentiated in the mind (and brain) in a framework especially if the core system by itself makes no distinctions between them and handles all of them the same way. Put another way how are linguistic systems, dialects, accents, languages, differentiated if they are not somehow identified by the mind in some way? This question of how to escape the confusion of the legendary Tower of Babel, where all languages are mixed up, was indeed posed in the last chapter. However, it has not yet been answered.

Leaving aside for the time being situations where languages *are*, either deliberately or unreflectingly, mixed up in speech, the easy and most obvious solution that comes to mind for keeping systems apart during spoken exchanges would be the *language tag* option (see e.g. Green 1998). This would have to involve giving any phonological or syntactic structure that is used when performing in a given language a special 'tag' to identify it as Hausa, Polish or Mandarin, etc. It would function like an index but be a separate system of 'language IDs'[4] specially

---

[3] It has seen a revival in recent years and is recognised now as a minority language, at least officially. Those supporting a revival of Scots claim that this once widely used language, and not Gaelic, the language of the North West of Scotland with about 57,000 speakers with some knowledge of it, should be the second language of Scotland. However, Gaelic is still a living language, whereas something that could be called standard Scots, some might argue, would be a reconstituted language built up from different dialects with no native speakers.

[4] This idea, which is not the preferred option, could be extended to mark structures according to style of register with tags like 'archaic', 'poetic', 'formal', 'informal' and even 'taboo'.

designed to identify any structure that belongs to a given language system. When processing, say Hausa or Polish, only structures tagged appropriately for Hausa or ones tagged for Polish will be selected. For example, variants of the sound 'od' ([od]) may be attached to the phonological structure /od/ but what happens next? Take a Polish-English bilingual, for example. The closest word in English that sounds like this is 'odd', which is an adjective as in 'an odd situation'. In this case, therefore, the most appropriate PS */od/* for this English word would be associated with the SS (syntactic structure) *Adj*, yielding the chain: */od/*⇔*Adj*⇔CS (meaning of 'odd'). In Polish, however, variants of a very similar sound 'od', which is *never* an adjective, could be associated in certain contexts with the preposition 'od' (meaning, roughly, 'from') as in 'od nas' ('from us'). How can we ensure that the right connections within the core language system are made to ensure consistent use of one language rather than the other so that the two languages can be kept apart and chains be produced in speech that are consistently either English or Polish? How can the 'od' sound consistently be associated with *Adj* and *CS* representing the meaning of 'odd' when the bilingual speaker is listening to or producing English rather than Polish?

Since, in the core language system, there is nothing especially English or Polish about syntactic structures like *Adj(ective)* or *Prep(osition)*, the 'identity tag' solution would mean having have a special type of index that functions as an identification code not specific to any one system. The job of this tagging system would just to be to promote the matching of structures (PS and SS) which belong to the same language system so that they bind together consistently across the working memories. In the case of the preceding example, the different interfaces can simply match up all the Polish-related structures and all the English-related structures and 'Babel speak' is thereby avoided. This idea, which can be applied to different varieties of a single language, including accents, could certainly be accommodated in the current framework. The question is, is this extra type of tag really necessary? Does the core language system have to 'know' what language system it is currently processing? The answer is no. The core language system need have no idea what it is processing; confusion can still be avoided.

Language system differentiation is accomplished entirely outside the core language system. In Sharwood Smith and Truscott (2014, 188–191) this was referred to as *conceptual triggering*. This means that association of a chain with the CS that represents the meanings 'English' or 'Polish', for example, will boost activation levels in such a way as to promote all the associated structures that will bring about the consistent use of one language (dialect, variety, register, etc.).

In Figure 15.1, where these options are displayed using the English word 'tiny' (very small), the second, preferred solution to the Babel problem is referred to simply as the 'conceptual' option showing that the introduction of a tagging system is not in fact necessary. Distinguishing Language A from Language B, Dialect A from Dialect B or Variety A from Variety B can be accomplished in another way. This is a natural consequence of spreading activation with initially small structural chains across working memories expanding further to form ever

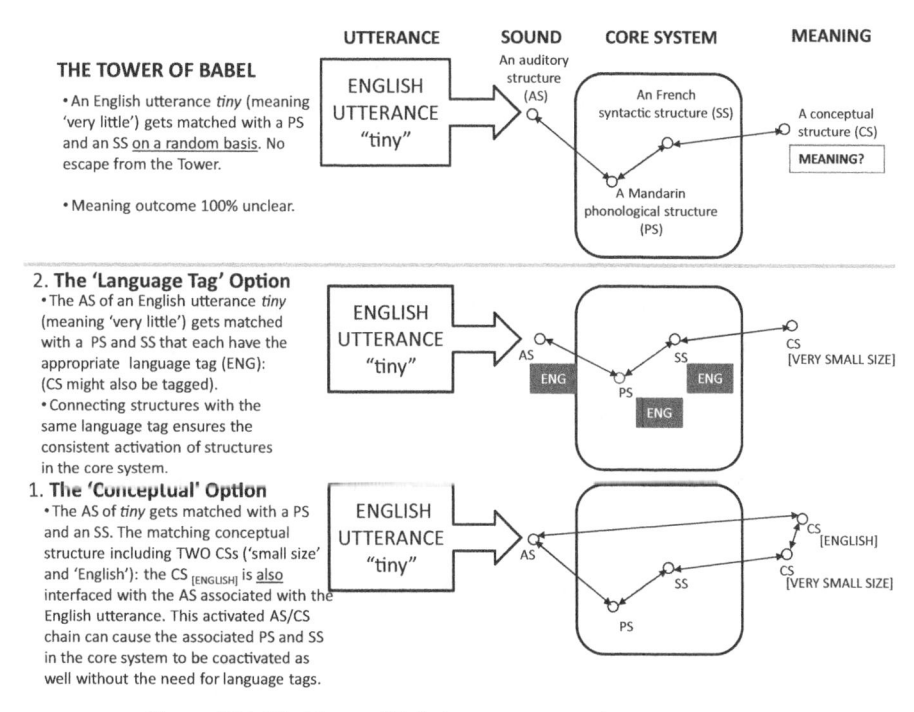

Figure 15.1 The Tower of Babel: two escape options.

wider networks of structure. A rich array of specific associations trigger each other which help to boost the activation of linguistic structures that happen to be associated with one language system rather than another via spreading activation. All this is possible even within a modular mental system. The sound of the English word 'tiny' will get matched with an auditory structure and that auditory structure will, given the right amount of exposure to the sound, will ultimately the trigger appropriate structures within the core system (PS and SS) plus the meaning of tiny in the conceptual system. If that auditory structure is *also* associated directly with the meaning 'English' identifying the sound as English, this should ensure that just that English-related PS/SS chain will be coactivated and not any other one that happens to be associated with the same concept (tiny).

The same story can be told about written language, i.e. the visual structures that represent the script: associations can arise from, for example, words in a written text that are or look like French and even sights and smells that are associated with French-speaking people such as billboards, road signs and the like.[5] This appears to offer a plausible account of how just one of the multilingual's languages can be selectively activated strongly enough to explain generally consistent patterns of comprehension and production.

---

[5] This relates to the notion of *linguistic landscape* (Landry & Bourhis 1997, 25). In the case of AS, we could by extension refer to a linguistic 'soundscape' (Sharwood Smith & Truscott 2014, 190).

Parents who bring up their children in two languages implicitly subscribe to this account when they decide that one parent will consistently use one language and the other parent the other so as not to confuse the child. In actual fact, although this may have some beneficial effect initially, children's minds are certainly adaptable enough for acquiring both languages when parents do not stick to this plan: conceptual triggering does not have to rely on just the parent's usage habits. Children just need enough exposure to each of the two languages for the right associations to be formed one way or the other. There will be other cues that will support the activation of consistent AS⇔PS⇔SS chains including topics of conversation, other monolingual children, grandparents and the like. We know that bilinguals are good at separating grammatical systems early on even while vocabulary remains blended, often very creatively sometimes obscuring from anxious parents that the basics of each language system have already been acquired (Meisel 2004, 98–100).

APT Applied to More Than One Language

In accordance with Acquisition by Processing Theory (Chapter 9) associations are gradually built up each time that utterances in the language in question are being interpreted by the listener. Recall that processing in this modular framework means that frequency of input means frequency of input *into a given module* and *not* frequency of the original environmental stimulus. The fact that the sound of a word vibrates in the ear or provokes a response in the eye does not mean that any internal system is automatically affected. Keeping that cautionary statement in mind, one can say that the resting levels of the structures involved in the interpretation process will climb with repeated stimulation.

A stretch of input that is unfamiliar may require novel combinations of structures: new chains will then grow across the various processing units both within and outside the core language system. Well-established structures and structural combinations, ones that have been in use for some time, will initially compete successfully with newcomers in the working memory areas involved. In the on-line formation of particular chains, any newcomers will typically be disadvantaged because of their low resting levels. They will often lose the competition so their nonappearance in observable performance will conceal the fact of their existence. Even if there are no competing structures that come close to matching the input, weakly established structures will still not appear because they have to be activated strongly enough to make it into working memory. If you have only just established a meaning for the word 'armadillo', in order for the sound or sight of this word to trigger a chain containing the appropriate conceptual structure the following day, its resting levels need to be at a sufficiently high level to make it accessible to working memory. The same goes for a newly acquired combination of any kind.

One might ask how, with all this opposition, can something newly acquired and having only a low resting level will ever make it into working memory at all. Several factors are in its favour however. Firstly, if we consider the acquisition of a new word, repeated acts of comprehension when confronted with the sound or sight of this new word will gradually raise the resting levels of the auditory and visual structures and this will have a knock-on effect on any core language chain (PS/SS) that has been associated with it. Secondly, the initial encounter establishing that chain will give the resting level a kick start although delayed and infrequent repetition will ensure this initial high level sinks to lower levels. This boost will reoccur on subsequent occasions, an effect that will diminish the longer the gap is between such occasions. Thirdly, during utterance comprehension, the conceptual triggering boosting all other structures associated with the language in question will also impact on the current resting level of the recently acquired word (see Figure 15.1). All of this assumes of course that the initial stages of constructing a new combination of structures has not undergone some exceptional boost as a result of, say, an intense *affective* association as happens with so-called flashbulb memories (see Chapter 8). In this case a much longer period of nonuse will be needed to reduce its accessibility. As argued earlier, affective factors will always influence the accessibility of a structure to a greater or lesser degree depending upon circumstances.

Applied in reverse, as *attrition* by processing (or rather by a lack of processing), APT says that infrequency of use will cause resting levels to decline: this will accordingly *reduce* the chances of successful competition for the structures concerned. The question now is how does this play out when more than one language system is involved?

Competition Revisited

Especially in the light of the preferred 'conceptual' option (see Figure 15.1), candidates in the *same* language system and those associated with *different* language systems will compete together and in the same way. For example, take a French-German bilingual thinking about or formulating an utterance about size and wanting to say that something is very small. In the process of doing this, the conceptual structure that encodes the meaning 'small size' will be activated. This CS will trigger the coactivation of all kinds of PS-SS pairs that are associated with small size. Rival chains will compete for a brief moment measured in milliseconds. For example, competing with the structural chain of structures belonging to the word 'small' will be other words with similar meaning in French like 'miniscule' and 'infime'. Also jostling for position will be chains associated with German related words like 'klein' and 'winzig' even though our bilingual will be thinking in French or planning to say something in French to French speakers in a totally French environment.

The psycholinguistic evidence comes out strongly in favour of the idea that all language systems are activated to a greater or lesser extent all the time, whatever the ultimate outcome is (Kroll et al. 2014). Even if there is no obvious effect of this crosslinguistic coactivation, subtle tests using response times, event-related potentials tracking brain activity as well as brain-imaging techniques such as fMRI all show the effects of general crosslinguistic coactivation. The brain seems to be bringing all its resources to bear all the time even where the language user might think they are not needed. All this boils down to the simple fact that along with each extra language system comes yet more of the simultaneous competition that already characterises monolingual processing. That bilinguals and multilinguals whose proficiency in each language is sufficiently developed are able to speak fluently and consistently in any one of their languages simply means that in such situations the competition is resolved in time and does not show itself in their outwardly observable behaviour.

Crosslinguistic Effects

Although multilinguals may be perfectly able to keep their languages apart in their observable performance, the very fact that they have at their disposal different language systems means, as was sketched out earlier, a source and intensity of competition during processing not shared by monolinguals. The internal chain reactions are simply greater. Also, when multilinguals interact, since they are usually perfectly aware of the language abilities of their interlocutors, there may be more mixing of languages during performance. Conceptually driven language switching may arise spontaneously, without any intention on the speaker's part. Alternatively, it may be the result of a deliberate conscious choice to switch. The conscious choice to switch will also be conceptually triggered and launch the same chain reaction, the only essential difference being that the CSs have been activated to a high enough degree to be projected into consciousness (as always via the perceptual group of systems).

As the general situational context is interpreted by the conceptual system, who the interlocutors are, what language(s) they are known to understand, what language is most frequently associated with the topic of conversation envisaged by the speaker, or its formality, or the extent to which the speaker wishes to convey solidarity with his or her interlocutors, and so forth, the activation levels of structures associated with the relevant languages are accordingly raised or else they decline: this facilitates or inhibits their use.

Language Modes

Temporary difficulty in recalling a word or expression with a particular meaning will also trigger the use of a more available equivalent in a language known by both or all participants in the exchange: this will mean a boost in the activation of items that are already coactivated to some degree anyway. This conceptually driven process can vary from moment to moment as the language user both subconsciously and consciously interprets the general context. At one point more than one language may be quite highly activated. Strictly speaking languages don't themselves get activated: what this actually means in terms of the framework is rather different networks of coactivated structure across the various systems each of which includes the CS that is associated with a given language. The selfsame identifying concept will of course match up with and identify other thing that are not linguistic as in French fashion, Russian dolls, Egyptian pyramids and Chinese philosophy. Where two language-related networks are coactivated to similar levels, switching between the two will be relatively easy. At another point, one language network will be dominant and the other(s) markedly less activated. This idea is captured by Francois Grosjean's notion of *language mode* (see Grosjean 2001). When, in the case of a bilingual, the current activation levels of two languages are close, that language user is said to be in a 'bilingual mode' as opposed to when they are not at all close and one language is currently dominant in which case the bilingual is said to be in 'monolingual mode'. Essentially the same distinctions hold for multilinguals with more than two languages. Note that being in the monolingual mode does not imply no competing activation at all but implies that the activation levels of one language are well ahead of those of the others. In such (monolingual mode) situations, switching from one language to another or mixing languages in some other way is going to be less likely and more costly in terms of processing time. Also, as already indicated, language modes do not have to depend on any conscious decision by the bi/multilingual to switch between one language system and another. And finally, language dominance is a relative matter, involving a *continuum* and not limited to a straightforward switch between complete dominance and zero dominance.[6]

Crosslinguistic Influence in Less Advanced Multilinguals/ Language Learners

Crosslinguistic influence is the term often used to cover different ways in which different languages affect learning and behaviour in the individual (Sharwood Smith 1983). Especially where suspected crosslinguistic influence is observable in an individual's speech and writing and in speech as a foreign accent, it has traditionally been called interference. Language 'transfer' is also a common term in the research literature. However, crosslinguistic influence covers more than transfer with its implied metaphor of carrying over something from one language to another: it also includes a whole different set of effects

---

[6] There is an interesting literature examining the processing cost of switching between dominant and non-dominant languages, in production and also in comprehension which will be dealt with in a following section.

ascribable to the influence of a competing language including the influence, in language attrition, of a second language on the native language and the deliberate avoidance of transfer by speakers, which can happen for various reasons, for example if a sound in the second language is difficult to pronounce, the speaker might choose a synonym or when a word or construction familiar from the native language is avoided in the second language because the speaker judges it to be unlikely that the two languages could possibly be so similar (Schachter 1974; Kleinmann 1977; Kellerman 1979). Apart from avoidance there are many less easily observed crosslinguistic effects that require clever psycholinguistic and neurolinguistic techniques to track down.

Grammatical Crosslinguistic Influence: The Case of Gender

Certainly, from the point of view of the framework, it should not be surprising as an individual is exposed to a new language that crosslinguistic influence is noticeable from the very start. Take, for example, grammatical gender, a notoriously difficult area of grammar for some second language[7] learners. *Grammatical* gender, for example masculine and feminine gender, should be sharply distinguished from *biological* gender. In principle, the grammatical gender of anything can be, say, feminine, i.e. not just women, girls and female animals, but chairs, electric razors and boarding passes and also abstract ideas like 'beauty' and 'gratitude'. English is a language that only has the vestiges of a grammatical gender system which for the most part has disappeared. It does mark gender in some personal pronouns, as in the distinction between 'he', 'she' and 'it', but parts of speech like nouns and adjectives are generally 'genderless'.

This absence of grammatical gender creates an obstacle for monolingual English speakers when learning a new language that *does* have a fully fledged gender system. This is because they have to regularly activate syntactic structures associated with gender that were simply not needed for the acquisition of their mother tongue. Suddenly, when producing or encountering a word in the new language, for chair, say, they must develop the ability to co-activate the gender structure associated with that particular noun. In the same way speakers of most Slavic languages, which do mark gender, also have to learn to co-activate a previously completely dormant syntactic structure every time they encounter the word 'chair' in English. This is nothing to do with gender but has to do with whether 'the', 'a' or nothing should precede it, a choice which simply does not occur in their own language since Slavic languages mostly have no articles (i.e. 'determiner' system). In such situations, crosslinguistic influence manifests itself in relatively long delays before the unfamiliar system is acquired along with errors that reflect misapplications of this system in the form of errors.

---

[7] Dealing with just two languages helps keep the examples simple but the principle remains the same with individuals with more languages, except of course that more structures are co-activated.

Crosslinguistic influence across languages that happen to *share* a system like grammatical gender but apply it in *different* ways naturally produces different results. Imagine now a situation in which a chair is in view and is being talked about. In the act of interpreting an utterance in a still fairly unfamiliar second language, you, the listener, may work out that a particular perceived fragment of speech probably refers to this chair. Maybe the speaker is looking at it or even pointing at it. This will immediately lead to the activation in your mind of the conceptual structure which represents the meaning of 'chair'. It will also trigger the rapid coactivation of all the various structures (in various memory stores) that are associated with that familiar concept. This will include phonological and syntactic structures and related conceptual structures in both the language of the speaker and your own, first language: say for the sake of argument that this is French.

Assume now that the language being spoken is German which obligatorily mark all nouns along with other parts of speech as well (like articles and adjectives) for gender. This is an advantage for you, the French speaker, but the ways in which gender is marked is not always the same and there is also an extra gender, neuter, to contend with.

'Chaise', the French word for 'chair', happens to be *feminine* as in '*une* grand*e* chaise' (a big chair): here, the italicised forms mark the gender as feminine: the feminine indefinite article 'une' and the feminine ending on the adjective 'grand' are selected because they have to 'agree' with gender of the noun. The syntactic structures that will therefore get most strongly coactivated together with the meaning of 'chair', will accordingly be *Noun* but also *feminine*. However, in German, the same conceptual structure is most likely to be associated with 'Stuhl', the German equivalent for 'chaise'. Even if you, the French-speaking learner, being sensitive to grammatical gender may well have previously identified some of the cues that signal *Masculine* gender in German, the resting level of the appropriate *masculine* gender feature will face strong competition from the well-established and now coactivated feminine structure belonging to the rival French network.

In this way, French acquirers of German will not face the same delays in acquiring German gender as English acquirers because the grammatical gender structures are for the most part already strongly established as a result of first language acquisition. However, misapplications of gender will occur: they will still need to develop the right forms to express gender and the right associations where the two languages actually differ as in the preceding 'chaise'/'Stuhl' example.

A sketch of the competition between these competing gender systems is shown in Figure 15.2, where a notional maximum resting level of activation is set at 100 and the very low one at 10. In the example displayed in the figure, the likelihood that the correct gender will be chosen in the performance of the developing French-German bilingual is very small but the expectation is that the successful acquisition of the German gender is very likely for this learner, given optimal

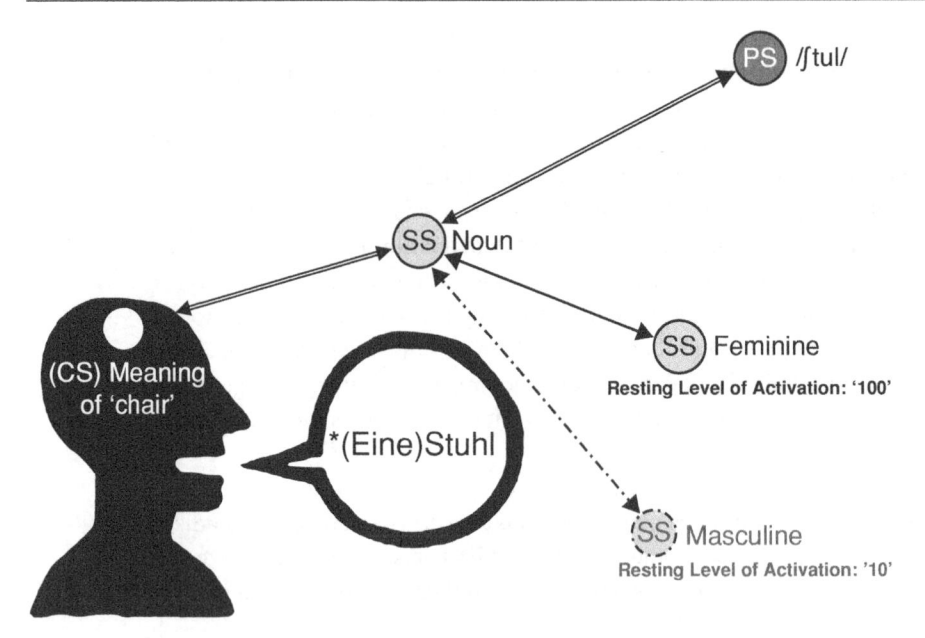

Figure 15.2 *Competition between alternative syntactic structures with hypothetical resting levels of activation.*

conditions (sufficient exposure, motivation, etc.) since the French native speaker at least has a fully developed grammatical gender system in place, albeit marked in different ways.

English learners of German who are less lucky since they have to develop a grammatical gender system in the first place to apply it in a nativelike fashion, they may fall back on conscious learning of some kind and learn each noun and its gender on a case by case basis. How well this might help stimulate the dormant, previously unused gender system is an open question. Difficulties associated with the acquisition of gender have stimulated a great deal of research, for example Grüter et al. (2012) and Hopp (2010), to quote just two examples.

Code-Switching and Code-Mixing

Previous sections have given instances of how structural combinations in one language can influence those in another in the developing multilingual. Fluent multilinguals who may be considered to have stopped developing to any significant extent, excluding vocabulary growth that is, very commonly exploit their multilingual resources, giving them arguably greater powers of expression and flexibility than their monolingual counterparts. The mechanisms keeping languages apart in production must be overridden in such circumstances. That is to say, although the core language system is neutral in this regard, there must be differences in the interface traffic across conceptual, affective and other systems that dictate language selection.

Milroy and Muysken call code-switching 'the alternative use by bilinguals of two or more languages in the same conversation' (Milroy & Muysken 1995, 7). This also covers the related term, 'code-mixing', a more important distinction for researchers being whether switches occur within the sentence or at sentence boundaries. Classic uses include switching from one language to another to signal a change in formality, to signal solidarity with the fellow bilingual or when dealing with a topic most closely associated to another of the speaker's languages not currently being used. The occasional use of a single word or expression from another language is often referred to as 'borrowing'.

In all cases, it would seem that the conceptual triggering option can help explain these phenomena. Changes in affective valence along with given shifts in conceptual and perceptual activity can shift the balance by bringing about increased activation of structures associated with the language not currently in use – 'Language B' – so that they can suddenly outcompete their rivals from the currently active 'Language A'. The precise way in which this is done is the object of study in this corner of bilingualism research (see e.g. Poplack 1980; Myers-Scotton 1993; MacSwan 1999; Truscott & Sharwood Smith 2016; as well as contributions to Milroy & Muysken 1995).

Research has also been done to study the cost, in processing terms, of switching between languages, in production and also in comprehension. There is some evidence to suggest that, in less proficient bilinguals at least, it is harder to switch back from their *dominant* language to their *less dominant* language than the other way around (Calabria et al. 2012). This would seem to be easily accounted for in terms of relative resting levels. A more dominant language network that by definition will have very high resting levels will sink back to those (high) resting levels that will then still pose a competitive ' threat' to the structures in a less dominant network that, when activated, have a long way to go to make it up to a winning position in their respective working memories.[8]

Note, in passing, that multilinguals' exploitation of their rich linguistic resources either intentionally or spontaneously has been presented here in a positive light even though negative views abound in society reflecting an attitude to 'inconsistent' use of one language as necessarily indicating laziness or just plain ignorance. There is no justification for this blanket judgement but, of course, the negative attitudes are interesting socio-psychological phenomena worthy of study in their own right.

---

[8] Researchers often appeal to the notion of inhibition to explain these phenomena (e.g. Green 1998). The dominant language can sometimes be harder to inhibit when switching to the less dominant one and this will manifest itself in slower response times although these may only be detectable when using psycholinguistic measuring instruments.

Knowing but Not Showing

Both learners and teachers normally qualify nonnative performance, especially when it is regular, as indicating a 'lack' of knowledge and as an example of 'incorrect' use of the language in question. We will return to this example when discussing explicit knowledge further on. However, one other thing to keep in mind here is that just because some anomalous feature showing a 'feminine' use of 'Stuhl' appears in some individual's regular observable performance does not always mean that a different and perhaps perfectly nativelike version of that particular syntactic feature is not simultaneously present in the individual's mind: it may just have not yet achieved a sufficient resting level of activation to break through and show itself in that individual's performance on a regular basis. In other words, absence need not signify ignorance. Someone can, as it were, 'know' two competing versions of a construction at the same time and still only provide observable evidence of one of them.

The amount of crosslinguistic influence especially in the earlier stages of becoming multilingual will differ for a number of reasons but one thing that researchers have noticed is that young children are able to start separating out the grammatical system very early on (Meisel 1989). The process seems to last a much longer time with older learners. This may be because very young learners have finely tuned perceptual skills, pay greater attention and are generally uninhibited about language having no fear of making mistakes. This is an area where controversy still rages, some of it having to do with the question of how much older learners have retained of Steven Pinker's 'language instinct' (Pinker 1994), but, within the current framework, part of the explanation will certainly involve talking about resting levels of activation and what boosts or inhibits them.

Finally, it is important to keep in mind that nonnative performance whether it is sporadic or regular is certainly not always caused by crosslinguistic influence. Research carried out since the early 1970s has made abundantly clear the fact that the transitional or permanent structural properties of nonnative language systems are also based on other factors (Selinker 1972; Krashen 1981). Space precludes anything like a full account of this.

Heritage Languages

'Heritage' languages provide an interesting case of crosslinguistic influence in early childhood. These are languages spoken by immigrants and their children. Children may grow up acquiring the language of the wider community plus the language spoken at home, i.e. the heritage language, at the same time. Alternatively, they may learn the language of home in advance of the language spoken in the wider community. This second language naturally becomes important once friends from that community are acquired, and of course, assuming that the heritage language is not used there, when children start school. In the end, children typically become more proficient at their second language than the home language they began with. Depending upon their particular circumstances, immigrants may vary widely in their use of the heritage language and of the language of the wider community (Montrul 2013).

Although the outside world makes these distinctions between different kinds of language acquisition situations, the mind's response remains the same. The same set of mental systems is engaged and the same principles are followed. The mind's core language system, for example has no way of distinguishing heritage languages from first, second or third languages or any other category of language. It simply works away with what it gets. If the immigrant's language has already been affected by, for example, exposure to the language of the host country and is therefore no longer identical to that same language spoken back in the country of origin, the effects will be felt in the way their children acquire this language. The language of the children will also show characteristics of the second language reflected in the language spoken by their parents and fellow immigrants to which they are exposed and which provides the 'input' for the first language acquisition. This also includes the lexical and stylistic repertoire of the parent's language which may well have shrunk or changed compared with what is spoken in the country of origin because of a reduction in the purposes for which the language is regularly used and the influence of convenient words and expressions from the host language to talk about life in the new country. Since they will probably be the principal source of evidence for their children, this means that the children will learn a different version of the language than they otherwise would have done if they were still in the country of origin (Montrul 2013, 176, 181, 184–185).

Given what was said about the role of affect, within the current framework, as the child grows up in the host community there may well be shifts in the value attached to the use of the two languages. All that needs to happen is for a relatively negative valence to get associated with the physical and conceptual attributes of the home language. This might include a negative evaluation of how the language *sounds* (encoded as a strong negative affective structure – AfS – attached to the related auditory structures – AS); it might also be related to *knowledge of speakers of the language* and to any *bad situations associated with using the language* (all involving AfS and CS and doubtless many others). It might involve the perceived *status* of the language in the peer group or in the community at large (encoded as CS). In this way, then, processing any concept like 'chair' along with the CS belonging to the language concerned (Spanish, Quechua, Hindi, Bulgarian, etc.) will also bring about coactivation of these other CS together with negative affective structures (AfS). The net result will be various forms of avoidance. If avoiding contact with all speakers is impossible, especially if it is the language of home, avoiding actually speaking the language where possible may be an option.

A similar result will occur if the home language is not negatively valued as such but where the culture and hence language of the host country is much more highly valued. If parents do not persist in speaking their language to their children because they never answer back anymore in that same language, the children's exposure to it will decline, resting activation levels of the relevant structures and their connections will decline and attrition thus set in as a result. Parents faced with the reluctance of children to cooperate actively with them in the heritage language might fear their persistence might make things worse and feel that the best thing is to give up speaking it to their children. Every family situation is different but one way or the other, together with frequency of exposure, the type of valence associated with the heritage language should have a big role to play in determining how, and how much this language will be acquired, used and maintained. The language of the host community can be highly valued relative to the heritage language but the reverse can also happen although it is much less likely since it requires some emotional and linguistic obstacle thing to withstand the powerful influence of the community at large, especially the heritage speaker's peer group in that community.

A superficially comparable example is provided by Schumann's Mexican subject Alberto, who, while he lived and worked in Los Angeles, kept himself immersed, whenever he could, in his native Spanish and never considered the United States as his permanent home (Schumann 1976). As a consequence of this his progress in English at an early stage of development. Because of the age of his arrival in the United States and his social circumstances, Alberto cannot be considered a heritage language speaker and the outcome is the reverse of the one that characterises this type of bilingual. Nevertheless the selfsame mechanisms are at work to produce cases such as his.

The Growth of Metalinguistic Knowledge in Multilinguals

Metalinguistic abilities, that is the ability to reflect consciously on language forms, is one characteristic that is often understood to be pronounced in multilinguals, even very young ones (see Bialystok 2001, 134–145). Young monolingual children become consciously engaged with language, playing with words in puns and rhymes even before the education system draws their attention to such strange things as 'accent', 'syllables', 'nouns', 'sentences' and grammatical rules. Bilingual and multilingual children clearly have an enhanced version of this conscious engagement with language and, as has been discussed earlier, this is centred on the conceptual system taking the form of conceptually encoded knowledge outside the core language system.

Although phonological and syntactic structure remain firmly hidden from conscious awareness, anything beyond the core is potentially open to some degree of inspection, the most obvious example being lexical, i.e. words and expressions. If one parent uses one word for 'window', say 'okno' (Polish) and the other parent uses a different word, say, 'venster' (Dutch), this is bound to catch children's attention: children prefer in any situation, monolingual or otherwise, to have one word for one concept. Note that while considering 'okno' as an example of a word in a particular language, the AS/PS/SS/CS chain is also activated. The core system is always ready to its job. The only thing is the object of our conscious awareness is not this chain but the sound, appearance (in writing or signing) and, above all, the *concept* of a word.

The desire for nothing to be ambiguous, to have one word with one concept, is strong enough to cause even monolingual children to invent words and expressions to preserve this one-to-one or 'uniqueness' principle even where they have no evidence for it. Annette Karmiloff-Smith (1978, 12; 1989), for example, notes that French children typically separate out the two related meanings of 'meme' (same-identical versus same-similar) by inventing a distinction that does not exist in French and therefore is something they have never heard anyone use. For the *identical* chair meaning, the word is 'la meme chaise', as in adult French, but for a *similar* chair, the child says 'la meme *de* chaise' (literally 'the same *of* chair'). They work the same ingenious trick on the singular article 'un(e)' which can either be a singular indefinite article ('a') or a number ('one') thereby inventing 'un(e) *de*' as in 'une *de* chaise' (one chair) which again is nonexistent in the French they are exposed to.

Since children in a multilingual context will be constantly faced with even more challenges to the uniqueness principle, it is not surprising that soon or later they become sensitised to the existence of two quite different codes such that they become consciously aware of it, talk and speculate about it. Even though the uniqueness principle can work subconsciously in children's minds, some of this sensitising process is certainly accompanied by metalinguistic awareness which is particularly strong in multilingual children. One five-year-old child, brought up thus far exposed to Polish, English and Dutch at home and playing happily by herself, suddenly exclaimed in surprise 'Daddy, *dlatego* is *why* and *why* is *waarom*!', a nice example of a spontaneous trilingual metalinguistic insight equating the meaning ('why') of three words, each in a different language and indicating that even without any prompting, metalinguistic knowledge is accumulated in the early years when multilinguals are involved.

One might speculate, since metalinguistic knowledge is based on conceptual structure in the framework, that the conceptual system might be the source of the ability to keep languages separate and to code-switch when required. Also, since conceptual triggering (Figure 15.1) may well be involved in all kinds of nonlinguistic switching behaviour as well, this might be one way of explaining the increased executive control[9] that is attributed to multilinguals, even in old age, the topic of the next section (Bialystok et al. 2010).

---

[9] *Executive control*, *cognitive control* and *executive function(s)* are all much used but somewhat slippery cover terms in psychology. They generally refer to what in the framework corresponds to processes that operate across the working memories and where conceptual processes plays a major role.

Conscious and Subconscious Control

'Executive control', 'cognitive control' and 'executive function(s)' are all much used but somewhat slippery cover terms in psychology. They generally refer to processes that, in the framework, corresponds to operations across the various working memories in a network of representations, where conceptual processes would seem to play a major role.

The fact that consciousness is not required for the operation of executive control does not *exclude* the possibility that conscious control can be involved in certain situations. To consider both options, conscious and subconscious control respectively, take translation for example, and even more compellingly, simultaneous interpreting. Here interpreters have to maintain two languages at levels of activation that are quite close to one another to facilitate *deliberate* switches back and forth between theme. Since there is no way of influencing the raising and lowering of these activation levels directly, the switches have to be controlled using the manipulation of conceptual structures that have the effect of shifting the balance of one activated network over to the other. This is essentially the same process that was described earlier when discussing conceptual triggering.

Translators and interpreters both have to 'think themselves over' to the other language to allow the appropriate conceptual triggering to take place. Especially in the case of simultaneous interpreters, listening to one language while at the same time translating it aloud, this will require a lot of practice. The switch that lowers the network associated with Language 1 so that the network for Language 2 can take over will soon have to be reversed. For this to happen, the activation levels need to be juggled in such a way as not to allow the levels of either of the two networks to sink too far down: the cost of switching back and forth must remain minimal so as to avoid disruptive delays and cause the interpreting process to breakdown. This juggling has to take place more or less at the same time as the input from one language continues: this keeps that language active, while the interpreter is trying to access the other language to produce the translated version and this is while, all the time, comprehension of the input must continue.

Compared with the situation of translators, who normally have much more time on their hands even when it is a rush job, the rapid language switching involved in simultaneous interpreting can hardly remain under conscious control. The interpreter has to focus on the content of the message being interpreted and the (hopefully similar) content of the attempted translation as well. In such situations, thinking over into the other language must be the result of skilled subconscious performance.

Multilingualism and the Ageing Mind

Something has already been said about age and acquisition. There is period of maximum sensitivity to language input in the first years of childhood when children can become proficient users, monolingual or multilingual within a period of two or three years with continuing refinements thereafter. With multilinguals, there will usually be slight delays in their early language development but they soon catch up with their monolingual peers. Their combined vocabulary repertoire in both languages will certainly not be the equivalent of that of monolinguals in each language but across both or all languages vocabulary size will be the normal size, possible more.

Quite recently, interest has grown in language ability in *later* life, especially multilingual ability. This interest owes much to pioneering research by Bialystok together with Craik and other associates providing evidence for the long-term effects of multilingualism and research on other skills like video gaming (Bialystok et al. 2010; Craik et al. 2010; Bialystok et al. 2012; Anguera et al. 2013). The dominant idea that has emerged from this research is that increased cognitive flexibility is conferred on those who have acquired more than one language from early childhood: this provides a cushion against the mental disabilities brought on by dementia and allows people who are affected to find a way, for a time, to compensate for the inroads that disease has made on their brains, and mind. The result is that they do not display the symptoms of their disease until much later. This cushion is referred to as *cognitive reserve*. More specifically those who are unlucky to get dementia will not suffer the effects of dementia until several years, four or more later.[10] Research carried out in Canada where both monolinguals and bilinguals were studied, has indicated that the average onset of Alzheimer's is four years later in bilinguals (Bialystok et al. 2012). Subsequent research by Bak and associates in India with nonimmigrant participants – of the 648, 391 of them were multilingual[11] – as well as replication studies in several other countries – has supported the Canadian findings (Alladi et al. 2013; Bak et al. 2014).

The research just referred to had to do with people who were multilingual from birth. The question then arises whether monolinguals acquiring another language *after* they had acquired their first language and continuing to use it regularly might also show some cognitive benefits as a result. One indirect way of researching this kind of question is to examine *brain reserve*. Brain reserve is a characteristic of the physical neural system represented on the right of Figure I.1 in the book's introduction, and not the subway map representing the mind system on the left (see, for a useful overview of research into these two types of reserve, Grant et al. 2014). Although relatable to cognitive reserve, brain reserve is different, having to do with observable features of the brain such as the density of neurons and the degree of synaptic connectivity. The ageing brain typically shows decline in these areas and, by using fast developing imaging techniques, makes it easy to spot changes across different groups of older individuals but younger individuals

---

[10] We do not know yet how early the physical (as opposed to behavioural) signs of dementia in any patient began to manifest themselves. They may have developed over many years so the beginnings of more easily observable behavioural change is what these studies are based on (E. Bialystok, pers. comm., 2015).

[11] As has been the case up to now 'multilingual' continues to be used here to include bilinguals.

can also be compared. For example, Pliatsikas and colleagues looked at the effects of bilingualism in learners who had already acquired a first language on the white matter structure of their brains (Pliatsikas et al. 2015). White matter could be called the brain's subway since it consists of millions of connections between different parts of the brain so damage there may have wide-ranging effects on brain and mind functioning. What they found suggested to them that acquiring and actively using a second language after childhood, can have effects on white matter which may last into old age, bringing with it cognitive benefits as well as resistance to the effects of dementia.

Growing new language systems combined with their regular use, since language engages so many systems in the brain, may be particularly beneficial even when compared to video gaming, but clearly research in this area is still in its infancy: increasing interest in ageing nowadays is such that more interesting insights will surely accrue into how language acquisition and many other tasks requiring mental flexibility may have effects that can be labelled beneficial.

Abutalebi et al. (2015) consider various studies reporting adaptive change in the neuroanatomical structure of brains of bilinguals and multilinguals that may be associated with the use of more than one language. They observe that combining the structural data with rich *behavioural* data will advance our understanding of the causal links between the two. This relates clearly to the potential benefits of a crossdisciplinary framework such as the one used in this book, facilitating collaborative research between, for example, theoretical linguists, psycholinguists and neurolinguists.

Summary

The existence of more than one language in the mind of an individual essentially means a further extension of a feature already present in the monolingual, namely the capacity to express meaning and understand utterances in more than one way. This capacity develops fast, especially in very young children, despite the tendency to avoid having two ways of saying the same thing.

With every new alternative system comes a cost, namely an increase in the amount of competition when processing language. Everything relevant to the comprehension and production of language competes all the time. However, control over these systems also develops so that generally it becomes possible to keep the systems apart in performance, or, alternatively, either deliberately or subconsciously exploit the resources of both at the same time as in code-mixing or code-switching. With changes of activation within the conceptual system, one or other language system can be effectively suppressed to keep just one in current use, or they can be coactivated more or less equally to make more than one language system available at the same time.

When one language system is still being developed or remains weakly established in relative terms, more strongly established systems will tend to show up one way or the other when individuals are performing in the weaker language. Even where new structural connections have been established that should in principle lead to nativelike performance in the language, the relevant linguistic behaviour will be prevented due to successful competition from equivalents in a more strongly established language system. This will give the false impression that the speaker completely lacks the relevant knowledge. Finally, having to deal with more than just one language system makes people metalinguistically more aware, especially young children and there appear to be cognitive benefits for both young and old alike.

Conclusion

Overview

To conclude, this final part of the book will provide an overview and some thoughts and suggestions, varying from the more cautious to the more speculative, on what mapping language and mind in this way can contribute to our understanding. As a preliminary to this reflective concluding part of the book, Figure C.1, where the 3D map could be taken as a 'prototype model' of the mind, shows the framework in its entirety but with the processors removed, so in other words all the memory stores and the interfaces that mediate between them. A map of the brain would look radically different but in principle the one should always be translatable into the other. This will be done in different ways according to whatever theoretical approach is adopted and these in turn must necessarily be aimed at explaining the results of past findings and directing further empirical investigations in all the different relevant research fields.

Fixed, Flexible and Dynamic

This map displayed in Figure C.1 is, despite initial appearances, a very simple one indeed if one considers all the things the human mind does. At the same time, it presents the human mind as a modular system of incredible flexibility allowing an enormous variety of tasks to be accomplished simultaneously. The myriad ways in which different systems can collaborate and the tremendous potential within each system to develop a variety of different ways of dealing with life is worth emphasising. Although the individual modular systems together with their various interfaces, taken as a whole, represent a fixed and stable system, there is also constant 'dynamic' change *within* that whole system: resting levels are continually on the move causing individuals to behave and respond differently. In that sense nothing stays the same. At the same time, moving away from the minute details of on-like processing, relatively stable states can emerge from all this: a new skill is acquired, a new language is learned and another one becomes inaccessible. To sum up, the fixed parts of mental and neural architecture do not inhibit change at all. Rather they promote an impressive amount of flexibility and adaptability. This is true of the mind and, in the light of recent findings on neural

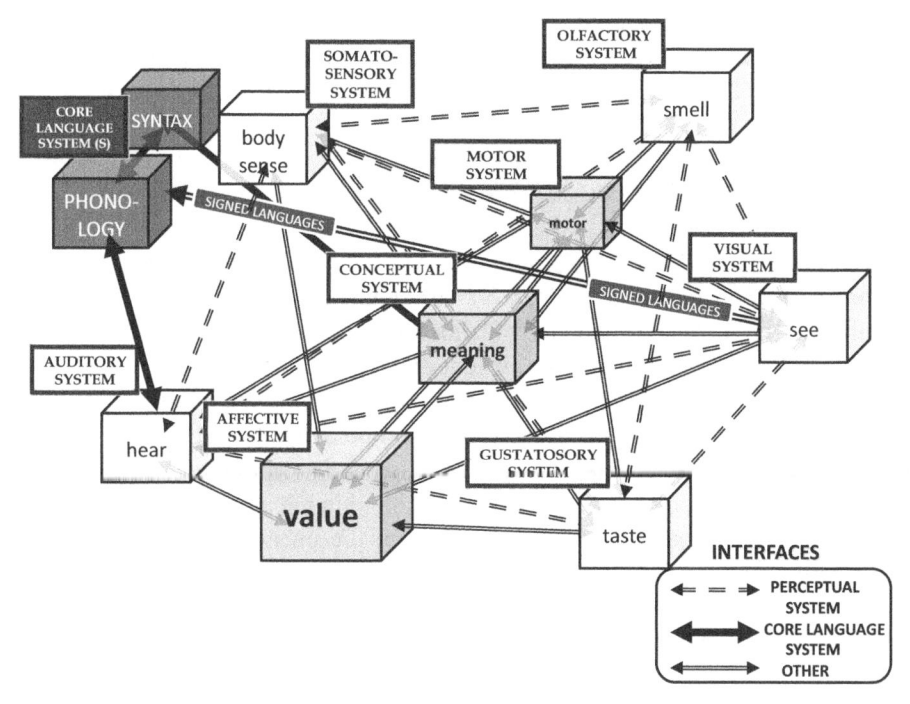

Figure C.1 *The framework: stores and interfaces.*

plasticity, the same can be said of the brain. There are no contradictions in seeing variation everywhere and maintaining a modular view. The two views are totally compatible.

The Relationship between Language and Vision

With regard to language, the interface between the visual system and the phonological system, if acceptable for the explanation of sign language processing might still be controversial with respect to the interpretation of written language. One might argue that the processing of written language should proceed indirectly via the auditory system (see the related discussion in Chapter 11 and Figure 11.2). Spoken language is, in the majority of cases, acquired first. Learning to read and write begins after the basics of the first language are already established so the visual patterns in written text may first be associated with the auditory structures of the same words when spoken aloud. These auditory structures will activate matching phonological structures. Even with writing systems with graphic symbols that bear little or no relationship with the sounds of speech, like Chinese characters, the symbols may still be matched with the structures representing associated sound patterns. As discussed in Chapter 11, however, sign language learned as a mother tongue by children with no or markedly impaired hearing ability cannot have any auditory structure available to play a role in processing, justifying for sign language use at least, the direct interface between vision and phonology in Figure C.1.

On the Myth of the Human Mind

In an article published in 2012, entitled 'The Original Sin of Cognitive Science', Stephen Levinson, renowned for his work on pragmatics and a supporter for the re-evaluation of linguistic relativity,[1] claimed that what he called the ideological myth of the human mind had been exploded by recent developments in cognitive science (Levinson 2012, 399). This complaint, containing some serious accusations, was born apparently from a feeling that anthropology was not being taken seriously by cognitive scientists. While making some laudable plea for more collaboration across disciplines, a theme which figured in the introduction to this book, he also fell into the trap of misrepresenting his presumed opponents and potentially perpetuating the division between areas which he claims ought to cooperate more, an error probably also perpetrated in the reverse direction by the other side. While it is beyond the scope to go into this particular crossdisciplinary quarrel, it would be interesting to see how the discussion would flow if such debates could be conducted within an overarching explanatory framework such as the one used in this book.

Social Context and the World Inside

In the introduction to this book, two important aspects of the framework used in this book were mentioned. Firstly, it was about the inner workings of the mind and not about the 'outside world'. Secondly, and just as important, the world outside was in no way irrelevant and it was 'outside' in one sense only. Each individual depends on upon the particular ways in which all humans, as opposed to other species, are able to perceive and internally represent the world outside. In addition, each individual's continual experience through his or her lifetime creates a whole internal cosmos, partly shared with other humans and partly unique. This cosmos undergoes continual change one way or the other.

---

[1] This goes back to the Sapir-Whorf hypothesis that claimed the language you grow up in – and this assumed a monolingual perspective – fundamentally influences your perception of the world: this makes people's minds different according to which is their native language. One famous example is the conception of time that Hopi gives Hopi Indians: Hopi has no way of expressing the same time distinctions used in most other languages. According to the hypothesis, their language dictates the way they are able to conceptualise time. This claim has remained highly controversial amongst linguists as well as anthropologists (Comrie 1985; Levinson 2012). The assumption in this book is a very mild version of this idea: language can bias the way you interpret aspects of the world, including abstractions such as time, but in most or all cases, such biases can easily be overcome.

It changes not only because of those internal changes in the mind and brain that may have no direct connection with social context; it also changes because experience with this outside world is continually changing and the effects of external events will be reflected in the world inside. For this reason research into the social context of language and research into the psychology and neurology of language cannot be carried out in strict separation from each other. For the student of mind, the focus is on how external events are processed and alter the configurations and resting levels of mental structures in the various stores and the connections established between them. This includes not only structures that could be called knowledge representations but also affective structures and motor structures as people change the way they assign values and respond emotionally to states and events as well as how they acquire new types and experience new levels of physical skill.

Closing Summary

The map of the mind is now complete. Let us finally review the main points. The mind comprises a network of modular 'expert' system each of which has a unique contribution to the whole. For sheer survival, we have a group of highly interactive perceptual systems to navigate us through our physical environment with an affective system assigning given values to virtually everything and enabling us to adopt appropriate avoidance or approach strategies. Add to that a motor system for physical responses and a conceptual system for interpreting the external world and manipulating it via reflection and planning and you have almost everything you need. To complete the picture, we have language. For this purposes we have two further experts to handle the organisation of phonology and syntax so that the physical world of sound and vision can be recruited for highly elaborate reflections and communication.

Although there is complexity and flexibility in how we can use this system we call the mind, its individual experts that collaborate with one another share the same basic design: a processor and a memory store. The contents of each specialised memory store, the primitives that are provided in advance plus all the various combinations, most of which are created through life experience, may be activated. Activation means rising towards the working memory area of the store which makes them candidates for participating in chains and networks of structure across the different systems and mediated via the connecting interfaces. This means there is no single working memory but combinations of different working memories collaborating of different ways. Participation always involves competition between rivals. The principle of activation by processing means the more something is activated in a memory store the better its future chances for fighting off its rivals when required. An important supporting role is played by the affective system so that highly valued representations get a boost in their accessibility.

Luckily for us, all this constant, ferocious competition, like most all mental processes, are hidden from conscious awareness. This allows many tasks to be carried swiftly and in parallel. Consciously controlled tasks are very resource intensive and can only be carried out relatively slowly and in sequence. A key role is played by the perceptual group which is the engine of consciousness.

Language fits into this scheme of things. Most language processing is carried out below the level of conscious awareness. Development in the phonological and syntactic system, the 'core language system', should not be confused with even the simplest technical knowledge about language which is developed in the conceptual system. In this way consciously acquired rules of grammar have no direct impact on the development of the subconscious grammar which must simply grow with an individual's attempts to use, and especially to interpret utterances in the language. We develop language ability in these ways whether as monolinguals or multilinguals and at any age although only acquiring language in the very early years absolutely guarantees what we might call complete success under normal circumstances and provided we have sufficient exposure to the language in question.

An enormous amount of specific detail has of course been left out. Work continues on the many different areas of research that have been touched upon but not necessarily in tandem. This framework is available as a shared platform and common reference point for those interested in collaborative research across disciplines.

Glossary

acquisition. *See* growth

Acquisition by Processing Theory (APT). Growth is the lingering effect of processing. APT is a specific claim made within the MOGUL framework and is supposed to be one principle that applies to *all* instances of cognitive development. Nevertheless, the specific nature of the growth is determined by the particular modular system in question. This APT for syntactic growth will be determined by the principles of the syntactic processor and not by some general cognitive set of principles. The same goes for conceptual growth, visual growth, auditory growth and so on. In each case, activation has the effect of raising the resting level of the structure concerned. This makes the structure more accessible and improves its chances of competing with rival candidates structures in working memory for participation in a current task. The more frequent, longer and more intense the activation of a given structure the greater is the resulting boost to its resting level. *See* attrition; resting level

activation. Structures (aka items in a memory store) are activated to various degrees during on-line processing and regularly compete with one other for selection by processors trying to make sense of input. The result of being activated may be appearance in working memory long enough to be used by some processing unit. For example, in speech perception, when sound is being processed, the interface processor between the auditory and phonological systems activates various PS, trying to find the best fit between a given AS and a PS. The phonological processor within the phonological processing unit will determine what the best fit is at the time as it attempts to build a phonological representation. It does this by manipulating activated PS that have appeared in its working memory. Some structures in working memory will not be used but be discarded that is, their activation levels will drop down again to a given resting level. Others will be selected and, as a consequence of this, undergo some change in their resting level so that they effectively become more accessible, that is, relatively more available for selection in the future. *See* resting level

affective structure (AfS). Affective structures are what underlie emotion. They are processed in the affective module and are represented in capital (block) letters, e.g. !DISGUST!, !FEAR!. AfS are understood to play a crucial role in cognition and this includes cognitive growth (development). Some connections between the affective system and other cognitive systems, important for the organism's survival, are understood to be *innate* while others are formed *as a result of experience*. Affect can be positive or negative so the AfS system includes the corresponding *value* structures. The function of these structures is to connect up with other structures assigning to them either a positive or a negative value. The number and characteristics of AfS depend on which theory of affect has been selected for instantiation within the MOGUL Framework. The neural substrate of AfS, traditionally referred to as the 'limbic' system, is distributed across various brain locations including the two amygdalae. *See* value

affective system. *See* affective structure

APT. *See* Acquisition by Processing Theory

attention. Attention has to do with intensive processing of any or all of the perceptual output structures (POpS). Attention does not automatically imply consciousness. If the activation levels of affected structures rise beyond a certain level they can become accessible to awareness (see also AfS). Experiments on blindsight, for example, show that we can attend to things without being aware of them.

attrition. A relative loss of accessibility of a given structural unit due to its infrequent involvement in building representations. Highly inaccessible items appear effectively to be 'lost' or 'forgotten' and to give credence to a 'use it or lose it' principle. Since they regularly fail to get selected, they never appear in overt performance (see also 'resting level' although they may reappear in a later stage in life as a result of ageing). This is Attrition by Processing, that is, APT in reverse. *See* Acquisition by Processing Theory

auditory structure (AS). Auditory structures are the output of the module that processes incoming acoustic input from the environment. AS provides input to, for example, the language modules, specifically PS, but only where PS is able to build phonological structure as a result. This AS that just happens to be used by the language module to build phonological structure is no different in other respects from the AS that 'represents' sounds like creaking doors, thunder and the rustle of leaves. AS supports the individual's experience of sound including sounds that are not triggered by input from outside, that is sounds that are imagined, sounds in dreams and auditory hallucinations. The traditional research domain of phonetics deals with the nature of AS_L, its articulation and perception and interaction with PS. In MOGUL, these auditory structures that are relevant for PS are accordingly represented in phonetic script with square bracket, e.g. [kʰæt]. More specifically, these structures will be represented following the conventions of the particular phonetic theory being applied. Non-linguistic AS are represented by a description of the relevant sound within square brackets, e.g. [sound of door creaking]. AS belong to a group of structures making up the perceptual system called POpS. *See* perceptual output structures

awareness. *See* attention; consciousness; perceptual output structures

coindexing. A process by which associations are created between representations in different stores/modules. Representations having the same index are said to be 'co-indexed': this relationship is traditionally indicated by means of subscript numbers or letters (representation A_1, representation B_1). When building a complex representation for a given input, the interface between the relevant processing units places a given index on certain representations with the result that they activate each other during processing. To take just two processing units as an example, English phonological structure /lip/$_1$ will become coindexed with syntactic structure N_1. In processing, indices first have to be created for given representations after which they function as described above. *See* index

competition. Competition is a major feature of all human processing. When comprehending or producing an utterance for example, the ultimate 'solution', i.e. the meaning we extract from the 'incoming' utterance or, alternatively, the utterance we finally produce to express our intended meaning, is only achieved after many competing candidate structures, within any of the processing units involved, have been reduced to a single chain of structures. The resolution of any competition is an interaction between the relevant working memories during on-line processing and the current resting levels of all the various items that have been activated. The system is always looking for a best-fit solution. *See* resting level

conceptual structure (CS). Conceptual structures may be thought of as meanings. This includes areas of meaning traditionally covered by the terms 'semantics' and 'pragmatics'. Meanings do not necessarily have to be linked up with the language module (PS and SS). The sound of a creaking door, for example, has a meaning. Non-linguistic conceptual structure is therefore also referred to as CS. Conceptual structure is sometimes referred to as 'mentalese' (Fodor 1975; Pinker 1994): we think (cogitate) in CS. That said, even though we are unaware of the structure of CS, its contents are accessible to awareness via POpS and, in this way, can be consciously manipulated. This means that we can go on to analyse the contents of CS in great detail and build up detailed knowledge of its properties. Knowledge about the world we live in is built out of CS. This includes metalinguistic knowledge. In MOGUL, conceptual structures are represented in capital (block) letters, e.g. DOG. *See* metalinguistic

consciousness. The phenomenon of conscious awareness in MOGUL is explained in terms of activation: When a representation reaches an extreme current activation level, it becomes the object of consciousness. These extreme levels arise naturally in the richly interconnected perceptual system. To become conscious of a meaning, for example, say the meaning of 'dog', one cannot be directly aware of the conceptual structure (DOG) that underlies this concept. Rather, the conscious awareness of this meaning is created by virtue of very highly activated perceptual output structures that are linked (co-indexed) with its conceptual structure. *See* attention; conceptual structure; metalinguistic; perceptual output structures

conventions. *See* MOGUL conventions

core language system. *See* language module; Universal Grammar

crosslinguistic influence (CLI). A generic term for a range of different effects attributable to an interaction between linguistic systems (in the language user's mind) understood to belong to different languages, for example various forms of transfer between two languages in language learners' performance, changes in an immigrant's use of the mother tongue due to influence from the dominant language in the community (so-called language attrition or language 'loss') and avoidance behaviour by learners attributable to a strategy of keeping different languages as distinct as possible or a perception of areas of difficulty in a nonnative language. *See* attrition; transfer

feature. *See* structure; primitive

growth. Also referred to as 'acquisition' as in 'language acquisition'; the growth of structural combinations within modules and structural associations between modules in response to environmental stimuli that have triggered internal processing operations within those modules. According to *Acquisition by Processing Theory* (APT), growth is marked by changes in the activation levels of the implicated structures. In the case of intuitive, subconscious language acquisition this will involve at the very least the language specific systems PS and SS and also associated CS. The shape of growth within a module is controlled by principles specific to that module. Hence growth in visual structures (VS) is controlled by the principles of the visual system. The same goes for growth in the phonological and syntactic module, and so on and so forth. *See* APT; attrition; interface; *see also* metalinguistic

gustatory structure (GS). Gustatory structures are perceptual output structures that relate to taste. *See* perceptual output structures

index. Indices/indexes are the formal mechanism by which elements in one module's memory store are chained together (placed in registration with/linked to) with elements in the memory store of an adjacent module (following Jackendoff). This should not be confused with the standard use of indices in generative linguistics to mark coreference or lack of coreference. For example, in MOGUL, the lexical item 'meat' involves the linking of a PS representation /mit/ with an SS representation indicating it is a noun thus: /mit/$_{23}$ ⇔ N$_{23}$ (using the number '23' as an arbitrary index). *See* coindexing; lexicon

input. 'Input' is a cybernetic metaphor used to describe what triggers a response from a particular part of the mental system. More specifically, it is what triggers the response of a particular module to activity in an adjacent system. More properly, the response to the trigger is actually mediated by an interface. For example, input to the syntactic module is when the interface between the phonological and the syntactic memory store pairs a phonological structure (PS) with a given syntactic structure (SS). By the same token, an auditory structure (AS) becomes input to the phonological module when the interface between the auditory and phonological memory stores establishes or activates a link between this AS and a given phonological structure (PS). Input in language acquisition studies has long been thought of as the language to which a language user is exposed and which is supposed to impact on the user's system in some way. If the impact in a long term one, it is sometimes referred to as 'intake'. In MOGUL, as in Carroll's Autonomous Induction Model, input that potentially has this long-term effect should be thought of more properly as resulting from a whole chain or network of separate inputs beginning with the organism registering an environmental event (the acoustic signal created by a spoken utterance, for example). This original acoustic event would be interfaced in various steps with the relevant modules ending up with the activation of a conceptual structure assigning a meaning to that utterance. At any point in the sequence of internal events, one of the interfaces may not take place in which case the possibility of language acquisition taking place is reduced.

interface. Interface systems link structures in modules to form chains of structure; a very simple example of a chain of three elements (PS-SS-CS) is /pig/⇔N singular⇔(meaning of PIG) (see also lexicon). The role of an interface system is to match certain structures in adjacent modules. This matching is also termed 'co-indexing' more or less as used in generative linguistics. Activation of a structure in one module will then trigger the activation of co-indexed structures in adjacent modules. Note that a word or lexical item does not exist in this system as such but is a principled linking (matching, indexing) of three structures via interfaces between three modules. *See* lexicon; index

item. *See* structure; primitive

language module(s). In MOGUL and following Jackendoff, 'language module' is a cover term for what is actually a *bimodular* system. That is, it consists of two independent modules (processing units), namely the phonological module and the syntactic module. This makes it different from the standard Chomskyan 'syntactocentric' conception of the language faculty. Together with their various interfaces, the two processing units (handling PS and SS) form the uniquely human core language system. Human language cognition covers a much wider area than the language module but it is this bimodular system which makes human language unique. Its essential structural properties are understood to be innate although the contents of its two memory stores will come to differ sometimes widely according to which languages are being used or acquired. Semantic and pragmatic structure lie outside the language module and are part of conceptual structure (CS). That said, semantic and pragmatic conceptual structures are created, and are therefore greatly influenced by their interaction with the core language system. *See* conceptual structure; Universal Grammar

lexicon. There is no general lexicon in the conventional sense. The 'lexicon' of a language is a metalinguistic notion useful for an analytic understanding of language but less helpful in understanding the actual way the mind works. Following Jackendoff, a lexical item can be seen in two alternative but compatible ways: (1) as a rule associating three separate and independent types of structure, a phonological structure (PS) a syntactic structure (SS) and a conceptual structure (CS). In processing terms, it is best thought of as (2) a chain of structures that have been activated and put in correspondence with one another: PS⇔SS⇔CS. Each structure is processed independently within its own processing unit (module) according to the principles of that module. The nearest thing to a lexicon in MOGUL is the unique memory store of structure that each module possesses, hence the phonological processing unit contains a phonological 'lexicon' in which only phonological structures are stored, either as independent elements, or typically in various combinations specific to some language or languages known to the individual language user and formed during exposure to that language.

memory (store). Memory in MOGUL is an essential component of a processing-unit. In other words, memory is modularised. This means that it is not to be seen as a 'common pool' that different parts of the mental system have access to. This goes both for long-term memory and working memory. In fact the distinction between long term and working memory is minimal and resides in different states of activation. 'Memories', as used in everyday language, will very often be built out of coalitions of items linked via interfaces across individual memory stores, a classic example being 'episodic' memories which do not exist under a separate rubric in MOGUL but which can reflect complex coalitions of memories involving various perceptual structures, conceptual structures and perhaps also motor structures and structures within the language module as well. *See* interface; store; working memory

metalinguistic. As with any kind of metacognition, knowledge about language, which can be raised to awareness, is created in conceptual structure and not within the language module. Raising such knowledge to awareness requires the mediation of the perceptual systems. *See* consciousness; POpS

module. In MOGUL, modules are also called 'processing units'. Each module operates with its unique code and unique set of principles. For example, phonological module operates with phonological code and phonological principles that are not shared or translatable into any other code. At the same time the basic structure of a module is generic and applies across the cognitive system as a whole. That is, any module consists of an integrative processor and a memory store. Memory stores are interfaced with one or more different modules allowing the formation of chains or networks of structure. In MOGUL, reflecting their status as the twin components of the human language faculty, PS and CS are informally referred to together as 'the language module' despite the fact that they form two separate processing units. *See* interface; language module; store

MOGUL conventions. The way various categories are represented in MOGUL may be illustrated as follows, in most cases using the dummy word 'cat' as a substitute term preceded by an equals sign and then the abbreviated term. To date, these category conventions are recommended (L, O and S subscripts are used for the convenience of the researcher to indicate structures associated with language and do not imply the existence of separate processing units)

    Affective structure = AfS
    1)   !FEAR or !fear!
    Auditory structure = AS:
    1)   a linguistically relevant AS: [kʰæt])
    2)   a representation of a sound made by cats
    Conceptual structure = CS: 1) **CAT**
    Gustatory structure = GS
    Motor structure = MoS
    Olfactory structures = OfS
    Perceptual Output Structures: POpS
    Phonological structure = PS
    Processing Unit = PU
    Somatosensory structure = SmS
    Syntactic structure = SS
    Visual structure = VS:
    1)   a linguistically relevant VS: *"cat"*
    2)   a representation of the image of a cat

motor structure (MoS). Motor structures control the articulation of body parts including those involved in linguistic activity (MoS_L), especially the production of speech, writing and sign language. For example, in speech production, PS are linked to those MoS that are responsible for the movement of the speech organs. Many body parts are multifunctional so the MS that control precise tongue movements during speech activity (the linguistic motor structures, MoS_L) exist alongside other MoS that control the articulatory activity associated with, for instance, tasting and swallowing. The neural correlates of MoS are distributed over various parts of the brain and notably the (primary, secondary and supplementary) motor cortices and related areas like the cerebellum and basal ganglia. The rich interconnectivity within the system as a whole means that motor structures may undergo some degree of sympathetic activation even where they are functionally irrelevant. One example would be the occurrence of minor movements in the vocal tract ('subvocalisation') when reading silently. *See* somatosensory structure

olfactory structure (OfS). Olfactory structures belong to a group of structures making up the perceptual system called POpS, in this case, having to do with the sense of smell. *See* perceptual output structures

perceptual output structures (POpS). A generic term covering all the structures (like auditory structures, AS, and visual structures, VS) that constitute the output of the perceptual systems. Of the various possible types of perceptual structure, only five have figured in the discussions and illustrations in this book: this has been simply for reasons of convenience. A crucial feature of POpS is the existence of strong interconnections between the individual memory stores so that, together, they form a well integrated system. POpS play a crucial role in the MOGUL account of awareness. They account for hallucinations, dreaming and self-initiated imagining as well. Whereas an acoustic stimulus occurring the environment, say a door chime, can activate a particular auditory structure and trigger the awareness of the sound of a door chime, the selfsame experience can arise from the activation of the auditory structure *alone*, i.e. without anything actually happening in the environment. POpS typically undergo high levels of activation: this has evolved in this way presumably since it is important for survival. This may also help account for differences occurring between species such that for example, in dogs, olfactory structures, the output of the sense of smell, play a greater role than is the case in human perception. Humans have highly developed visual systems so that it is much easier, if asked to, to imagine an object (recreate the experience without any environment stimulus) than imagine a smell or a touch. Although this is a very simplified account it gives an idea of the innate biases in the functioning of different types of perceptual output structure (POpS). The characteristics of POpS and the number of different types (corresponding to the number of senses) naturally depend on which theory of perception has been selected for instantiation within the MOGUL framework. *See* auditory structure; gustatory structure; olfactory structure; somatosensory structure; visual structure

phonetics. What might otherwise be called 'phonetic' structures in MOGUL do not exist independently from auditory structures (AS) as a whole, i.e. as a separate type of POpS. This means that phonetic strings, traditionally represented using square brackets (e.g. [kæt]) are actually auditory strings, i.e. auditory structures (AS) that *happen* to have been created specifically as a result of interaction with the language module and as a result of *listening* experience (see also the discussion in the section on orthography). If it is convenient to identify auditory structures that are phonetic, this can be done by adding the optional subscript L which serves only to act as a reminder of their association with language, thus: AS_L. *See* auditory structure

phonological structure (PS). The storing and processing of phonological structure is carried out within a closed-off expert system or module: even though we can become aware of features of auditory structure with which PS is linked (like stress, rhythm sibilants etc., we remain completely unaware of the structure of PS itself; cf. Jackendoff 1987, 88), its contents are inaccessible to awareness and therefore cannot be consciously manipulated in any direct manner. Phonological structures in MOGUL are represented following standard phonological convention in simple phonetic script e.g. /kæut/. More specifically, phonological structures will be represented following the conventions of the particular phonological theory being applied. *See* auditory structure; phonetics

primitive. Primitives are the essential building units that make up representations. They are supplied in advance, i.e. they are innately given. They are used either independently or in combination with other primitives. The principles of combination are determined entirely by the given processing unit in question, for example, visual primitives combine in ways determined uniquely by the visual processor. The actual combinations however will be greatly influenced by the individual's processing history which explains, for example, why a Chinese speaker's phonological memory store contains combinations not shared by a Hausa speaker's memory store. Even though the same set of phonological primitives are available to both of them, the individual's processing history has meant that the shared stock of primitives has been configured in different ways. This is a general principle and holds for all types of structure. *See* growth; Universal Grammar

processing unit (PU). A key component of this highly modularised (Jackendovian) view of cognition. A processing unit has a dedicated processor and a dedicated memory store, akin to a lexicon, containing only structures specific to that processing unit/module. Although the more general term 'module' is also used to characterise this component of MOGUL architecture, 'processing unit' is the specific term used in this framework to designate a processor-store combination: the definition excludes interfaces between stores. All PUs have the same basic structure but each one is also unique in that it cannot deal with structures in another 'alien' memory store. A syntactic processor for example cannot handle phonological structures. The store in a given processing unit is interfaced with one or more other stores: the activation of a structure in its own memory store will then trigger the activation of a given structure or structures in the stores of those other processing units. The degree of encapsulation of a module is related to the amount of access it has to the memory stores of that modules or those modules with which it is interface. *See* interface; module

representation. A structure in the memory store of a processing unit. Representations are manifested in two ways in MOGUL, statically, as simple or complex structures stored within a memory with particular resting levels, or dynamically, that is, during on-line processing, as activated structures, again of greater or lesser complexity. A single structural item in a memory store can be thought of as a 'representation'. During processing, structures are chained together to form a representational chain or network in working memory. One example would be a sentence like 'Benjamin hid the watch' which is built out of individual representations activated in, respectively, the SS, PS and CS stores. The term 'representation' must be understood flexibly because strictly speaking structures do not 'represent' anything (Jackendoff 2002, 20). *See* structure; primitive; memory store

resting level. The particular base level of a given structural unit: this can be higher or lower relative to the resting level of other units; the higher the resting level, the more accessible it is and, all other things being equal, the better chance it has in any competition to be selected when a representation is being built on line. Frequent selection has the effect of raising the resting level. Items that are not selected will experience a decline in their resting level. *See* activation

somatosensory structure (SmS). Somatosensory structures are the output of a group of sensory systems relating to touch, pain, temperature, body position and sense of the body generally. *See* perceptual output structures

store. Another name for a facility which stores structures of a particular type, some of which will be primitives and others combinations of structures within that store that have been formed through experience. The totality of an individual's memory is the complete set of all these various specialised memory stores and the connections between them. Given this modular view of memory, there is, therefore, no single all-encompassing memory facility. *See* memory; primitive

structure. Structure is the most neutral name to describe what can also variously be called 'representation', (structural) 'element', (structural) 'feature' or (structural) 'item'. Structures are the contents of the memory stores that form part of each processing unit. A structure, when activated, causes those structures that are co-indexed with it also to be activated. The result is coindexed chains or networks of activated structures (representations, elements, units) ranging across different memory stores. Within a given memory store, as a result of the individual's earlier experience, structures may be combined together in various ways to form complex structural units. The original structural elements in any store, its 'primitives', form the basis for such combinations. *See* index; memory; primitive; representation

transfer. This is a term conventionally used in language acquisition studies to describe the modelling of structures in a developing language on the patterns of some structure in another language known to the user. Transfer is one type of crosslinguistic influence. Transfer is thought to be either a transitory phenomenon associated with on-line processing strategies or a longer term phenomenon whereby the structure in question is actually incorporated into the new language system. In MOGUL, this distinction is a relative one depending especially upon the resting level activation involved. *See* crosslinguistic influence

UG. *See* Universal Grammar

Universal Grammar (UG). UG is a cover term for principles unique to the design of natural grammars, i.e. the grammars of any human language. It is supposed to be part of our biological inheritance and unique to our species. UG does not constitute a grammar in the traditional sense but is rather a 'toolbox' or 'limited set of properties' out of which a particular grammar will only select some of the available options. Knowing what the options are makes it possible for the (unconscious) mind to work out how the grammar works. The precise nature of UG is determined by the current version of whatever linguistic theory is using this notion. In MOGUL, this means the principles underlying the innate structure of the language module including the primitives in PS and SS that constrain and dictate the way linguistic structure is constructed on line and stored. The processors that do the constructing in these two modules embody the principles of UG. UG is in principle available at any age – topic that has generated much debate – but it shows itself in its purest form in the way the young child acquires the grammar of a language when exposed to sufficient linguistic input in the course of day-to-day life and without the aid of any correction or the conscious analysis of rules. UG is largely irrelevant as far as the acquisition of vocabulary, rules of usage in different contexts. In other words UG is not about the acquisition of language in the wider sense. *See* language module; primitive

value. A crucial aspect of the affective system has to do with assigning positive or negative value. Value is about what matters to us. It has its roots in the basic need of every organism to avoid potentially harmful things, like predators, and seek potentially beneficial things, like food and sex. But in the complex human mind/brain, it has naturally taken on a much broader role, namely evaluation of everything we experience in terms of positive/negative and intensity. Mental representations in general are connected to representations of positive and/or negative value. The intensity of the valuation is the resting activation level of the index that is the connection. Value is the foundation of emotion and plays a crucial role in all aspects of cognition and behaviour, including the acquisition and use of a second language. Positive and negative value structures combine with other AfS to represent a whole range of emotional states. In Truscott's book on consciousness (Truscott 2014), positive and negative value are represented by, respectively, the affective structure !val! and the affective structure !harm! *See* affective structure

visual structure (VS). Visual structures are the output of the module that processes incoming visual input from the environment. VS is interfaced with, amongst other systems, the language module. This means that 'orthographic' structure is a variant of VS_L (visual structures involved in language). Orthographic structures are also referred to as VS_O (orthographic visual structures) indicating a particular type of VS that happens to be used by the language module and which are interfaced with PS. By the same token, sign language involves the development of specialised visual structures, VS_S, that will also serve as input to PS. VS supports the individual's complete visual experience including the experience of visual events that are not triggered by input from outside, i.e., sights that are imagined, in dreams and visual hallucinations. In MOGUL, VS_O are represented in italics between double inverted commas, e.g. "*dog*" and VS_S are represented as follows *sign for dog*, or **dog**. Otherwise VS are simply referred to by means of a paraphrase for example 'the visual memory/ representation of a dog'. VS belong to a group of structures making up the perceptual system called POpS. *See* perceptual output structures

working memory. MOGUL follows the line of thought that sees working memory as patterns of highly activated structures in given memory stores roughly along the lines proposed by Cowan (1993, 2001). This means there is no fundamental distinction between long and short (or working) memory. Rather, the distinction is explained as a difference in the level of current activation of particular stored items. In some models, working memory is represented as a blackboard or sketchpad separate from long-term memory. In both ways of representing working memory, structures very briefly held in working memory are used to build cognitive representations on-line. *See* memory; store

References

Abutalebi, J., Guidi, L., Borsa, V., Canini, M., Della Rosa, P. A., Parris, B. A., & Weekes, B. A. (2015). Bilingualism provides a neural reserve for aging populations. *Neuropsychologia*, 69, 201–210.

Acredolo, L. P., Goodwyn, S. W., Horobin, K., & Emmons, Y. (1999). The signs and sounds of early language development. In L. Balter & C. Tamis-LeMonda (Eds.), *Child psychology* (pp. 116–139). New York: Psychology Press.

Alladi, S., Bak, T., Duggirala, V., Surampudi, B., Shailaja, M., & Shukla, A. K. (2013). Bilingualism delays age at onset of dementia, independent of education and immigration status. *Neurology*, 81(22), 1938–1944.

Amaral, L., & Roeper, T. (2014). Multiple grammars and second language representation. *Second Language Research*, 30(1), 3–36.

Anderson, J. R. (1982). Acquisition of cognitive skill. *Psychological Review*, 89, 369–406.

Anguera, J., Boccanfuso, J., Rintoul, J., Al-Hashimi, O., Faraji, F., Janowich, F., Kong, E., Larraburo, Y., Rolle, E., Johnston, C., & Gazzaley, A. (2013). Video game training enhances cognitive control in older adults. *Nature*, 501, 97–101.

Antoniou, M., Gunasekera, G., & Wong, P. (2013). Foreign language training as cognitive therapy for age-related cognitive decline: A hypothesis for future research. *Neuroscience and Biobehavioral Reviews*, 37, 2689–2698.

Baars, B. (1997). *The theater of consciousness*. Oxford: Oxford University Press.

Baars, B. (1988). *A cognitive theory of consciousness*. New York: Cambridge University Press.

Baars, B., & Franklin, S. (2007). An architectural model of conscious and unconscious brain functions: Global Workspace Theory and IDA. *Neural Networks*, 20, 955–961.

Baddeley, A. (2012). Working memory: Theories, models, and controversies. *Annual Review of Psychology*, 63, 1–29.

Baddeley, Alan D., & Hitch, G. (1974). Working memory. In G. Bower (Ed.), *The psychology of learning and motivation: Advances in research and theory* (pp. 47–89). New York: Academic Press.

Bak, T., Nissan, J., Allerhand, M., & Deary, I. (2014). Does bilingualism influence cognitive aging? *Annals of Neurology*, 75(6), 959–963.

Balda, R. P., Pepperberg, I. M., & Kamil A. C. (1998). *Animal cognition in nature: The convergence of psychology and biology in laboratory and field*. New York: Academic Press.

Balsby, T., Vestergaard Momberg, J., & Dabelsteen, T. (2012). Vocal imitation in parrots allows addressing of specific individuals in a dynamic communication network. *PLoS ONE*, 11, e49747. doi:10.1371/journal.pone.0049747

Barlow, H. (1961). Possible principles underlying the transformation of sensory messages. In W. Rosenblith (Ed.), *Sensory communication* (pp. 217–234). Cambridge, MA: MIT Press.
Barsalou, L. W. (2008). Grounded cognition. *Annual Review of Psychology*, 59, 617–645.
Bates, E., & MacWhinney, B. (1982). Functionalist approaches to grammar. In E. Wanner & L. Gleitman (Eds.), *Language acquisition: The state of the art* (pp. 173–218). New York: Cambridge University Press.
Berridge, K., & Winkielman, P. (2003). What is an unconscious emotion? (The case for unconscious "liking"). *Cognition and Emotion*, 17(2), 181–211.
Bialystok, E. (1997). The structure of age: In search of barriers to second language acquisition. *Second Language Research*, 13(2), 116–137.
Bialystok, E. (2001). *Bilingualism in development: Language, literacy, and cognition*. Cambridge: Cambridge University Press.
Bialystok, E., Craik, F., & Freedman, M. (2010). Delaying the onset of Alzheimer disease: Bilingualism as a form of cognitive reserve. *Neurology*, 75(19), 1726–1729.
Block, N. (1995). On a confusion about a function of consciousness. *Behavioral and Brain Sciences*, 18(2), 227–287.
Brown, R., & Kulik, J. (1977). Flashbulb memories. *Cognition*, 5(1), 73–99.
Calabria, M., Hernández, M., Branzi, F. M., & Costa, A. (2012). Qualitative differences between bilingual language control and executive control: Evidence from task-switching. *Frontiers in Psychology*, 2(399), 1–10.
Carroll, S. E. (1999). Putting "input" in its proper place. *Second Language Research*, 15, 337–388.
Carruthers, P. (2006). *The architecture of the mind*. Oxford: Oxford University Press.
Chapman, R., & Bragdon, H. (1964). Evoked responses to numerical and non-numerical visual stimuli while problem solving. *Nature*, 203, 1155–1157.
Chomsky, N. (1965). *Aspects of the theory of syntax*. Cambridge, MA: MIT Press.
Chomsky, N. (1980). *Rules and representations*. Oxford: Basil Blackwell.
Chomsky, N. (1995). *The minimalist program*. Cambridge, MA: MIT Press.
Chomsky, N. (2000). *New horizons in the study and language and mind*. Cambridge: Cambridge University Press.
Chomsky, N. (2004, May 17). *Biolinguistics and the human capacity*. Lecture delivered at MTA, Budapest.
Comrie, B. (1985). *Tense*. Cambridge: Cambridge University Press.
Cook, V. (1992). Evidence for multicompetence. *Language Learning*, 42, 557–591.
Cook, V. (2013). *Second language learning and teaching* (4th ed.). Abingdon, England: Routledge.
Cook, V., & Newson, M. (2007). *Chomsky's universal grammar: An introduction* (3rd ed.). Oxford: Wiley Blackwell.
Cosmides, L., & Tooby, J. (1992). Cognitive adaptations for social exchange. In J. Barkow, L. Cosmides, & J. Tooby (Eds.), *The adapted mind: Evolutionary psychology and the generation of culture* (pp. 163–222). New York: Oxford University Press.
Cowan, N. (1993). Activation, attention, and short-term memory. *Memory and Cognition*, 21, 162–167.
Cowan, N. (2005). *Working memory capacity*. New York: Psychology Press.

Cowan, N. (2008). What are the differences between long-term, short-term, and working memory? *Progress in Brain Research*, 169, 323–338. Retrieved from http://www.ncbi.nlm.nih.gov/pmc/articles/PMC2657600/

Cowan, N. (2010). The magical mystery four: How is working memory capacity limited, and why? *Current Directions in Psychological Science*, 19(1), 51–57.

Craik, F. I. M., Bialystok, E., & Freedman, M. (2010). Delaying the onset of Alzheimer disease: Bilingualism as a form of cognitive reserve. *Neurology*, 75, 1726–1729.

Crick, F. (1994). *The astonishing hypothesis: The scientific search for the soul.* New York: Charles Scribner.

Crick, F., & Koch, C. (2007). A neurobiological framework for consciousness. In M. Velmans & S. Schneider (Eds.), *The Blackwell companion to consciousness* (pp. 567–579). Malden, MA: Blackwell.

Damasio, A. (1994). *Descartes' error: Emotion, reason, and the human brain.* New York: Putnam.

Damasio, A. R. (1999). *The feeling of what happens: Body and emotion in the making of consciousness.* New York: Harcourt Brace.

Damasio, A. R. (2010). *Self comes to mind: Constricting the conscious mind.* New York: Pantheon Books.

De Bot, K., Lowie, W., & Verspoor, M. (2007). A dynamic systems theory approach to second language acquisition. *Bilingualism: Language and Cognition*, 10, 7–21.

Dehaene, F. (2014). *Consciousness and the brain.* New York: Viking.

D'Esposito, M., & Postle, B. (2015). The cognitive science of working memory. *Annual Review of Psychology*, 66, 115–142.

Dewaele, J.-M. (2010). *Emotions in multiple languages.* Basingstoke, England: Palgrave Macmillan.

Doherty-Sneddon, G. (2008). The great baby signing debate. *Psychologist*, 21(4), 300–303.

Dörnyei, Z. (2001). *Teaching and researching motivation.* Harlow: Longman.

Dörnyei, Z. (2003). Attitudes, orientations, and motivations in language learning: Advances in theory, research, and applications. In Z. Dornyei (Ed.), *Attitudes, orientations and motivations in language learning* (pp. 3–32). Malden, MA: Blackwell.

Dörnyei, Z., & Ottó, I. (1998). Motivation in action: Process model of L2 motivation. *Applied Linguistics*, 4, 43–69.

Eimas, P. D. (1975). Speech perception in early infancy. In L. B. Cohen & P. Salapatek (Eds.), *Infant perception: From sensation to cognition* (pp. 193–231). New York: Academic Press.

Ekman, P. (1972). Universals and cultural differences in facial expressions of emotions. In Cole, J. (Ed.), *Nebraska Symposium on Motivation* (pp. 207–282). Lincoln: University of Nebraska Press.

Ekman, P. (2004). *Emotions revealed: Understanding faces and feelings.* Phoenix, NJ: Phoenix Press.

Farrell, L. O', Lewis, S., McKenzie, A., & Jones, L. (2010). Charles Bonnet syndrome: A review of the literature. *Journal of Visual Impairment & Blindness*, 104(5), 261–275.

Fitch, W. T., Hauser, M. D., & Chomsky, N. (2005). The evolution of the language faculty: Clarifications and implications. *Cognition*, 97, 179–210.
Fodor, J. A. (1975). *The language of thought*. Cambridge, MA: Harvard University Press.
Fodor, J. A. (1983). *The modularity of mind: An essay on faculty psychology*. Cambridge, MA: MIT Press.
Fodor, J. A. (2000). *The mind doesn't work that way*. Cambridge, MA: MIT Press.
Foucart, A., & Frenck-Mestre, C. (2013). Language processing. In J. Herschensohn & M. Young-Scholten (Eds.), *A handbook of second language acquisition* (pp. 394–416). Cambridge: Cambridge University Press.
Friederici, A., & Weissenborn, J. (2007). Mapping sentence form onto meaning: The syntax-semantic interface. *Brain Research*, 1146, 50–58.
Frijda, N. (1986). *The emotions*. Cambridge: Cambridge University Press.
Fromkin, V., Rodman, R., & Hyams, N. (2013). *An introduction to language* (10th ed.). Boston: Wadsworth.
Gardner, R., & Lambert, W. (1972). *Attitudes and motivation in second language learning*. Rowley, MA: Newbury House.
Gathercole, S., & Alloway, T. (2007). *Understanding working memory: A classroom guide*. London: Harcourt Assessment.
Gladwell, M. (2006). *Blink: The power of thinking without thinking*. London: Penguin.
Gómez Milán, E., Iborra, O., de Córdoba, M. J., Juárez-Ramos V., Rodríguez Artacho, M. A., & Rubio, J. L. (2013). The Kiki-Bouba effect: A case of personification and ideaesthesia. *Journal of Consciousness Studies*, 20(1–2), 84–102.
Grant, A., Dennis, N., & Li, P. (2014). Cognitive control, cognitive reserve, and memory in the aging bilingual brain. *Frontiers in Psychology*, 5, Article 1401.
Green, D. W. (1998). Mental control of the bilingual lexico-semantic system. *Bilingualism, Language, and Cognition*, 1, 67–81.
Groh, J. M., Krause, A. S., Underhill, A. M., Clark, K. R., & Inati, S. (2001). Eye position influences auditory responses in primate inferior colliculus *Neuron*, 29, 509–518.
Grosjean, F. (2001). The bilingual's language modes. In J. Nicol (Ed.), *One mind, two languages: Bilingual language processing* (pp. 1–22). Oxford: Blackwell.
Grüter, T., Lew-William, C., & Fernald, A. (2012). Grammatical gender in L2: A production or a real-time processing problem? *Second Language Research*, 28(2), 191–215.
Harrar, V., & Spence, C. (2013). The taste of cutlery: How the taste of food is affected by the weight, size, shape, and colour of the cutlery used to eat it. *Flavour*, 2(21), 1–12.
Hauser, M. D., Chomsky, N., & Fitch, W. T. (2002). The faculty of language: What is it, who has it, and how did it evolve? *Science*, 298, 1569–1579.
Hauser, M., Newport, E., & Aslin, R. (2001). Segmentation of the speech stream in a non-human primate: Statistical learning in cotton-top tamarins. *Cognition*, 78, B53–B64.
Hayes, B. (2008). *Introductory phonology*. Oxford: Blackwell.
Herschensohn, J. (2007). *Language development and age*. Cambridge: Cambridge University Press.
Heyes, C. (2010). Where do mirror neurons come from? *Neuroscience and Biobehavioral Reviews*, 34, 575–583.

Hickok, G. (2014). *The myth of mirror neurons: The real neuroscience of communication and cognition.* New York: W. W. Norton.

Hopp, H. (2010). Ultimate attainment in L2 inflection: Performance similarities between non-native and native speakers. *Lingua*, 120(4), 901–931.

Hyltenstam, K., & Abrahamsson, N. (2000). Who can become native-like in a second language? All, some, or none? *Studia Linguistica*, 54(2), 150–166.

Hyltenstam, K., & Obler, L. (1989). *Bilingualism across the lifespan: Aspects of acquisition, maturity, and loss.* Cambridge: Cambridge University Press.

Izard, C. E. (1979). Emotions as motivations: A evolutionary-developmental perspective. In R. A. Dienstbier (Ed.), *Nebraska Symposium on Motivation, 1978* (Vol. 26, pp. 163–200). Lincoln: University of Nebraska Press.

Jackendoff, R. (1987). *Consciousness and the computational mind.* Cambridge, MA: MIT Press.

Jackendoff, R. (1990). *Semantic structures.* Cambridge, MA: MIT Press.

Jackendoff, R. (2002). *Foundations of language.* Oxford: Oxford University Press.

Jackendoff, R. (2011). What is the human language faculty? Two views. *Language*, 87(3), 586–624.

Jackendoff, R., & Pinker, S. (2005). The nature of the language faculty and its implications for evolution of language (reply to Fitch, Hauser, and Chomsky). *Cognition*, 9, 211–225.

James, W. (1884). What is an emotion? *Mind*, 9, 188–205.

James, W. (1894). The physical basis of emotion. *Psychological Review*, 1, 516–529.

Johnson, J. S., & Newport, E. L. (1989). Critical period effects in second language learning: The influence of maturational state on the acquisition of English as a second language. *Cognitive Psychology*, 21, 60–99.

Kahneman, D. (2011). *Thinking, fast and slow.* New York: Farrar, Straus, and Giroux.

Kanwisher, N., McDermott, J., & Chun, M. (1997). The fusiform face area: A module in human extrastriate cortex specialized for the perception of faces. *Journal of Neuroscience*, 17, 4302–4311.

Karmiloff-Smith, A. (1978). The interplay between syntax, semantics and phonology in language acquisition processes. In R. N. Campbell & P. T. Smith (Eds.), *Advances in the psychology of language* (pp. 1–23). London: Plenum Press.

Karmiloff-Smith, A. (1979). *A functional approach to child language.* Cambridge: Cambridge University Press.

Kegl, J. (2004). Language emergence in a language-ready brain: Acquisition issues. In L. Jenkins (Ed.), *Biolinguistics and the evolution of language.* Amsterdam: John Benjamins.

Kellerman, E. (1979). Transfer and non-transfer: Where we are now. *Studies in Second Language Acquisition*, 2(1), 37–57.

Kihlstrom, J. (1999). The psychological unconscious. In L. A. Pervin & O. P. John (Eds.), *Handbook of personality: Theory and research* (2nd ed., pp. 424–442). New York: Guilford Press.

Klein, W., & Purdue, C. (1997). The basic variety (or: couldn't natural languages be much simpler?). *Second Language Research*, 13, 301–347.

Kleinmann, H. H. (1977). Avoidance behaviour in adult second language acquisition. *Language Learning*, 27, 93–107.

Krashen, S. (1976). Formal and informal linguistic environments in language learning and language acquisition. *TESOL Quarterly*, 10, 157–168.
Krashen, S. D. (1981). *Second language acquisition and second language learning*. Oxford: Pergamon.
Kroll, J., Bobb, S., & Hoshino, N. (2014). Two languages in mind: Bilingualism as a tool to investigate language, cognition, and the brain. *Current Directions in Psychological Science*, 23, 159–216.
Kutas, M., & Hillyard, S. (1980). Reading senseless sentences: Brain potentials reflect semantic incongruity. *Science*, 207, 203–208.
Lakoff, G., & Johnson, M. (1980). *Metaphors we live by*. Chicago: University of Chicago Press.
Lamme, V. (2003). Why visual attention and awareness are different. *Trends in Cognitive Science*, 7(1), 12–17.
Landry, R., & Bourhis, R. (1997). Linguistic landscape and ethnolinguistic vitality: An empirical study. *Journal of Language and Social Psychology*, 16(1), 23–49.
LeDoux, D. (1996). *The emotional brain*. New York: Simon and Schuster.
LeDoux, J. (2002). *The synaptic self*. Harmondsworth, England: Penguin.
Lenneberg, E. (1967). *The biological foundations of language*. New York: John Wiley.
Lehrdahl, F., & Jackendoff, R. (1983). *A generative theory of tonal music*. Cambridge, MA: MIT Press.
Levinson, S. C. (2012). The original sin of cognitive science. *Topics in Cognitive Science*, 4(3), 396–403.
Long, M., Vega-Mendoza, M., Sorace, A., & Bak, T. (2015, September). *Language learning as cognitive training: Attentional improvement after a one-week intensive Gaelic course*. Poster presented at the 2015 AMLaP conference on Architecture and Mechanisms of Language Processing, Valetta, Malta.
Lyons, J. (1968). *Introduction to theoretical linguistics*. Cambridge: Cambridge University Press.
Lyons, J. (1991). *Natural language and universal grammar: Vol. 1. Essays in linguistic theory*. Cambridge: Cambridge University Press.
MacSwan, J. (1999). *A minimalist approach to intrasentential code-switching*. New York: Garland.
MacWhinney, B. (1987). The competition model. In B. MacWhinney (Ed.), *Mechanisms of language acquisition* (pp. 249–308). Hillsdale, NJ: Erlbaum.
Maher, J., & Groves, J. (2007). *Introducing Chomsky*. 3rd ed. Cambridge: Icon Books.
McGurk, H., & MacDonald, J. (1976). Hearing lips and seeing voices. *Nature*, 264(5588), 746–748.
McNeill, D. (1970). *The acquisition of language*. New York: Harper and Row.
Meisel, J. (1989). Early differentiation of languages in bilingual children. In L. Obler & K. Hyltenstam (Eds.), *Bilingualism across the lifespan: Aspects of acquisition, maturity and loss* (pp. 13–40). Cambridge: Cambridge University Press.
Meisel, J. (2004). The bilingual child. In T. Bhatia & W. Ritchie (Eds.), *The handbook of bilingualism* (pp. 91–113). Oxford: Blackwell.
Milroy, L., & Muysken, P. (1995). Introduction: Code-switching and bilingualism research. In L. Milroy & P. Muysken (Eds.), *One speaker two languages: Cross-disciplinary perspectives on code-switching* (pp. 1–14). New York: Cambridge University Press.

Miyake, A., & Shah, P. (Eds.). (1999a). *Models of working memory: Mechanisms of active maintenance and executive control.* Cambridge: Cambridge University Press.

Miyake, A., & Shah, P. (1999b). Towards unified modules of working memory: Emerging consensus, unresolved theoretical issues and future research directions. In A. Miyake & P. Shah (Eds.), *Models of working memory: Mechanisms of active maintenance and executive control* (pp. 442–458). Cambridge: Cambridge University Press.

Molenberghs, P., Cunnington, R., & Mattingley, J. (2009). Is the mirror neuron system involved in imitation? A short review and meta-analysis. *Neuroscience & Biobehavioral Reviews*, 33(1), 975–980.

Montrul, S. (2013). Bilingualism and the heritage language speaker. In W. Ritchie & T. Bhatia (Eds.), *The handbook of bilingualism* (pp. 174–189). Malden, MA: Wiley-Blackwell.

Morsella, E., Godwin, C., Jantz, T., Krieger, S., & Gazzaley, A. (2015). Homing in on consciousness in the nervous system: An action-based synthesis [Online first]. *Behavioral and Brain Sciences.*

Mortimer, J., Alladi, S., Bak, T., Russ, T., Mekala, S., & Duggirala, V. (2014). Bilingualism delays age at onset of dementia, independent of education and immigration status. *Neurology*, 82(21), 1936.

Myers-Scotton, C. (1993). *Dueling languages: Grammatical structure in codeswitching.* New York: Oxford University Press.

O'Grady, W. (2005). *Syntactic carpentry: An emergentist approach to syntax.* Mahwah, NJ: Erlbaum.

Öhman, A., Flykt, A., & Lunquist, D. (2000). Unconscious emotion: Evolutionary perspectives, psychophysiological data and neuropsychological mechanisms. In R. D. Lane & L. Nadel (Eds.), *Cognitive neuroscience of emotion* (pp. 296–327). Oxford: Oxford University Press.

Osterhout, L., & Holcom, P. (1992). Event-related brain potentials elicited by syntactic anomaly. *Journal of Memory and Language*, 31(6), 785–806.

Osterhout, L., & Nicol, K. (1999). On the distinctiveness, independence, and time course of the brain responses to syntactic and semantic anomalies. *Language and Cognitive Processes*, 14, 283–317.

Owen, S., Coleman, M., Bolys, M., Davis, M., Laureys, S., & Pickard, J. (2006). Detecting awareness in the vegetative state. *Science*, 313(5792), 1402.

Paivio, A. (1986). *Mental representations: A dual coding approach.* Oxford: Oxford University Press.

Palmer, H. (1921). *The principles of language study.* New York: World Book Company.

Pavlenko, A. (2005). *Emotions and multilingualism.* Cambridge: Cambridge University Press.

Pinker, S. (1987). The bootstrapping problem in language acquisition. In B. MacWhinney (Ed.), *Mechanisms of language acquisition.* Hillsdale, NJ: Erlbaum.

Pinker, S.(1997). *How the mind works.* New York: W. W. Norton.

Pinker, S. (1994). *The language instinct.* New York: Morrow.

Pliatsikas, C., Moschopoulou, E., & Saddy, J. D. (2015). The effects of bilingualism on the white matter structure of the brain. *Proceedings of the National Academy of Sciences*, 112(5), 1334–1337.

Poeppel, D. (2013). The maps problem and the mapping problem: Two challenges for a cognitive neuroscience of speech and language. *Cognitive Neuropsychology*, 29(1–2), 34–55.

Polich, J. (2003). Overview of P3a and P3b. In J. Polich (Ed.), *Detection of change: Event-related potential and fMRI findings* (pp. 83–98). Boston: Kluwer Academic Press.

Poplack, S. (1980). Sometimes I'll start a sentence in English y termino en español: Toward a typology of code-switching. *Linguistics*, 18, 581–618.

Posner, M., & Rothbart, M. (2007). Research on attention networks as a model for the integration of psychological science. *Annual Review of Psychology*, 58, 1–23.

Posner, M., & Rothbart, M. (2012). Attentional networks and consciousness. *Frontiers in Psychology*, 3, 64.

Prinz, W. (1997). Perception and action planning. *European Journal of Cognitive Psychology*, 9, 129–154.

Pryke, S. (2009). Is red an innate or learned signal of aggression and intimidation? *Animal Behaviour*, 78, 393–398.

Ramachandran, V., & Hirstein, W. (1998). The perception of phantom limbs. *Brain*, 121, 1603–1630.

Ramachandran, V. S., & Hubbard, E. M. (2001). Synaesthesia: A window into perception, thought and language. *Journal of Consciousness Studies*, 8(12), 3–34.

Rumelhart, D. E., Hinton, G. E., & McClelland, J. L. (1986). A general framework for parallel distributed processing. In D. E. Rumelhart, J. L. McClelland, & the PDP Research Group (Eds.), *Parallel distributed processing: Explorations in the microstructure of cognition: Vol. 1. Foundations*. Cambridge, MA: MIT Press.

Sacks, O. (2012). *Hallucinations*. London: Pan Macmillan.

Sandler, W. (1989). *Phonological representation of the sign*. Dordrecht, Netherlands: Foris.

Savage-Rumbaugh, E. S., & Lewin, R. 1996. *Kanzi: The ape at the brink of the human mind*. New York: John Wiley.

Schachter, J. (1974). An error in error analysis. *Language Learning*, 24, 205–214.

Schumann, J. (1976). Second language acquisition: The pidginization hypothesis. *Language Learning*, 26(2), 391–408.

Schumann, J. H. (1997). *The neurobiology of affect in language*. Oxford: Blackwell.

Schurger, A., Pereira, F., & Cohen, J. (2010). Reproducibility distinguishes conscious from non-conscious neural representations. *Science*, 327(5961), 97–99.

Selinker, L. (1972). Interlanguage. *International Review of Applied Linguistics*, 10, 209–231.

Semendeferi, K., Lu, A., Schenker, N., & Damasio, H. (2002). Humans and great apes share a large frontal cortex. *Nature Neuroscience*, 5(3), 272–276.

Senghas, A., & Coppola, M. (2001). Children creating language: How Nicaraguan Sign Language acquired a spatial grammar. *Psychological Science*, 12(4), 323–328. Retrieved from http://www.columbia.edu~as1038/pdf/SenghasCoppola2001.pdf

Sharwood Smith, M. (1983). Crosslinguistic aspects of second language acquisition. *Applied Linguistics*, 4, 192–199.

Sharwood Smith, M. (2014). Can you learn to love grammar and so make it grow? On the role of affect in L2 development. In L. Aronin & M. Pawlak (Eds.), *Essential topics in applied linguistics and multilingualism: Studies in honor of David Singleton*. Berlin: Springer.

Sharwood Smith, M., & Truscott, J. (2014). *The multilingual mind: A modular processing perspective*. Cambridge: Cambridge University Press.

Singleton, D. (1989). Language acquisition: The age factor. Clevedon, UK: Multilingual Matters.

Sipler, P., & Fischer, S. (Eds.). (1990). *Theoretical issues in sign language research*. Chicago: University of Chicago Press.

Stanovich, K. E., & West, R. F. (2000). Individual differences in reasoning: Implications for the rationality debate. *Behavioral & Brain Sciences*, 23, 645–665.

Stokoe, W. (1960). *Sign language structure: An outline of the visual communication systems of the American deaf* (Studies in Linguistics Occasional Papers, Vol. 8, 2nd ed.). Silver Spring, MD: Linstok Press. Retrieved from http://citeseerx.ist.psu.edu/viewdoc/download?doi=10.1.1.129.9024&rep=rep1&type=pdf

Styles, E. (1997). *The psychology of attention*. Hove, England: Psychology Press.

Styles, E. (2005). *Attention, perception and memory*. Hove, England: Psychology Press.

Tallerman, M. (2015). *Understanding syntax* (4th ed.). New York: Routledge.

Truscott, J. (2014). *Consciousness and second language learning*. Bristol, England: Multilingual Matters.

Truscott, J., & Sharwood Smith, M. (2004). Acquisition by processing: A modular perspective on language development. *Bilingualism: Language and Cognition*, 7(1), 1–20.

Truscott, J., & Sharwood Smith, M. (2016). *The internal context of bilingual processing and acquisition*. Unpublished manuscript.

Tucker, M., & Ellis, R. (1998). On the relations of seen objects and components of potential actions. *Journal of Experimental Psychology: Human Perception and Performance*, 24, 830–846.

Ullman, M. T. (2001). A neurocognitive perspective on language: The declarative/procedural model. *Nature Reviews Neuroscience*, 2, 717–726.

Van Boxtel, J., Tsuchiya, N., & Koch, C. (2010). Consciousness and attention: On sufficiency and necessity. *Frontiers in Psychology*, 1, 217.

VanPatten, B. (1996). *Input processing and grammar instruction in second language acquisition*. Norwood, NJ: Ablex.

Vouloumanos, A., Hauser, M., Werker, J., & Martin, A. (2010). The tuning of human neonates' preference for speech. *Child Development*, 81(2), 517–527.

Warrington, E., & Shallice, T. (1984). Category specific semantic impairments. *Brain*, 107, 829–854.

Watt-Smith, T. (2015). *The book of human emotions: An encyclopaedia of feeling from anger to wanderlust*. London: Profile Books.

Whalley, L., Deary, I., Appleton, C., & Starr, J. (2004). Cognitive reserve and the neurobiology of cognitive aging. *Ageing Research Reviews*, 3, 369–382.

Whong, M. (2011). *Language teaching: Linguistic theory in practice*. Edinburgh: Edinburgh University Press.

Wilson, D., & Carston, R. (2007). A unitary approach to lexical pragmatics: Relevance, inference and ad hoc concepts. In N. Burton-Roberts (Ed.), *Pragmatics* (pp. 230–260). Basingstoke, England: Palgrave Macmillan.

Wu, Y.-J., & Thierry, G. (2012). How reading in a second language protects your heart. *Journal of Neuroscience*, 32, 6485–6489.

Yerkes, R., & Dodson, J. (1908). The relation of strength of stimulus to rapidity of habit-formation. *Journal of Comparative Neurology and Psychology*, 18, 459–482.

Zajonc, R. (2000). Feeling and thinking: Closing the debate over the independence of affect. In J. P. Forgas (Ed.), *Feeling and thinking: The role of affect in social cognition* (pp. 31–58). New York: Cambridge University Press.

Index

Abrahamsson, 171, 215
Abutalebi, 192, 211
Acredolo, 211
activation
   spreading activation, 14, 15, 40, 72, 75, 119, 176, 177
affect, 11, 40, 43, 45, 54, 56, 57, 58, 59, 60, 61, 62, 67, 79, 81, 90, 91, 95, 133, 134, 135, 136, 138, 139, 141, 142, 143, 146, 147, 149, 161, 162, 169, 173, 181, 187, 218, 219, 220
affective structure, xvii
age, 3, 38, 53, 134, 139, 142, 152, 153, 155, 157, 160, 161, 171, 172, 188, 189, 190, 192, 198, 211, 212, 217
Al-Hashimi, 211
Alladi, 167, 191, 211, 217
Allerhand, 211
Alloway, 166, 214
Amaral, 175, 211
Anderson, 126, 211
Anguera, 191, 211
Antoniou, 211
apes, 17, 53, 54, 100, 122, 154, 157, 158, 172, 218
Appleton, 219
APT, 87, 88, 89, 90, 149, 163, 172, 178, 179
Aronin, 219
Aslin, 214
attention
   attend, 36, 79, 161
auditory structure, xvii
awareness. *See* consciousness

Baars, 78, 211
Baddeley, 69, 71, 211
Bak, 191, 211, 216, 217
Balda, 50, 211
Balsby, 154, 211
Balter, 211
Barkow, 212
Barlow, 212
Barsalou, 34, 212
Bates, 14
Berridge, 59, 212
Bialystok, 167, 171, 188, 189, 191, 212, 213
Block, 82, 212

Bobb, 216
Boccanfuso, 211
Bolys, 217
Borsa, 211
Bourhis, 177, 216
Bower, 211
Bragdon, 140, 212
brain versus mind, 5
Branzi, 212
Brown, 89, 212
Burton-Roberts, 219

Calabria, 185, 212
Canini, 211
Carroll, 57, 152, 212
Carruthers, 25, 212
Carston, 114, 219
chain, 26, 27, 28, 29, 35, 47, 72, 73, 74, 75, 77, 96, 102, 104, 107, 109, 112, 114, 117, 119, 122, 136, 138, 141, 145, 150, 165, 166, 176, 178, 179, 180
Chapman, 140, 212
Chomsky, 6, 13, 17, 97, 98, 212, 214, 215, 216
Chun, 215
Clark, 214
Cohen, 213, 218
coindex. *See* index
Coleman, 217
Comrie, 196
conceptual structure, xvii
conceptual triggering, 176, 178, 179, 185, 189, 190
connectionism, 12
consciousness, 1, 11, 31, 34, 52, 55, 56, 61, 62, 78, 79, 80, 82, 84, 95, 125, 130, 131, 133, 141, 166, 167, 172, 180, 211, 212, 213
   A-consciousness, 82
   P-consciousness, 82
   subconscious, 6, 45, 55, 57, 58, 59, 78, 79, 80, 126, 127, 129, 140, 146, 147, 166, 174
Cook, 16, 127, 175, 212
Coppola, 218
cortex, 2, 8, 10, 22, 42, 43, 47, 50, 53, 79, 143, 218
Cosmides, 25, 212

Index

Costa, 212
Cowan, 68, 71, 166, 212, 213
Craik, 191, 212, 213
Crick, 3, 79, 213
Cunnington, 217

D'Esposito, 213
Dabelsteen, 211
Damasio, 10, 56, 57, 213, 218
Davis, 217
de Bot, 16, 213
de Córdoba, 214
Deary, 211, 219
Dehaene, 71, 213
Della Rosa, 211
Dennis, 214
Dewaele, 134, 213
Dienstbier, 215
Dodson, 220
Doherty-Sneddon, 157, 213
Dörnyei, 134, 213
dualism, 6
Duggirala, 211, 217

Eckman, 213
Eimas, 152, 213
Ellis, 34, 219
Emmons, 211
emotion, 1, 37, 56, 57, 58, 59, 62, 70, 83, 133, 144, 212, 213, 217
event-related potential, 180
expert system, 12, 24, 26, 27, 28, 67, 76, 100

Faraji, 211
Farrell, 213
Fernald, 214
Fischer, 120, 219
Fitch, 214, 215
flashbulb memory, 89, 91, 179
Flykt, 217
Fodor, 25, 214
Forgas, 220
Foucart, 140, 214
Franklin, 78, 211
Freedman, 212, 213
Frenck-Mestre, 140, 214
Friederici, 141, 214
Frijda, 56, 214
Fromkin, 214
fusiform gyrus, 24

Gardner, 133, 214
Gathercole, 166, 214
Gazzaley, 211, 217
Gladwell, 136, 214
Godwin, 217

Gómez Milán, 37, 214
Goodwyn, 211
Grant, 191, 214
Groh, 214
Grosjean, 181, 214
Groves, 16, 216
Grüter, 184, 214
Guidi, 211
Gunasekera, 211
gustatory structure, xvii

Harrar, 36, 214
Hauser, 153, 214, 215, 219
Hayes, 103, 214
Hernández, 212
Herschensohn, 171, 214
Heyes, 46, 214
Hickok, 46, 215
Hillyard, 140, 216
Hinton, 218
Hirstein, 218
Hitch, 69, 71, 211
Holcom, 140, 217
Hopp, 184, 215
Horobin, 211
Hoshino, 216
Hubbard, 37, 218
Hyams, 214
Hyltenstam, 171, 215, 216

Iborra, 214
Inati, 214
index, 27, 29, 48, 71, 72, 74, 77, 113, 164, 167, 175
indices. *See* index
input, 9, 23, 24, 27, 28, 31, 33, 38, 39, 40, 42, 75, 79, 96, 97, 98, 99, 101, 104, 108, 109, 110, 111, 113, 116, 117, 122, 135, 142, 151, 152, 153, 154, 158, 159, 160, 161, 163, 165, 167, 169, 170, 171, 172, 178, 187, 190, 212
interface, 24, 27, 28, 29, 39, 40, 42, 48, 51, 53, 63, 67, 68, 70, 71, 74, 85, 90, 97, 102, 103, 104, 107, 108, 112, 116, 120, 136, 143, 145, 160, 168, 185, 195, 214
Izard, 57, 215

Jackendoff, 9, 13, 17, 52, 95, 97, 100, 102, 111, 169, 215, 216
James, 56, 58, 59
Janowich, 211
Jantz, 217
Jenkins, 215
John, 17, 37, 100, 215
Johnson, 34, 171, 215, 216
Johnston, 211
Jones, 213
Juárez-Ramos, 214

Index   223

Kahneman, 58, 59, 80
Kamil, 211
Kanwisher, 24, 215
Karmiloff-Smith, 189, 215
Kegl, 170, 215
Kellerman, 182, 215
Kihlststrom, 215
Klein, 161, 171, 215
Kleinmann, 182, 215
knowledge, 2, 5, 8, 10, 11, 12, 19, 50, 52, 58, 59,
    67, 70, 73, 78, 79, 85, 86, 87, 88, 91, 108,
    124, 125, 126, 127, 129, 130, 131, 135, 138,
    139, 142, 148, 166, 173, 175, 186, 187, 188,
    189, 193, 197
Koch, 79, 81, 213, 219
Kong, 211
Krashen, 127, 186, 216
Krause, 214
Krieger, 217
Kroll, 180, 216
Kulik, 89, 212
Kutas, 140, 216

Lakoff, 34, 216
Lambert, 133, 214
Lamme, 81, 216
Landry, 177, 216
Lane, 217
Larraburo, 211
Laureys, 217
LeDoux, 56, 57, 59, 133, 216
Lenneberg, 171, 216
Lerdahl, 216
Levinson, 196, 216
Lewin, 157, 218
Lewis, 213
Lew-William, 214
Li, 214
linguistic landscape, 177
Long, 155, 161, 216
Lowie, 213
Lu, 218
Lunquist, 217
Lyons, 100, 216

MacDonald, 216
MacSwan, 216
MacWhinney, 14, 216, 217
Maher, 16, 216
Malcolm, 214
Martin, 219
Mattingley, 217
McClelland, 14, 218
McDermott, 215
McGurk, 37, 216
McKenzie, 213
McNeill, 161, 216

Meisel, 178, 186, 216
Mekala, 217
memory, 8, 9, 10, 14, 22, 24, 25, 26, 27, 28, 31,
    32, 33, 38, 40, 42, 48, 52, 53, 65, 66, 67, 68,
    69, 70, 71, 72, 73, 74, 75, 76, 77, 84, 85, 88,
    89, 90, 91, 96, 97, 102, 106, 107, 108, 114,
    117, 130, 132, 146, 148, 159, 160, 164, 166,
    169, 171, 176, 178, 189, 190, 194, 211, 212,
    213, 214, 217, 219
  short term memory, 68
  working memory, 24, 27, 28, 29, 66, 68, 70, 71,
    76, 85, 88, 89, 97, 107, 108, 160, 164, 166,
    178, 217
Milroy, 185, 216
Mind versus brain. *See* brain versus mind
Minimalist Program, 13
Miyake, 69, 71, 217
module, 14, 15, 17, 21, 22, 23, 24, 25, 26, 27, 28,
    31, 38, 40, 43, 52, 66, 70, 74, 76, 79, 87, 88,
    91, 96, 97, 100, 101, 102, 105, 106, 107, 129,
    159, 162, 167, 169, 178
  language module, 100
MOGUL, 5, 13, 33, 122
Molenberghs, 217
Montrul, 187, 217
Morsella, 34, 217
Mortimer, 217
Moschopoulou, 217
multiple encoding, 12
motor structure, xvii
Muysken, 185, 216
Myers-Scotton, 217

Nadel, 217
Newport, 171, 214, 215
Newson, 16, 212
Nicol, 140, 214, 217
Nissan, 211

O'Grady, 15, 217
Obler, 171, 216
Öhman, 56, 57, 58, 217
olfactory structure, 28
Osterhout, 140, 217
Ottó, 134, 213
Owen, 47, 217

Paivio, 12, 217
Palmer, 127, 217
Parris, 211
Pavlenko, 134, 217
Pawlak, 219
Pepperberg, 211
Perceptual Output Structure, xvii
Pereira, 218
Pervin, 215
Phonological structure, 103

Pickard, 217
Pinker, 16, 52, 97, 163, 186, 215, 217
Pliatsikas, 192, 217
Poeppel, 7, 218
Polich, 140, 218
Poplack, 185, 218
Posner, 81, 218
Postle, 71, 213
primitive, 25, 26, 32, 60, 61, 62, 66, 67, 77, 96, 97, 102, 103, 105, 106, 107, 112, 122, 148, 149, 153, 154, 163, 197
Prinz, 46, 218
processing unit, 21, 35, 76, 102, 108
Pryke, 40
Purdue, 161, 215

Ramachandran, 37, 218
representation, 6, 8, 9, 10, 11, 15, 27, 28, 30, 31, 40, 42, 51, 67, 70, 71, 73, 75, 79, 86, 89, 103, 104, 106, 108, 113, 122, 145, 150, 164, 166, 211, 218
  dispositional representation, 10
resting level, 70, 77, 88, 89, 90, 114, 144, 159, 164, 183, 186
Rintoul, 211
Ritchie, 216
Rodman, 214
Rodríguez Artacho, 214
Roeper, 175, 211
Rolle, 211
Rosenblith, 212
Rothbart, 81, 218
Rubio, 214
Rumelhart, 14, 218

Sacks, 38, 218
Saddy, 217
Salapatek, 213
Sandler, 159, 218
Savage-Rumbaugh, 17, 157, 218
Schenker, 218
Schneider, 213
Schumann, 134, 188, 218
Schurger, 79, 218
Selinker, 11, 186, 218
Semendeferi, 53, 218
Senghas, 218
Shah, 69, 71, 217
Shailaja, 211, 217
Shallice, 40, 219
Sharwood Smith, 1, 5, 33, 81, 87, 100, 173, 176, 177, 181, 218, 219
Shukla, 211
Singleton, 171
Sipler, 120, 219

somatosensory structure, xvii
Sorace, 216
Spence, 36, 214
Stanovich, 58, 219
Starr, 219
Stokoe, 159, 219
Styles, 81, 219
subconscious. *See* consciousness
Surampudi, 211, 217
synapses, 12
Syntactic structure, xvii, 105

Tallerman, 105, 219
Tamis-LeMonda, 211
thalamus, 8, 22, 42, 43, 59
Thierry, 145, 220
Tooby, 25, 212
Truscott, 1, 5, 33, 37, 60, 78, 81, 87, 100, 102, 173, 176, 177, 219
Tsuchiya, 81, 219
Tucker, 34, 219

Ullman, 126, 219
Underhill, 214
Universal Grammar, 97, 102, 212, 216

Van Boxtel, 81, 219
VanPatten, 219
Vega-Mendoza, 216
Velmans, 213
Verspoor, 213
Vestergaard, 211
visual structure, 28
Vouloumanos, 153, 219

Warrington, 40, 219
Watson, 3
Watt-Smith, 219
Weekes, 211
Weissenborn, 141, 214
Werker, 219
West, 58, 108, 175, 219
Whalley, 53, 219
Whong, 219
Wilson, 114, 219
Winkielman, 59, 212
Wong, 211
working memory, 68
Wu, 145, 220

Yerkes, 220
Young-Scholten, 214

Zajonc, 56, 59, 220